Domesticating Information

Managing Documents Inside the Organization

Carol E. B. Choksy, Ph.D., CRM

D1563451

The Scarecrow Press, Inc.
Lanham, Maryland • Toronto • Oxford
2006

ROWMAN & LITTLEFIELD PUBLISHERS, INC.

Published in the United States of America
by Rowman & Littlefield Publishers, Inc.
A wholly owned subsidiary of The Rowman & Littlefield Publishing Group, Inc.
4501 Forbes Boulevard, Suite 200, Lanham, Maryland 20706
www.rowmanlittlefield.com

PO Box 317
Oxford
OX2 9RU, UK

British Library Cataloguing in Publication Information Available

Library of Congress Cataloging-in-Publication Data

Choksy, Carol E. B., 1956–
   Domesticating information : managing documents inside the organization / Carol E. B.
Choksy.
     p. cm.
   Includes bibliographical references and index.
   ISBN-13: 978-0-8108-5190-0 (pbk. : alk. paper)
   ISBN-10: 0-8108-5190-3 (pbk. : alk. paper)

  1. Records—Management. 2. Business records—Management. 3. Information
resources management. I. Title.
HF5736.C4546 2006
651.5—dc22

                               200619490

Printed in the United States of America

∞™ The paper used in this publication meets the minimum requirements of American
National Standard for Information Sciences—Permanence of Paper for Printed Library
Materials, ANSI/NISO Z39.48-1992.

For Jamsheed and Darius, who order pandemonium.

Contents

Figures

Tables

Preface

I have been fortunate to have performed records management consulting projects in many different types and sizes of organizations. I have experienced nearly every industry including pharmaceuticals, law firms, insurance, brokerages, banks, manufacturing, construction, engineering, architecture, local government, state government, and federal government. I have also had the luck to address every aspect of the life cycle from conception to death certificate and archives.

Like Darwin, I have dissected nearly every "barnacle" of records management and have drawn some conclusions about my observations. My first observation was that books on records management are aimed at a very low level of personnel within an organization. They are how-to books on filing, creating a filing system, or setting up a system of retiring records, not unlike books published a century ago that resulted from the importation of scientific management into the office. At best, a manager might read them and glean useful tips. Those books have no guiding principles, no broader observations, and no preliminary conclusions for how to go forward.

This book is intended to advance the profession of records management by lifting the level of principle, observation, and conclusion to at least the level of executive management. I am quite certain that others in my profession will find fault with some part of what I write here and would advance rigorous arguments about why I am wrong. Indeed, I fervently hope that hundreds of thoughtful articles and books will be published demonstrating the inadequacies of my offering. Only in that way can we hope to achieve recognition for our profession.

Another purpose for this book is to provide tools for professionals. At no other time have our skills been more needed. The captured information within our organizations has never provided more adverse evidence at trial. This is the result of our increased ability to capture information, the ease with which we can create new documents, and the social change of our society from oral/aural communication to "digital" (as in fingers) and visual communication. Oh, yes, and our completely mislaid trust that the computer was minding the store.

The calamities of corporate compliance in the 1990s and now the 2000s are documented by our computers. They caught us doing and saying things we should not have. When we tried to destroy the evidence, our computers documented that activity as well. Once information technology (IT) professionals admitted they were helpless before this problem and upper-level executives realized the extent of the problem—seeing, for example, Frank Quattrone going to jail for sending an email that files be cleaned up—they began to remember the folks in the subbasements of their organizations, the records managers. Covered in dust and fungus, we must now make ourselves presentable to upper-level executives.

We must also learn several new sets of jargon. The most important is not that of technology, but of strategic management. The vocabulary is easy: compliance—both for regulatory agencies and litigation—is a goal or at least an objective for many organizations. An objective and a goal are ordained by the strategic management process. What we must learn about strategic management is how it works. Then we must learn how to measure our successful execution of the goals and objectives that pertain to our portfolios.

For information technology (IT) we must learn some of the jargon of their profession. For example, a repository is a location where documents sit and can be quickly retrieved. We might call that a file room, a set of cabinets, a desk drawer, or a pile on a desk. IT would be referring to a hard drive, a RAID, a jukebox, or even a smart phone. An archive is a location where documents sit, but require a little time and possibly even personnel for retrieval. We might call that off-site storage. IT would be referring to a room or a storage site filled with tapes or optical platters.

We must also learn another set of jargon from IT, the one that refers to our activities. That jargon set changes about every three to five years. Some of the most recent labels are document management, knowledge management, content management, business process management (BPM), we must learn even what they mean when they use the term "records management." The vendors all change their marketing material and even the names of their products. They may even add some functionality. They will never call everything they do records management, even though that is precisely what they are doing, albeit in a compliance-challenged manner.

This book is also intended for academics in library and information science and archives who for too long have assumed they knew what records management was and how it fits into their academic world. Records management is a hybrid of business and information science, its form of classification resembles the methods used in biology more than it does libraries. We must worry about statutes, regulations, and case law. We do not worry about culture or what scholars will need. We often, to our detriment, do not worry about how information is created or used, even though we do worry about how it is affixed and distributed.

The title of this book is for the academics. The first written documents were business documents. The tokens, bullae, and then tablets of the ancient world were business contracts. The oldest archives are records rooms. Information was captured and used by humanity to perform work, not for history, scholarship, or art. What humanity has done with information is to learn to catch it and use it, just as we learned to catch horses, dogs, and wild grain and use them. Information evolved with our understanding of it, just as horses, dogs, and grain have evolved. Just as we domesticated animals and plants, we domesticated information.

My advisor, Jonathan Z. Smith, taught all of his students that much of the basis of living is working: religion is work, dreams are work. Creating and capturing information is also work. This book is about captured information put to work for organizations to continue existing and for individuals to earn a living.

Acknowledgments

I could not have written this without relationships with some extraordinary people and firms to guide me along the way. I owe a debt of gratitude to my mentors: Lou Covotsos, Jean Ciura, Fred Diers, and the late Russell Gureasko, for their generosity of spirit, patience, and offers of opportunity. I am also greatly appreciative for the opportunities Doculabs offered to me and still offers to me to get a more thorough understanding of "the technology" in action inside many different organizations. I am thankful for being surrounded by the brilliance of a group of people called "records managers" who have no idea how intelligent and creative they are.

I am deeply indebted to Blaise Cronin, Debora (Ralf) Shaw, and the faculty at the School of Library and Information Science at Indiana University, Bloomington for giving me two years as a Visiting Lecturer to read and listen. I was supposed to be teaching, but I believe I learned much more than I taught. Blaise especially was helpful in recommending books and articles, each of which opened a new dimension of understanding. Now as an adjunct professor at IUB, find I am still in wonderment about the breadth of library and information science.

This was not the first book I expected to write after graduate school, and I am not sad that it was. Most of my analytical skills were learned under the tutelage of my dear advisor, Jonathan Z. Smith. Analyzing the culture of an organization is not so different from analyzing the culture of an entire society. William Robertson Smith, Durkheim, and Louis Dumont certainly understood more about organization and classification than many modern authors.

My editor and dear friend, Linda Andrews, has taken my words and made them sound professional. I cannot thank her enough for raising the level of my work to what I had dreamed it could be. I would also like to thank Mark Frankena of the Early Office Museum, www.officemuseum.com, for use of several photos from his site.

Finally, I need to thank my husband and son, Jamsheed and Darius Choksy, for believing in me, for their support, and for their patience.

Introduction

Few concepts are as ubiquitous, important, or inchoate as information. Much of human history and endeavor can be seen as a continuous effort to create and harness information. As we grapple with the advent of the "Information Age," few activities are more urgent than clarifying what information is and how we master it. In recent events, we have seen instances where actions undertaken with insufficient information either threatened or brought dissatisfaction with the ruling parties of major political powers.[1] Our social, political, and physical infrastructure and the regular conduct of business have been threatened or interrupted by information "graffiti artists"—hackers who corrupt, destroy, or prevent access to our information through various WORMS, viruses, and social engineering.

This book is entitled "Domesticating Information" to reflect what humans do with information: capture it, add to it, copy it, refer to it, transmit it, retrieve it, make decisions with it, show it, describe it, organize it, study it, and manage it, among many other things.

Professionals in the fields of library science and information science study information as an element of culture, library science focusing primarily on libraries and museums and information science on scholarly collaboration and use of information. This book argues that both of these approaches present limitations. Most significantly, such a narrow focus completely misses the study of information as a tool to perform work. Both humans and animals make tools. Likewise, both humanity and animals use information as tools. However, while a footprint or spoor can be read by a human or a fox, only the human has the capacity to make a cast of the footprint or chemically analyze the spoor.

The difference between humans and animals, then, is not tool-making, but technology-making. We create tools as part of a larger technology to perform work.[2] We created specialized flint tools for the technology of the hunt. Other specialized flint tools led to the creation of another tool, animal hide, part of in the technology of providing material for clothes. Yet another technology was agriculture, in which humans set aside some of their seeds for planting rather than eating them.

Our greatest technological creation was language. With language, we could communicate more directly with each other and, supposedly, with our gods. We could enjoy the sounds and the images it created for us. We could elaborate on emotion. Language helped us to perform work more efficiently — work such as barter and agreement, trial and sentencing. Language also helped us to create larger associations of humans with common interests such as religious and business organizations and enabled us to govern larger numbers of humans.

The subsequent ability to encode language in writing allowed us to communicate with others even when we were not present. Writing conquered the linguistic problems of time and space: how to be "heard" when we are many miles away or after we are dead. It also permitted us to perform work by creating lasting monuments to our agreements on clay, sheepskin, papyrus, paper, and now the computer screen.

All of these are documents. Records management did not, however, spring from the field of documentation. It sprang from the needs of business in the late nineteenth and early twentieth centuries through the application of "systematic" or "scientific" management techniques to offices. These were the same techniques that Frederick W. Taylor, the popularizer of scientific management, had applied to the factory floor.[3] The rise of records management was integral to the rise of management.

Records management is concerned with the use of information tools within organizations — business, government, non-profit organizations, etc. — as part of several different technologies. Records management is a form of business analysis. What we analyze as records managers is how information can best be used as a tool within a particular organization. For records managers, documents are not cultural objects but business objects. Claude Lévi-Strauss's observation that women in culture are objects of exchange — business objects, not cultural objects[4] — may have been more shocking generally, but the observation that documents, *records*, are business objects might be rejected by most of library and information science. Certainly, women cook, sew, nurture, etc., but they are, or were, for the society, objects of barter. Documents are objects of exchange, too. Certainly, they perform other functions — to heal, to broaden awareness, to dictate, to calculate, and so forth — but their original and primary purpose is to memorialize a commercial exchange. Every document, every record, performs work.

For the field of records management, the very nature of documents is different than it is for library and information science. This fundamental difference lies at the apex of the classification system in the same way the kingdoms of animals and vegetables are differentiated in the Linnean system.[5] That difference results in two different cultures of understanding: records management is pragmatic, utilitarian, and rigorous; library and information science are creative and open to exploration.

Just as the fundamental nature of documents is different, so are the functions documents perform. Documents within organizations are created to serve usually only one function: they are business objects. Library and information science manage and utilize documents for reference by scholars or citizens—for everything but that one function.

Records managers do not "appraise" information in the sense that archivists do because we are unconcerned with culture. We are only concerned with work. We evaluate and assess information, the tools used to encode it, and the technologies for which it is used. We do not reflect upon the value of information's content to a particular project as an employee performing work would do. Rather, we reflect upon that value for the organization generally. We are concerned with the health and overall functioning of an organization, rather than on a particular business process or division.

Because records managers are primarily analysts, we are busy doing. What is of value to us are snapshots of problems, recommendations for a particular circumstance. Hence, our literature is filled with "how-to" books. We rarely sit back and reflect on *how* we do what we do—i.e., we rarely analyze our analysis in publications in the form of books and periodicals.

Unlike the archivists, we have not encountered any major shifts in how we practice our profession. In the 1980s and 1990s, archivists were faced with what could almost be called a paradigm shift in custodianship. Electronic records are maintained by those who create them. Nor are electronic records necessarily all kept by the same electronic record keepers because different knowledge is required for different applications.[6] The corresponding archives literature demonstrates a deep reflection of what this shift means and how archives practices must change—for instance, by finding common standards such as XML and DOD 5015.2, as well as educating end users in what is necessary. Records managers in many nations have read this literature and have been deeply affected by it—without reflecting, however, on whether the shift to a noncustodial method or archival practices actually addresses what we do at all.

Records managers have rarely had custody of records. Sometimes a records manager's portfolio includes being the custodian of records when quick access to them is no longer needed, but it is the organization that is responsible for maintaining them. Records managers are much more concerned with the entire life cycle of those records—the life cycle that ranges from the "family planning" phase (policies and procedures for creation of information) all the way to the "ashes and headstone" phase (complete destruction with certificate of destruction).

In contrast, archivists function as caretakers of cultural and political artifacts; ultimately, they work for scholars and citizens. Records managers are concerned with how information is used within a particular active system; they work for organizations. The major area of difference is that records managers are primarily business analysts. What records managers analyze may be strategic or tactical, enterprise, departmental, workflow, or single employee-based. What records managers do may address information systems security, compliance with regulations or statutes, business practices, intellectual property, industry practice, legal practice, human resources practices, human-computer interaction, or helpful hints. Records management in some instances may require a policy directive from the CEO and board of directors, or it may require an individual to change the position of the staple on a particular document type from the left to the right.

This is not "organizational informatics," as informatics addresses solely human interaction with computers—although it is difficult to see how an organization uses a technological artifact, as it is humans who are doing the actual using! To perform our activities successfully, we must analyze every aspect of the organization, including its functions, its corporate culture, its industry sector, its regulatory environment, its compliance environment, its risk management environment, its security environment, the various business processes within the organization, the employee's level of knowledge about information, and how information in the form of records can become an intangible asset within a particular organization.

In writing this book, my hope is to contribute a very different type of work to the field of records management. While I want to apply critical thinking to records management and to place records management within the academy, I also want this book to be of use to records managers and to information technology (IT) managers. Current works by records managers are written for records managers; seminars and conferences on records management are intended for the same audience. While we have practiced communicating to ourselves, we have not learned to communicate well with our employers or with our colleagues in information technology, even as the need to serve those employers and to find ways to use our organizations' information technology to serve our employers' purposes has become critical. Many of our employers are being exploited through specious document subpoenas that cost more to comply with than the potential fine or settlement.

Meanwhile, archivists and librarians have aggressively issued publications on documents and records, some even purporting to deal with records management. While those publications have been fruitful for broadening awareness of some records management issues, such as preservation, they have also confused the very grounds of our field through grand definitions of documents and records, the invention of terms to cover concepts already well documented (such as the renaming of records management as the records continuum), and misplaced emphasis on the last phases of the life cycle.

This confusion has also now spread to information technology, the organizational unit that currently bears responsibility for the very documents and systems that cause the most trouble in litigation: back-ups, cache, and partially deleted documents. According to prevalent definitions, including that of the International Organization for Standardization (ISO) 15489,[7] information technology (IT) is doing its job. The amount of money that companies are paying for electronic discovery, however, suggests that IT is creating more expensive problems than it is fixing.

I wanted to write a work that could help scholars of the fields of information science and informatics to understand not only how records management differs from archives and library science, but also how it could contribute positively to all of those fields.

To this end, I have approached my subject from several angles, to meet the needs of not only records managers, but also IT, legal, and compliance officers. Chapter 1 is concerned with the history of records management. This may seem like a cultural activity, but it places the rise of modern records management clearly in the same line of development and thinking that gave rise to modern U.S. business. Chapter 2 takes up the role of context in records management. Chapter 3 addresses primarily a realistic definition of what we are required by law to manage, as well as the criteria that can and cannot go into that definition. In Chapter 4, I look at the context of what goes into the making of records as complex objects. Chapter 5 addresses the concept of the records life cycle and the relationship between records and business processes. Finally, in Chapter 6, I take up the value of information within the organization and how records management manages the value of information. Throughout this book, my objective has been to reach all of the constituencies within today's organization that have a role to play in managing records, and in protecting and enhancing an organization's information assets.

NOTES

1. U.K. Iraq intelligence estimate as Blair government's justification for war. The document was not saved as a new document, so a curious reader looked at the author and version tracking and discovered the document had actually been authored by U.S. intelligence experts and reformatted for the United Kingdom. This discovery made clear that the U.K. had not performed its own assessment, but had relied entirely on U.S. intelligence.

2. The primacy of work in human life is little emphasized, even when what we study is work. I am grateful to my Ph.D. advisor, Jonathan Z. Smith, for never letting me lose sight of this. My area of study, government and business, is less prosaic than what we studied together: religion and culture. Many of the technologies, and tools within those technologies, for studying *homo operarius:* human the worker, I learned from him.

3. Frederick W. Taylor, *The Principles of Scientific Management* (New York: Harper Brothers, 1911).

4. Claude Lévi-Strauss, *Les structures élémentaires de la parenté* (Paris: Mouton & Co., 1967).

5. The reader will recall the layers of the Linnean system are kingdom, phylum, class, order, family, genus, and species.

6. See, for example, David Bearman, *Electronic Evidence: Strategies for Managing Records in Contemporary Organizations* (Pittsburgh, PA: Archives & Museum Informatics 1994), 41–42.

7. ISO 15489, "Information and documentation—Records management" (Geneva: ISO, 2001).

Chapter One

History of Records Management

Writing a history of records management, however brief, is difficult, because most of what we know comes from snapshots created for us by archaeologists and historians. Management is an activity that is not easily captured in the snapshots of archaeology. We must interpret what we see as representative of activity, so there is always a danger that what we are seeing is happenstance, not intentional. Intention is a complex issue better discussed by rabbis and jurists. What I mean by "intention" is similar to what a paleontologist does when looking for fossils and making a distinction between the shapes an animal or plant left and the shapes created by other forces of nature.

Another issue that skews our ability to create a history is how we understand representations of tabular information, also called structured information (as opposed to semistructured forms and unstructured documents). Is a calendar a document? Is a table of values a document? While I would side with those who answer "yes" enthusiastically, I find it helpful to trace the history of this information separately, as this history helps us to understand many of the problems we currently have managing digital or electronic records.

We can identify a number of important transformations in history as being essential to records management. Several of those transformations are lost in time and probably took tens of thousands of years to develop: the intentional capturing of information, such as the notches on a bone, the creation of language, the memorializing of actions through language such as in a contract or grant of rights, the standardization of media formats, the standardization of language to memorialize action, making copies of those memorials, and arranging memorials in an orderly way in a storage room for later reference. Others of those historical transformations took place within the past thousand years, so we have better documentation and histories to count on: the changing dependence on written records, the rise of archives to maintain written records, the rise of mass literacy, and the invention and dissemination of printing presses.

The most recent changes occurred within the past two hundred years and include the rise and spread of the post office, the change in size and geographic spread of business, the invention of machines that could read information, the invention of tools to print ad hoc documents such as letters, the invention of tools to copy ad hoc documents such as the gel-press, the ability to record voice, the ability to send information over wires and without wires, the rise of machines to process tabular information, and the rise of machines to process documentary information. We cannot cover all of these in detail, but each was a revolutionary development in tool-making in the aid of different technologies. One observation we can make about our history from this synopsis is that our use of information as a tool has increased exponentially in recent history.

A BRIEF HISTORY OF HUMAN USE AND MANAGEMENT OF INFORMATION

Information captured by humans has always been divided between tabular information (what we would call a table or a database) and documents. The oldest consistently encoded information we have by far is tabular information from the Paleolithic period about 100,000 BCE (Before Common Era, equivalent to BC): notches on bone are collections of discrete units of information captured—i.e., tabular data.[1] Notches on bones were most likely markers or tallies that represented an instance of something. As signifying artifacts created by humans, these are documents or records.

We associate tabular data most often with numbers. Our modern numbers were not completely developed until around 850 CE (Common Era, equivalent to AD) in India and in the Middle East with the invention of zero and the place-value system of representing numbers.[2] These numbers were used in India at that time for exploring the mysticism of numbers and astronomy through calculation, but were used in poetry to describe the incalculable, imperial inscriptions, and charters.[3] Numbers as tools to perform work were not fully developed until the Iranian al-Khwarazmi (783–850 CE) formalized and developed the basic methods for solving equations with unknowns, algebra (from *al jabr*), in the ninth century in Baghdad at the court of the caliph al-Ma'mun. (Our word "algorithm" is derived from al-Khwarazmi's name.) The numbers 1 through 9 and arithmetic methods arrived in Europe around 970 CE when Gerbert of Aurillac (945–1003 CE), later Pope Sylvester II, brought them from Islamic Spain to France.[4] Zero and algebra arrived in Europe in approximately 1202 when Leonard of Pisa (1170–1250 CE), also known as Fibonacci, wrote a book about what he had learned from his travels in North Africa and the Middle East.[5]

The first records we have with identifiable writing were contracts. Those first contracts used representations of the objects involved in the contract, such as pictures of sheep or cattle, to memorialize a transaction. Historically, the objects were represented as pictures on clay; they were first represented as separate tokens, like tiny clay figures, and then representations: "The main debt of the token system to Paleolithic and Mesolithic tallies consisted of the principle of abstracting data."[6] Tokens were developed around 8,000 BCE.

Writing as we understand it arose with the creation of records used to memorialize business transactions around 3100 BCE when it became "possible to record and communicate the name of the sponsor/recipient of the merchandise, formerly indicated by seals."[7] Later, writing was used by rulers to record deeds such as battles, or to record tribute from conquered peoples. One of the most important durable documents we have is money. In many instances, coins are the only memorial to a long-dead king.

The substrate used to write on and its characteristics have always dictated how the document was used and preserved. Caves, bones, animal hide, stone, clay tablets, metal, papyrus, flax, cotton, and trees all have particular characteristics that demand different treatment. Caves are not portable. The size of a stone tablet dictates whether it was portable or not. Clay tablets could be portable, but could also break or be damaged with long exposure to water. Much of the papyrus we now have was dug up from garbage heaps, indicating that the documents were considered trash by their owners. Other documents were carefully protected and preserved, such as the Dead Sea scrolls which had been sealed in jars and stored in caves. In many instances, however, the only material we have with which to date a document are the coins found near them, because the practice of dating documents was inconsistent.

For as long as humans have used information within their technologies, there has been a need to manage the records created. Early examples where sets of documents needed managing are easy to find, but how those documents came to be where they were found and how they were managed are difficult to establish. Archaeologists estimate that records management has been around for at least five thousand years: "By the third millennium B.C. recordkeeping had gone beyond an experimental stage of trial and error, and had become a professional system of documentation."[8] Documents had standardized shapes and content, forms had standardized language, and the archives appeared to have been placed in order, with like tablets placed together.[9] Ancient archives also appear to have contained primarily commercial transactions, receipts, legal documents, and real estate transactions.[10] Records retention was also practiced; summary documents were created and the detailed, lengthy originals were destroyed.[11]

Figure 1.1 is an example of a cuneiform contract, dated 2024 BCE. It reads, "9 lambs, 43 sheep, 23 large goats from the herd of the governor of Girsu, [and] 70+ sheep, all delivered as tax [and] transferred from Na-lu-5 to Dull-ga [in the] 5th month of the year the ship [named] "Ibex of the Abzu" was caulked [Signed] Su-Sin-2." It would have been sealed inside a clay envelope with the seals of Su-Sin-2 and possibly another witness. Any document that required an added layer of credibility, such as a legal document or contract, was sealed inside a clay envelope with seals applied.

Because few people could write, literacy was associated primarily with the scribes of monarchs and their associated religious organizations. This permitted the use of information as a technology for concentrating power.[12] Monarchs used writing produced by scribes and priests as a tool to control resources and their distribution. If you could not read, how could you know whether the mark on the tablet meant that you had paid your debt in full, or whether it indicated you still owed something? Despite the improvements in

Figure 1.1.   Babylonian Cuneiform Contract 2024 BCE.
Photograph courtesy Archive J. K. Choksy

writing materials—from the scroll to the codex, from clay tablets to papyrus and then linen- and cotton-based paper—as well as improvements in ink, only a small percentage of persons ever learned to read, much less to write.

This situation held sway in Western Europe until around the thirteenth and fourteenth centuries, when literacy became more common. M. T. Clanchy argues that this rise in literacy in England occurred because of the change from oral to written as official records from the eleventh to the fourteenth centuries: "[T]his growth in the uses of literacy is indicated by, and was perhaps a consequence of, the production and retention of records on an unprecedented scale."[13] Clanchy traces the growing popularization of the use of written documents, including points at which oral records (*recordationem*) and written records existed alongside each other, to the general acceptance and use of written records, even by peasants who could not read them at the beginning of the process, but could at the end.[14]

The first official records of proceedings at the British court to have been created in written form, in 1176 and 1182, are agreements, called *chirographs*.[15] Copies of those agreements were often made in triplicate, each one being as acceptable as the others. One of those copies was ordinarily written in a bound book so that it would not get lost quite so easily.[16] Clanchy convincingly describes the need to read with the rise in popularity of the written over the oral record. On page 6 is a copy of a wage account of a Robyn Hod (not necessarily the legendary one). Mr. Hod would have wanted to know how to read so he could ensure his wages were correctly registered.

Another innovation was the rise of the visual representation of tabular information in the seventeenth and eighteenth centuries. The increased accuracy of maps through surveys and the representation of tables as graphs permitted us to take pages and pages of readable but uninterpretable information and make it understandable to literate persons as pictures or lines on a graph.[17] Essentially, we took tabular information and turned it into pictures. Those pictures could be included in the text as hand-colored engravings. Only very recently have we been able to unify the process of including tabular information, pictures, drawings, maps, and photographs in the same work process, with the use of computer-aided typesetting. Previous to this, the two were separate (and they remain so, in high-quality print work).

The rise of the printing press in the middle to late fifteenth century certainly made some types of information more readily available, but not all information. We are all aware that the first book printed was the Bible, a religious text. This development is actually contrary to the trend of the preceding 4,000 years, in which business requirements motivated changes in document technology. The information that records managers manage—i.e., information inside the organization, such as contracts, letters, summary information,

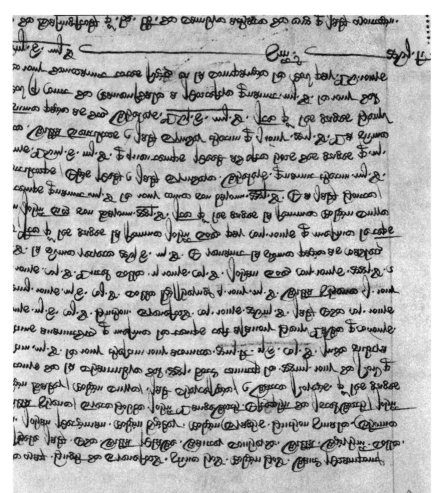

Figure 1.2. Wage Account of "Robyn Hod," a Porter in the King's Chamber 1324, British National Archives.
Photograph courtesy Art Resources

and tabular information—continued to be hand-written until the invention of carbon paper in 1823 and the mass production of the Remington typewriter in 1874.

The years between the invention of the printing press and the typewriter were filled with advances in the handling of tabular information. Georges

Ifrah's book *The Universal History of Computing: From the Abacus to the Quantum Computer*[18] records the mind-numbing number of inventions required for the advent of the computer as we know it: keyboards, calculating machines, analog machines, mechanization of all arithmetic functions, and fully programmable machines, among others. A remarkable amount of this work actually occurred in the seventeenth and eighteenth centuries. We will not examine the development of computers as machines, as this has been well documented.[19]

The reader should be made aware, however, that computers were originally designed to deal either with calculating complex formulae quickly and accurately, or with managing tables of similar and discrete information—tabular information. Indeed, "tabulating gear has always been the heart of data processing's pre-computer history and is the computer's most direct ancestor. The reason was simple, unlike typewriters or calculating machines, which were single units of equipment that handled small amounts of information in a restricted fashion, tabulating gear operated on thousands, even millions of pieces of data. . . . The important difference between this technology and others was that it dealt with a *system* that processed information quickly and in high volume. Reliance on such equipment by a large number of organizations laid the foundation for computers because the first users of computers were primarily those who had experience with punched card tabulating gear."[20]

Tabular information and numbers have always represented a very specific form of information: they answer questions that require keeping track of and counting things. What we consider to be records or documents—verbal analysis, contracts, recorded thoughts, recorded deeds, etc.—locate us as actors within society. Neither is more objective, as both records and documents are social constructs; but the first describes the relationships of concepts, and the second describes the relationships of people.

This is a nontrivial distinction. For thousands of years, until recent developments in computers, we did not expect the same technology to manage tabular and documentary information. The printing press was not designed for counting, and the abacus was not designed for printing or displaying documents. The history of the computer begins with counting and tabulating devices, not with attempts to display documents. Early attempts to use the computer for documents, such as SuperWylber, required the end user to bring up a single line of text in the same way a programmer would bring up a line of code—a laborious method for writing any document. When word processors were created and documents became digitized, we began to use the same technology—computers—to create and manage both. Interestingly, what originally made personal computers attractive was not their ability to manage documents, but to manage tabular information. It was VisiCalc—a spreadsheet application, not Word or WordPerfect—that was the "killer app," the application that everyone just had to have on their PC. As such, the rise of the computer would appear to have proceeded along the same lines as the earliest known encoded information—those early notches on bone.

THE RISE OF RECORDS MANAGEMENT PRACTICES
IN U.S. BUSINESS

The following account of records management focuses on the U.S. I found some evidence of the rise of records management in the United Kingdom that parallels America, but not to the degree to which I found evidence in the U.S. Conversations with scholars from several other European countries indicates that records management is an Anglophone invention. I surmise this is a result of the radically different company laws in Anglophone countries and the subsequent rise of management in those countries. Records, however, are not, so there will be points in later chapters where we will turn to definitions from other countries to illustrate how we must define records (and documents).

One of the reasons for the dearth of technological innovation in business from the earliest traders to the middle to late nineteenth century is that commercial ventures, i.e., business, had not undergone dramatic changes in size. The owner still oversaw daily operations, receiving and passing most information verbally. Letters were written to agents and accounts were expected in return, but on a miniscule scale. Risk and opportunity came primarily from outside the organization. According to Alfred D. Chandler, Jr., even in the early nineteenth century, recordkeeping of information within the organization was irrelevant: "The business information the merchants wanted came from external sources not internal records."[21] Before the rise of newspapers, coffeehouses were the main sources of this information. Indeed, Lloyds of London began in 1675 as a coffeehouse. In 1696, recognizing the importance of having information ready at hand for his customers, Lloyd created a broadsheet and "filled it with information on the arrivals and departures of ships and intelligence on conditions abroad and at sea"[22]—thereby providing the external sources of information that commercial enterprises needed.

We can clearly date improvements in methods of managing information within the organization to the rise of large companies that employed many people and were spread over large geographic areas. Alfred Dupont Chandler, following Joseph Litterer,[23] dates these improvements to the rise of systematic management in the late nineteenth and early twentieth centuries, when we see wholesale attention being paid to information and management: "Structure can be defined as the design of organization through which the enterprise is administered. This design, whether formally or informally defined, has two aspects.

It includes, first, the lines of authority and communication between the administrative offices and officers and, second, the information and data flow through these lines of communication and authority. Such lines and such data are essential to assume the effective coordination, appraisal, and planning so necessary in carrying on the basic goals and policies and in knitting together the total resources of the enterprise."[24] Litterer focuses much more on information: "With the increase in the size of the firm, there occurred an increase in the amount of detailed information necessary for efficient operation. To complicate the matter further, this information was now spread among many people instead of being possessed by one central executive as formerly."[25]

JoAnne Yates, in her book *Control through Communication: The Rise of System in American Management*, measures the rise of our current methods of creating and managing documents from several catastrophic train crashes in 1841: "As early as 1841, a series of collisions on the Western Railroad (running between Worcester and West Stockbridge, Massachusetts) prompted its managers and directors to investigate and to tighten managerial control. . . . Downward communication, including the published schedule and rules as well as specific written orders, was formalized as a managerial tool. Furthermore, the final report also established rudimentary records and upward reporting procedures by which management could create a body of knowledge about railroad operations to aid both middle and top management in learning from past mistakes."[26] The creation of records as a tool of management rather than as a memory aid or transaction memorial is thus not created until the late nineteenth and early twentieth centuries. The railroads were the first type of organization to be geographically spread widely enough, to have enough complexity of function and enough employees to require business processes to rise above dependence upon individual and verbal communication.

Where before this time the only crucial business information came from sources external to the company, now an increasing amount of business information, such as what time a train will be at a particular location and for how long, was internal. Yates describes what role records played within systematic management: "In the past only transactions with the external world had been documented; now the systematic management movement suggested that internal practices and procedures also be documented."[27] The role of records was to make each employee a role rather than a personality: "The literature of systematic management proposed many different administrative systems. At the bottom of all of them, however, lay the need to transcend the individual worker and manager in favor of systems institutionalized through records and flows of written communication."[28] To make a profit, it became necessary to have consistent and thorough business information inside the company.

Furthermore, the kind of information within these records was fundamentally different from what previous businesses had created. As Chandler observes in *The Visible Hand*, "Nor did the managers of the first large roads borrow directly from the practices and procedures of military or other
non-business bureaucracies."[29] This is a point of view very different from that
of Max Weber, who noted that all types of routinized organizational behavior
sprang from the rise of bureaucracy in government: "The development of
modern forms of organization in all fields is nothing less than identical with
the development and continual spread of bureaucratic administration. This is
true of church and state, of armies, political parties, economic enterprises, interest groups, endowments, clubs, and many others."[30]

Weber may be forgiven for not understanding the differences between the
rise of large businesses in continental Europe and the United States. According to Litterer, two of the most dramatic differences between business as it
was conducted during the nineteenth century in continental Europe and in the
U.S. are the division of labor within the U.S. that permitted companies to pay
higher salaries to employees, yet maintain a lower cost of goods, and the use
of more and more refined machines in the U.S.[31] Management had to be more
knowledgeable, as well, to manage more complex structures: "In order to
carry out this more extended division of labor, develop more specialized
equipment, and handle larger volumes of production within more restricted
product lines, executives had to be more aware of and more skilled in the exercise of the managerial function."[32] Weber lived in a place and time that was
only beginning to embody this type of division of labor within business.

Conversely, businesses in the U.S. knew only a very tiny federal government until the presidency of Franklin D. Roosevelt—a sharp contrast to Europe, which had seen large governments from the time of Rome. Chandler's
Strategy and Structure is devoted to describing the complex structures necessary to manage this increased division of labor within American businesses
and the correspondingly increased need to manage information: "With the increase in the size of the firm, there occurred an increase in the amount of detailed information necessary for efficient operation. To complicate the matter
further, this information was now spread among many people instead of being possessed by one central executive as formerly."[33]

The enormous increase in information required to run the organization also
meant dividing labor yet again to ensure an employee role for managing information: records managers. As James R. Beniger points out in *The Control
Revolution: Technological and Economic Origins of the Information Society*,
"The shop-order system of accounts based on routing slips developed in the
mid-1870s to control material flows through factories, but by the 1890s a
growing hierarchy of timekeepers and specialized clerks had become neces-

sary to control not these throughputs themselves but their controlling flows of information."[34] W. H. Leffingwell's *Scientific Office Management*, published in 1917, did for records management what Frederick Winslow Taylor's *Principles of Scientific Management,* published in 1911, did for factory management. Leffingwell took Taylor's model of time and motion studies and applied it to information management within the office. By 1917, enough technology and principles of information management had been created to codify them into a field of study. We even find the title "record manager" used in a representation of a 1919 organizational chart for the DuPont Company's sales department;[35] indeed, this is the first use of the professional title I have found.

THE RISE OF RECORDS MANAGEMENT PRACTICES IN U.S. GOVERNMENT

Whether governments were large enough to need records management, complaints within the U.S. government until the late nineteenth century were primarily concerned with the issue of space for storing inactive documents. As Clanchy notes, the notion that a government needed to have an archives came only after the switch from memory to writing to memorialize social, governmental, and commercial events. Archives as repositories of working documents, not books, are a fairly recent idea in human history.

By the late nineteenth century, the government of the U.S. was drowning in documents and was foundering in its efforts to make change. The government's first clear notice of the need for records management was the 1877 fire in Washington, D.C., in which several government buildings full of documents burned. Records management has always been associated with disaster. In response to this particular disaster, President Rutherford B. Hayes appointed a commission, the Hayes Commission, "to examine the several public buildings in this city and determine the nature and extent of their security against conflagration, and the measures to be taken to guard the buildings and their contents from destruction or damage by fire. The records of the government constitute a most valuable collection for the country, whether we consider their pecuniary value or their historical importance, and it becomes my duty to call your attention to the means suggested for securing these valuable archives, as well as the buildings in which they are stored."[36] The analysis and solution recommended by the Hayes Commission do not focus on business processes, but on the creation of new, fireproof buildings and the retrofitting of others: "Navy Department.—Naval Observatory.—The buildings are old and so much worn as not to be susceptible of being remodeled into fireproof structures. The preservation of the valuable instruments and documents in this observatory would seem to demand that a new fire-proof building should be constructed at an early day for the accommodation of the institution."[37]

Recognizing the rapidly increasing volumes of documents under storage, the commission considered destroying documents that were no longer required, but providing more space won out over the management of information:

> What provision, if any, should be made for the custody and safety of files not in constant use. While in some of the departments there are files in constant use that date back to the earliest days of the government, there are in all the departments large numbers of papers no longer needed for constant reference that only add to the quantity of combustible material in the structures, and the consequent danger from fire. The number of papers is increasing rapidly, and in the consideration of the care and preservation of the files this commission has met with the suggestion that many of the papers could well be destroyed. After a careful examination of this question, we do not consider it advisable to recommend this course with any of the records, however unimportant they may appear. Every paper worthy at any time to be recorded and placed on the public files may be of value at some future time, either in a historical, biographical, or pecuniary way, to the citizen or the nation. Papers seemingly of the least importance have been connected with the proof of false demands against the government, and it is scarcely possible to arrive at a decision of what is important to be preserved and what is useless to be destroyed. We therefore recommend, for the relief of the overcrowded buildings, and in view of the rapid increase of the public records, that a fire-proof building of ample dimensions be constructed for the accommodation of the archives of the government no longer required for constant use. This structure should be built in the most approved and thoroughly fire-proof manner, with walls of brick, and so designed that additions can be made from time to time without impairing the general architectural features. Its location should be so remote from all other buildings as to place it beyond danger from exterior fires.[38]

Ten years later, the U.S. Senate appointed another commission, whose objective was to examine business processes to: "Inquire into and Examine the Methods of Business and Work in the Executive Departments, etc., and the Causes of Delays in Transacting the Public Business, etc."[39] The commission's report, published March 8, 1888, looks exhaustively at the myriad activities taking place in the government, particularly bookkeeping. For today's records manager, it is a revealing peek at the way offices were run more than one hundred years ago. Consider, for instance, how copies were made in the War Department: "Copying Letter-press copies into Records. In the examination of these sundry reports it was found by your committee that there were in the different Departments sundry employees engaged in copying from the letter-press copy-books, and from letter-press copies into large record-books, the utility and importance of which work were questionable."[40] Copies of letters were made by pressing them onto a tray filled with a type of gelatin to make a negative copy, and then pressing a blank page on the gelatin to receive a positive copy. Those positive copies are then put in a type of binder with other copies in chronological order. Employees in the War Department were hand-writing copies of those gel copies and keeping them in yet another book. Even then, this was considered to be unnecessary: "In the opinion of your committee there is no necessity for the copying of letters from letter-press books into the large record-books, or from the letter-press copy sheets into such records, and that the letter-press copies when the originals are written with best quality of inks, upon the best quality of paper, and the press copies therefrom taken upon the best quality of paper, are sufficiently durable and permanent for the records of the Government, and consequently much labor and the time of many employees are expended to no beneficial purpose. And such work should be discontinued."[41]

Unfortunately, no experts existed to help with the resolution of this and other problems; solutions are created by individuals who may be bright, but have no training. As the report recommends: "The most feasible and practical remedy your committee can suggest, is for the Secretary of the Treasury and the Secretary of War to select a committee or commission of three competent, industrious, painstaking officers or employees of their respective departments most familiar with the existing methods of business therein, and with correct, proper, and prompt methods of business methods generally, and not wedded to the idea that the age of the existing methods has made them the only correct and proper ones, or that any change therein will be an improvement."[42]

One solution created for pension files is described in detail because of the dramatic improvement in work being performed by the department: "The reforms in the system and methods of business introduced by Dr. F. C. Ainsworth since he took charge of the record and pension division of the Surgeon-General's Office, in the December, 1886, are most manifest and most commendable. He has reduced the entire work of the division, one of the largest in any of the departments—having by law 280 employees—to a uniform method and an exact system seldom found in any branch of the government service, and yet remarkably plain and simple in operation and accurate in its results, enabling each employee to perform the maximum amount of work in the minimum of time, and enabling him, as chief of the division, to know daily the exact condition of all the work in his office, and the amount and character of work performed by every employee, and where the delays

occur."[43] The key to the solution is the creation of an index for the multitudi-
nous documents:

> But the most prominent feature in his system is the application of the well-known
> library-card-index system to a card-index record, which is a card containing not
> only an index to every hospital record book wherein a soldier's name appears, but
> also containing the entire record of such soldier, and is therefore properly de-
> scribed as a "card-index record." Upon the nearly 19,000 volumes of hospital
> records over 7,000,000 of names are entered of record, the name of the same sol-
> dier often occurring many times not only on one record-book but some times on
> several. In addition to answering the 9,511 calls on hand December 13, 1886, he
> has caused to be answered promptly the current calls from day to day in most
> cases in two and three days after receipt of call. And still, in addition to this, he
> has prepared the cards and introduced his card-index-record system, and had,
> since April up to December 17, 1887, made 600,000 card-index records, nearly
> one-tenth of the entire work of making card-index records of all the 7,000,000 of
> soldiers' names appearing on the hospital records. And as the names on each hos-
> pital record are transcribed therefrom to the card-index record, the amount of
> work to complete the card-index-record system of all the records is reduced, and
> the means for answering promptly all calls for such records increased. All this
> work has been done not only without any increase of force, but with a reduction
> of the number of employees in the division on the work. It is reasonably certain
> that this system, with the present force allowed by law, can be completed within
> eighteen to twenty-four months, and then we will have a card-index record con-
> taining the name of every soldier appearing on any of the hospital records in that
> office, and showing the record where it appears, however often it may have been
> written, and also containing an exact transcript or copy of all the entries therein
> of record, arranged by regiments in alpho-alphabetical order. These card-index
> records dispense with the necessity of any reference whatever to the original
> record, except only in case of a dispute as to their correctness, and can and should
> be, as soon as completed, printed in book form.[44]

An example of the records created by this process is included. Ainsworth created and included metrics to demonstrate the effectiveness of his method. The
efficacy of this project may be suspect, however, as it was self-reported via a
letter from Ainsworth and not checked by the members of the commission.

This example makes reference to the "library-card-index system," which
was indeed invented by and for librarians. Ainsworth called his cards a "card-
index-record system" presumably because he was creating a new document,
the card, which has as much value as the original. What this method constitutes, however, is the abstraction of relevant information from a document,
that abstraction then written on a card and placed in an order different from
the order the document is kept in. The documents can then be accessed from

different angles. This is a remarkable technology. Rather than creating a summary report, the features of the document are dissected in order to make it more useful—so useful that the card itself has an intrinsic value.

The Senate report includes descriptions of other interesting and detailed processes for the Customs Department, Mail and Files Division,[45] the State Department, Bureau of Indexes and Archives,[46] and the Post-Office Department, Clerks of Files and Records.[47] Unlike what Ainsworth reported above, these accounts demonstrate how clerks were used to register all correspondence by routing all correspondence, incoming and outgoing, through them. In most of the examples above, however, the clerks in the offices in question are bottlenecks.

Unlike the Hayes Commission, which was loath to destroy inactive records, this Senate report not only recommends destroying records, but quotes precedent in the budgets of previous years for doing so:

> Upon an examination of the laws now existing in reference to any sale or other disposition of such valueless papers, it was found that in "An act making the appropriations for the legislative, executive, and judicial expenses of the Government for the fiscal year ending June 30, 1882, and for other purposes," approved March 3, 1881, on page 412, 21 Statutes, is the following provision: "That the Postmaster-General is hereby authorized to sell as waste paper, or otherwise dispose of, the files of papers which have accumulated or may accumulate in the Post-Office Department that are not needed in the transaction of current business and have no permanent value or historical interest; and the proceeds of said sales he shall pay into the Treasury and make report thereof to Congress." And that in "An act making appropriations for sundry civil expenses of the Government for the fiscal year ending June 30, 1883, and for other purposes," approved August 7, 1882, is the following provision: "And it shall be the duty of the Clerk and Door-keeper of the House of Representatives and the Secretary and Sergeant-at-arms of the Senate to cause to be sold all waste paper and useless documents and condemned furniture that have accumulated during the fiscal year 1882, or that may hereafter accumulate in their respective departments or offices under the direction of the Committee on Accounts of their respective houses, and cover the proceeds thereof into the Treasury; and they shall at the beginning of each regular session of Congress report to their respective houses the amount of said sales." These were the only provisions of law found by your committee in regard to sales or other disposition of such files and papers.[48]

The reader will recall that in the nineteenth century, paper was quite valuable and not thrown away, but recycled. While this does not constitute a retention schedule, it certainly reflects an understanding that documents become useless and can be destroyed.

The Taft report, a Congressional report issued in 1913 by the U.S. House of Representatives, began a trend within government reports on records, as it wistfully reflected that the private sector has the records problem solved: "After careful detail inquiry the commission has been led to the conclusion that in the office of the Adjutant General there has been an insistent attachment to this elaborate method of carding and cross referencing the great volume of current correspondence handled by the office, which has stood in the way of the introduction of improved office practice which has been so marked in recent years in private corporations. . . . The Adjutant General's Office is some 25 years behind the times."[49] The "carding" system referred to is one in which the correspondence itself is folded, a brief description of the topic is written on the fold, then a copy of the correspondence is copied onto an index card—all by hand. At this time, typewriters, gel press copies (see drawing below), and carbon paper were in common use in industry. The report contains descriptions of aspects of records management within eight agencies within the federal government, but primarily of the Adjutant General's office—a complex discussion that consumes 480 pages out of a total 923-page report, covering many different offices and sets of records. It includes discussions of the cost of real estate taken up by files,[50] as well as of measures of efficiency.[51]

Figure 1.3.   1886 Bailey's Gel Press with Moistening Attachment.
Courtesy Early Office Museum

In many instances, the argument that the Taft report gives for doing things differently is the practice in industry; for example, the government practice of folding, then filing correspondence: "The universal practice in commercial concerns is to file correspondence flat, and this likewise is the practice in most of the offices of the Government;"[52] writing notes on the back of folded correspondence (briefing): "Briefing is unheard of in commercial concerns, and is fast being discontinued in the executive departments;"[53] making duplicates of all correspondence on index cards (writing of record cards): "With the installation of modern filing systems, both in outside business concerns and in the offices of the Government, the practical necessity of such record, either book [registers] or card [record card], is rapidly disappearing;"[54] and on the use of forms: "It is the custom in many offices of the Government, as well as in most commercial concerns, where incoming correspondence or reports have to be made the subject of routine corrective action."[55]

One of the more interesting discussions of the Taft report and in a legal brief presented in Appendix III of the report is whether one technology, gel press copying, makes a document more authentic for legal purposes than carbon copying. Court rulings indicate that at this time the gel press is considered of secondary evidentiary value to the original (meaning that an explanation of why the original cannot be found must be produced), whereas the carbon is considered to be of primary evidentiary value. The gel press copy (see example in figure 1.3) is believed, by the same Adjutant General's Office cited above, to be a superior copy because it has a signature on it, whereas the carbon copies do not. Despite the presence of the signature, it is still a copy. The carbon copy is considered superior as evidence in court because it is made at the same time and by the same method as the original: "By the overwhelming weight of judicial authority, however, the carbon copy, being made by the same process and at the same time as the original, is regarded as primary evidence, and therefore introduceable [*sic*] as such without notice to the other side."[56] The report also provides a look into the filing systems of the government of the time as well as the solutions implemented by business at the time, including methods of filing, tracking with the use of indexes, the legality of copies, and basing the management of people and space using economic terms.

It should be noted that, of the cases cited in the Taft report's Appendix III legal brief concerning the adequacy of gel press copies versus carbon copies for the Adjutant General's office, most of the examples cited are commercial cases. Indeed, the Taft report provides little evidence that records management had its origin in government. The continual references to "commercial concerns" and "business concerns" indicates that businesses were far in the lead and in many instances appear to have served as the model for a government seeking practices to manage its records. Chester L. Guthrie demonstrates this quite well. He documents no advances provided by government in records management until after World War II. However, Guthrie's article does not give convincing evidence that the government contributed anything of significance even after World War II. I will describe below how government archivists "completed" records management into what we know today.[57]

THE RISE OF RECORDS MANAGEMENT AS A DISCIPLINE

As mentioned previously, the first use of the term "records management" I have identified is in the organizational chart for the Sales Department of the DuPont Company for 1919–1921. The "Sales Record Manager," along with other administrative roles, reports to the Wilmington Office Bureaus, headed by the General Director of Sales.[58] The next documentation I have found is in the title of a set of catalogs by the Acme Visible Records, Inc., "Trade catalogs on card-based filing systems for records management in business . . ."[59] dating from 1931. I have been unable to locate periodical literature dating before World War II that uses the term. After that, the next listing for a book in the Online Computer Library Center (OCLC) catalog to have "records management" in its title is the *Procedure Manual for Records Management* for the United States Department of Agriculture, Office of Plant and Operations, published in 1942.[60] After World War II, however, the term appears to have entered common parlance.

Before the term "records management" became common, our activities were regarded as a part of the systematic management movement, falling under the rubric of "the office" and usually referred to by terms such as filing and indexing. One of the earliest products of this trend was J. William Schulze's book, *The American Office: Its Organization, Management and Records,*[61] published in 1913. From the beginning of the application of systematic management, office documents were referred to as records. Schulze's book is among those most often quoted on this subject. The chapters of this book describe the different types of records to be handled: correspondence, purchasing and storeroom records, production order systems, records for credit and collection departments, records for advertising and sales departments, and for other office systems.

One of the most striking themes of the book is how records are treated as part of a business process. Management of documents is described in the context of each department and activity. For example, in the chapter titled "Purchasing and Storeroom Records,"[62] Schulze describes the various systems: requisition system, perpetual inventory, order system, and receiving system.

In each section, he describes the purpose of each workflow and the method of authority, and gives examples of the types of forms and how they would be used.

Another theme is the seriousness with which Schulze recommends records be taken and the training of employees who handle records. He recommends an order of magnitude increase in salary for the person managing records, as well as a particular course of study: "The fundamental reason [there is considerable confusion in the filing departments of most business concerns] is the fact that usually an office boy or an $8 a week girl, with absolutely no training in classification and filing, is assigned to the important position of file clerk. . . . It is worth from $75 to $200 per month, depending upon the size of the concern, so that any papers in the files can be produced at a moment's notice. A capable young woman or young man with library training should be employed and should be given complete responsibility for the proper handling of the files."[63]

Schulze also describes the various technologies used, in chronological order of development, to hold files: "The first file we know anything about was the stick or spindle file with its sharp point sticking in the air. This was followed by the box file, containing the index of 25 or 26 pieces of manila paper, tabbed with the letters of the alphabet and fastened into a box at one side, the papers being filed between these sheets. The flat file came next. This was based on almost the same principle as the box file except that a drawer was used and only one division of the alphabet placed in each drawer. These divisions were further subdivided to allow for closer range in filing. The latest development for filing is the vertical file and it would seem that this efficient method of filing correspondence has come to stay for some time, although some concerns still use the pasteboard, cloth covered box files. Except in isolated cases the vertical file cabinet either in wood or metal has become the standard equipment."[64] The vertical file was considered such a marvelous invention that it was displayed as a grand improvement in technology at the 1893 World's Fair in Chicago. (The reader will recall that the Taft report recommended "flat filing" over folding and filing.) The difference between the flat file and the vertical is that the documents were kept on end in a drawer, whereas the flat file was kept on its broad side.

Schulze also dealt with the various types of systems: Straight Alphabetic, Subject or Topical Alphabetic, Geographic, Chronologic, Numeric, Subject Decimal, and Combined Alphabetic and Numeric. He describes each of these and the relationship each has to card indices. He differentiates Decimal filing systems from other numbering systems because of their relationship to the Dewey Decimal library system. In those systems, groups of files are differentiated by subject, just as in the library system. Each subject is further differentiated. He gives the example of a railroad classification: General, Executive, Finance and Accounts, Railway, Equipment and Shops, Transportation and Storage, Traffic, Local Facilities and Affairs.[65] Interestingly, he does not recognize that the divisions within the railroad system cited here happen to correspond to function. This is striking, as the concurrent reorganizations of the major corporations described by Chandler are all focused on function. For example, DuPont tried organizing along geographical lines, along product lines, and finally settled along lines representing major business activities. This method of classification continues today.

What we call records retention was termed "transferring" by that era. According to Schulze, correspondence was transferred to the lower drawers of a four-drawer vertical cabinet at the end of the year, then to storage boxes; the location of the boxes is not indicated. These are then destroyed at the end of seven years, according to the statute of limitation in the state in which the business is located. Schulze further indicates that not all documents from a set must be destroyed together.[66] It is important to note that Schulze used the term "records" to refer to all sets of documents within the organization. Most of his remaining chapters on the various office systems include sample business forms to be used, as well as descriptions of how the business processes work and how the documents fit in.

The period from 1913 through 1919 saw the creation and publication of many manuals on filing and indexing. *Indexing and Filing: A Manual of Standard Practice,* by E. R. Hudders,[67] published in 1916, covers geographic filing, subject filing, information and data files, catalog and pamphlet filing, purchase records, sales records, credit records, sales invoices, purchase invoices, checks and vouchers, electrotypes and cuts, legal filing, architectural filing, and accountant files in addition to transferring, lost papers, classing and grouping of records and index card systems.

W. H. Leffingwell's *Scientific Office Management,* published in 1917, is a more general study of the office.[68] Leffingwell had worked with Frederick Winslow Taylor (author of *Principles of Scientific Management*, published in 1911) and was the first to publish on the application of systematic or scientific management to the office. The book deals with correspondence, "files that really remember," "when to use card files," and "saving thousands with standardized forms." Leffingwell includes an extract from the Westinghouse Electric and Manufacturing Company filing manual.[69] This last inclusion is another piece of evidence that it was the application of systematic management in "business concerns" which led to the development of the field of records management.[70]

During that period, many more books were written from varying perspectives; for example, William David Wigent's *Modern Filing and How to File:*

Figure 1.4.   1886 Shannon Cabinet File from the Schlicht Field Co., Rochester, NY.
Courtesy Early Office Museum

A Textbook on Office System[71] appeared in 1920. Wigent's book was primarily a description, with pictures, of the many different types of technologies used in filing: box files, loose-sheet cabinets, "Shannon"[72] board files (spindled files) see figure 1.4 , "Shannon" drawer and perforator, vertical files and compressors, vertical folders and guides, copying books used with gel press (letter press), letter press, and the rapid roller copier (another gel press). One of the more interesting technologies is the various card systems illustrated that include metal follow-up indicators, the predecessors of today's "tickler" files.

Another topic Wigent covers is "Document and Check Filing,"[73] in which he describes the filing of "documents." According to Wigent, the term "document" refers to how the paper is folded: "The term 'document' is usually applied to a folded paper measuring about 4 × 10 inches." These are primarily records that are associated with major personal and business activities, some needing to be recorded with the government, including "insurance policies, leases, vouchers, affidavits, legal notices, and papers filed with government officials, such as copies of mortgages, certificates of incorporation and many others are in this class."[74] This use of the term "document" is somewhat indicative of how in the U.S. the terms "record" and "document" differ even today. Wigent does not use the term "record," but we use it to refer to everything we handle, whereas we use the term "documents" to refer to captured information with a separate importance to business or personal activity that may or may not be part of a large set of documents.[75] Similar to Schulze, Wigent also deals with "transferring," which he defines as "clearing out the original file to make room for the current papers, and putting the old papers in storage or transfer cases." He does not indicate that records are destroyed.

James N. McCord's *A Textbook of Filing,* published in 1920,[76] covers similar ground, including the routing of mail. McCord also treats the destruction of records, suggesting that each company needs to deal with this on its own. He suggests, for example, evaluating correspondence according to statutes of limitation and to the collection of debt as a guide (see figure 1.5).[77]

Ethel E. Scholfield appears to have been a records manager, holding the professional title of "File Systematizer" at DuPont and National Aniline and Chemical Company. She published *Filing Department Operation and Control: From the Standpoint of the Management* in 1923.[78] This text appears to be the first to have been published by someone who actually worked in records management. Her work is notable in that it is a more complete treatment that includes assessing and training employees. In a section on Transferring, she differentiates the status and value of records for consideration of destruction: "1. Records which treat of policy and standard practice. These are the law. They must be kept indefinitely as a basis of authority. . . . They

Figure 1.5. 1886 U.S. Document File Cabinet, Office Specialty Manufacturing Co., Rochester, NY.
Courtesy Early Office Museum

may be considered permanent. 2. Records which are in the nature of sum-
maries and reports. . . . The value of statistics depends very largely upon the
length of time over which comparisons may be made. The time these should
be kept in the files depends upon their nature and the record system in use.
But as a class, this type of material is semi-permanent. 3. Records which deal
with specific cases and routine matters. Orders, routine sales and manufacturing memoranda, etc., come in this class. Daily and weekly routine reports
are also usually put into this class, because if they are of lasting interest they
are usually summarized in reports covering longer periods. These as a class
may be considered of temporary value."[79]

Scholfield also makes comments on the classification plan for a business—
comments that are of interest today, as we have many of the same miscon-
ceptions wherein master classification plans are incorrectly made according
to organizational charts: "It has been the custom for years to build the file
classification on the same lines as the organization chart, putting each small
unit as a subdivision of the next larger unit. This is most natural and logical,
but it presents many unnecessary mechanical difficulties which are easily
avoided if the less familiar but more practical scheme outlined is adopted."[80]
Her first reason for using the simplified scheme is identical to reasons given
today concerning the need for stability in the schedule: "1. The filing arrangement is more stable. It does not reflect company organization to such an extent that file numbers have to be changed or material transferred every time
there is a change in business organization. In this connection it is well to remember that a healthy business is a live and growing thing, and as such, is
ever in a state of flux with, it seems, ever-shifting lines of responsibility."[81]
Scholfield's simplified scheme is to use the functions of the corporation as a
guide.

Another work by a records manager is *Filing Methods* by Eugenia Wallace,
published in 1923.[82] Wallace was the supervisor of library and bond filing at
Guaranty Trust Company of New York. Her work was written for the file specialist, not for the manager. Wallace was the first to define "records," a term
which "includes not only every record used in either the commercial or professional world, but also all other types of special records which are kept for
reference." She includes index cards, whether used as indices or as records
themselves.[83] While not commendable as a definition per se, this definition is
notable for its inclusion of things which even today some would exclude.

Not to be outdone, the Library Bureau, the company begun by Melvil
Dewey in 1876 to design library furniture, also created a textbook, *Progressive Indexing and Filing for Schools,* published in 1927.[84] This work is most
notable for the number of photographs of filing technologies and the quality
of its illustrations.

In the 1930s, there were fewer filing manuals and more general business manuals. These business manuals were a continuation of the business advice and business texts of the earlier part of the century. Each of them includes a section on filing and correspondence. Like Leffingwell's 1917 study of the office, these publications emphasize the business owner's or the manager's point of view. Some, such as Charles W. Gerstenberg's *Principles of Business,* published in 1918, limit their discussion of filing practices to chapters on office management.[85] Others, such as Frank C. McClelland's *Office Training and Standards* published in 1919, have several chapters devoted to the subject of filing and correspondence.[86]

The first textbook to use the term "records management" in its title was Margaret K. Odell and Earl P. Strong's *Records Management and Filing Operations,* published in 1947.[87] Odell was a records manager who had worked for the office equipment manufacturer Remington Rand. Strong also worked at Remington Rand, in the Typewriter Division's Utilization Department. By this time, the concept of "transferring" had become known as "retention," and all the activities previously described by Scholfield are included under the rubric of records management.

As these books show, the basics of filing, the need for and use of indices, overall systems of classification, retention or transferring, different treatments for different types of records, the need for trained personnel, and a concern for the appropriate use of technology are all found before 1925. What was lacking, however, was a framework to tie all of these activities together. Each activity addressed a different phase of what we now call the life cycle, but the notion of the life cycle and the risk management side of records had yet to be explored.

THE U.S. GOVERNMENT'S ROLE:
PROVIDING THE FRAMEWORK

As we have seen in the U.S., records management developed first in business in the late nineteenth and early twentieth centuries, with the invention of office management. Government began to appropriate the successful practices of business in its management of records, following a series of Congressional commissions. It was not until 1934 that the U.S. National Archives Records Service (NARS) was established by congressional act, in recognition of the increasingly critical need for a central repository for the nation's increasing volume of records. At this stage of the history of records management, it was government archivists who made their own significant contributions to the discipline, creating the framework that had been missing in "filing and indexing."

In the late 1930s and early 1940s, a number of archivists were publishing articles in the *American Archivist* on the problem of records. Many of these archivists had either worked for the U.S. National Archives or were staff liaisons; Emmett Leahy, for example, was the Navy staff liaison, and Helen Chatfield was the Treasury liaison. It was Chatfield who coined the term "life cycle management" in 1940, as part of an article describing why records needed the application of management skills, not administration.[88] Chatfield lists three phases of the life cycle: "1. The period of accumulation and current use; 2. The period of infrequent governmental use; and 3. The period of historical use."[89] Despite the fact that the concept of life cycle is one of our most important tools, even now most texts do not discuss it in detail (see chapter 5 for further discussion of the life cycle concept and its role in records management).

One of the greatest challenges for employees of the National Archives "was the development of principles and procedures for tackling the mammoth record problem. The accumulation of more than a century and a half totaled nearly 10,000,000 cubic feet of records scattered throughout the country. . . . Most of these records, of course, did not possess values sufficient to warrant their continued preservation, and therein lay the greatest task before the staff: the appraisal of thousands of series to determine which records could, with the approval of Congress, be disposed of and which of the residue could be accepted by the National Archives."[90] When records management developed in the U.S. government, it did so because the U.S. government was inundated with records.

The notion of retention and disposition schedules appears to have been created by employees of the National Archives in 1941 as a way of managing this problem.[91] They were the first to address the problem of "transferring" using the concept of schedules. Of course, the National Archives did not have the authority to manage this problem, as it—i.e., the volumes of records— was created within the branches and agencies of government. Rather, the "mammoth record problem" was simply inherited by the National Archives.

One of the solutions was to enlist the aid of the Training Division of the Civil Service Commission, which would invite persons from each agency to a meeting to discuss "records administration." That committee, the Interdepartmental Committee on Records Administration, came together to address: "1. Interchange of ideas of various members of the committee on records procedures and problems, 2. Discussion of the principles of filing, 3. Review and analysis of the systems of records management in the various Agencies, 4. Drawing up of materials for filing manuals, 5. Planning for the training of records clerks and supervisors."[92] The subcommittees were divided into groups to study mail or correspondence management; filing and charge-out systems; classification, retirement, and disposal; space, forms, and equipment standards; personnel tracking and standards; and organization and administration. The "retirement and disposal" section makes reference to "disposition schedules" that had been developed within the Department of Agriculture, Office of Plant and Operation, and which were outlined in its manual and published in 1941.

By 1947, when Odell and Strong published their records management textbook, the expression "retention and disposition schedule" had become a term of art and had the same meaning which we give it.[93] What made the schedule work was the tracking of the classification of records to their disposition rather than just to finding them via their function within the business: "One of the greatest factors in the saving of overhead expense is the proper classification and indexing to provide for the segregation of vital and important records from temporarily useful records and grading them according to their life value."[94] The methods for creating the schedule, the executive authority required to execute the program, and the records committees for oversight are the same. The textbook does not outline a vital records program, but it does ask about the value of records that are vital.[95]

Odell and Strong also define records, but they do so with the knowledge that business concerns and government both must manage records: "Records provide the facts necessary for successful management of an individual's affairs, a government agency, a profession, an institution, or a business. A description of every important action, transaction, or policy is written on paper. Papers are records, or the source of records, which are filed to furnish administrative management with information about previous activities and the results obtained by actions taken."[96] Again, this is not a commendable definition *qua* definition, but it points in the direction of actions taken within business. Unfortunately, however, it points more to "documents" as outlined above: insurance policies, mortgages, etc., than it does to the captured information within an organization. The reason for the odd definition is perhaps because Odell came from the world of business, and Strong had previously been chair of the Interdepartmental Committee on Records Administration, noted above. While on the Committee, he worked for the Training Division of the Civil Service Commission, the U.S. Office of Education, and then Remington Rand, where he met Odell.

Odell and Strong created a set of competencies required by a records "administrator": "1. Routing incoming mail; 2. Rendering a decision as the correct subject title for a record; 3. Training the personnel to select the correct filing caption; 4. Indexing, cross-referencing, sorting, and arranging records; 5. Assigning work and fixing responsibility for quality and quantity of work performed; 6. Producing immediately the records required or knowing who has the records; and 7. Effecting disposition of records."[97] These are the same basic competencies required today, with the additional requirements of more communication, technology, management, and understanding of legal issues which raise the bar much higher for current records managers. Interestingly, Odell and Strong provide no section on classification. In the index listing for "Classification of records," the reader is directed to "Indexing."[98] Under "indexing," there is no reference to classification—although there is a section labeled "Indexing (Classifying) the Records," in which many issues are jumbled together, including alphabetical filing rules and subjects and functions.[99] Odell and Strong's work was very much a "how-to" book, as many of its predecessors and successors were and continue to be.

The greatest impact on government records came with World War II when an unprecedented number of documents of a truly transitory nature were created and the volume of the records maintained by the U.S. government grew from eleven million cubic feet to nineteen million cubic feet. By the end of the second world war, government archivists were pleading for authority and procedures to staunch the flow of documents into the archives, as well as for authorization to destroy documents of no continuing value to the government, the citizens, or to future scholars. One of the outcomes of this special pleading was a report written in 1949 by Emmett Leahy as part of what is currently called the first "Hoover Commission Report" on records management in the U.S. government.[100] This report shares many of the objectives of the Taft report of 1913, but it focuses primarily on the Navy and to a lesser degree on other military agencies, as well as the Tennessee Valley Authority (TVA), which, as a large federal public works project, was generating a considerable volume of records.

Leahy's recommendations reflect the previous fifty years of records management in industry. His list of recommendation reads like the table of contents for Robek, Maedke, and Brown, third edition: copy control, automation, correspondence control, forms control, reports management, active records, micrographics, mailroom management, vital records, and retention schedules.[101] His discussion includes many of the arguments for records management, such as the elimination of more than 50 percent of records from office and plant.[102] What caught the eye of business, the government, and legislators were the retention schedules consigning records management to the management of retired documents, which Leahy laments in the second Hoover Commission report.

Leahy himself considered this change of emphasis to retired documents to be lamentable, and he addressed this issue in 1955 in the second Hoover Commission Report,[103] which he also wrote. The report was written in two parts, "Records Management" and "Paperwork Management," because, as Leahy regretfully acknowledged, records management is by that date too strongly associated with the retirement, destruction, or archiving of records.[104] Leahy either invented or borrowed the term "paperwork management" to describe the creation, distribution, and active use of documents that includes correspondence management, forms, reports, directives, active records, and mail management.[105] Part II of the report, concerning the paperwork that citizens and companies create for the government, covers what we currently understand by "paperwork."

According to Schellenberg, private business began the management practice called records management in the U.S. through the control of the creation of records: "In the United States, business firms were the first to inaugurate formal programs for standardizing and simplifying paper work."[106] Writing in 1956, by "paper work" Schellenberg is referring to what we now regard as the first part of the life cycle.

RECENT DEVELOPMENTS IN THE
HISTORY OF RECORDS MANAGEMENT

The practice of records management remained fairly stable until the early 1960s, when the federal government's increased used of computer technology resulted in a requirement for the preservation of either whole databases or backup tapes, along with all the other software and hardware to read them. Despite some spectacular losses, such as the entire 1960 set of Census data, the people assigned muddled through.[107] Private business destroyed, migrated, or converted their data continuously. Indeed, some applications created in the 1960s are still in use and may even be running on a mainframe or are emulated on a PC.[108]

On the whole, it should be said that NARS, and then the National Archives and Records Administration (NARA; the name was changed to reflect the need for employees of the National Archives to have some say in the role of records when they are active) have done an admirable job with these "electronic records." What they recognized early on with respect to this new format was that the document was the entire system. Just as we need eyes and appropriate ambient environment to read a paper document, the entire system is required for the machine to read the database and interpret it for us to read. In 1964, IBM produced a typewriter that could store input to electronic tape and then replay it again. The activity performed by this typewriter/tape system was called "word processing." In 1969, IBM introduced magnetic cards that were the same shape and size as computer punch cards, but were magnetic. These were used primarily for form letters for which additional information, such as name and address, had to be added manually.

In the 1970s, the proliferation of mini-computers made computation available to small and medium-sized companies. The major purpose for those computers was computation of tables of numbers, not the production of documents. While products were available that permitted the creation and editing of text documents, even those who had access to such machines often preferred the "smart" typewriters that had become available. The two types of machines, data processing and word processing, remained separate until the early 1980s.

In 1972, Lexitron introduced machines that performed word processing, but with a cathode-ray tube for viewing the output and then sending it to print. Vydec introduced a word-processing system in 1973 that used floppy disks, increasing the number of pages that could be stored per unit of magnetic storage from one page to approximately one hundred. All of these products were hard-wired—i.e., the hardware and software were one. The amount of storage on a floppy drive meant that individual applications could reside on a floppy disk and be uploaded for use inside a computer, a development that introduced the opportunity for a computer to run both data-processing and word-processing applications on the same piece of hardware. WordStar, first released in 1979, was the first commercially successful word-processing application to run on microcomputers. The final output of all these word processors were hard-copy versions of the electronic file. Essentially, word processors were typesetting products. Databases functioned the same way, producing a hard-copy report or a form as their output.

Microcomputers first became commercially viable in the early 1980s. As noted previously, what made them "must-have" devices was the spreadsheet application VisiCalc, not their word-processing capabilities. To share information on a computer, people worked from terminals linked to the same computer, and sharing electronic copies generally meant sharing floppy disks. Separate computers, such as PCs, did not really get linked together until the late 1980s, using local area networks (LANs). While LANs took some of the sharing and storage burden away for databases as well as documents such as manuals, they added devices capable of storage. This development had the unintended effect of creating more electronic copies—for instance, one on the C-drive, one on removable disk, and one on the server.

The Internet email that linked universities to enable researchers to collaborate and share their work became popular among many faculty and administrators for correspondence and collaboration. Inside some companies, this capability was mimicked using internal applications that were accessible only within the company; unlike the universities, companies could not send or receive email outside the organization. Word processing did not change significantly in its purpose; it was still a typesetting product for creating hard copy.

The commercial availability of facsimile (fax) machines made it possible for people to send images of documents to anyone else who had a fax machine. Copying machines using xerographic technologies began to be sold at prices that were sufficiently reasonable that most organizations could afford them, making copies an affordable and easily to acquire technology. Overall, the information and communications technology of this decade is notable for having set the stage for the unintended consequence of the proliferation of copies.

In the early 1990s, the World Wide Web (a technology that uses a browser and hypertext markup language [HTML] to represent text, pictures, and links to permit creating virtual relationships among documents), was added to the Internet and made available to anyone who had a computer, browser, phone line, and Internet service provider. This permitted nearly anyone to use email. Package delivery, courier services, and facsimile systems were still used to deliver documents. We were still composing in word processing and spreadsheet applications, but instead of printing those documents and sending them, we began to send them as attachments, whereupon the recipients printed the "attached" documents. But the World Wide Web was also responsible for yet another paradigm shift in computing. Because anyone with Internet access could access any Internet server, companies began making applications available on the web. Completing web forms, making inquiries via "customer self-service," then purchasing—electronic commerce—became common activities.

Until the late 1990s, computers essentially made electronic copies of hardcopy documents. The electronic documents were kept on individual computers and disks because sharing the files was complicated. Many companies had very poor back-up procedures, so few copies existed there. Because the electronic copies were not stored on servers, there was very little identifying information (metadata). Because the electronic copies were ordinarily in the possession of the author, there was not much need for electronic copies. In the late 1990s, however, email became a composition, message transportation, and delivery technology that also permitted the attachment of documents, and the proliferation of copies began to increase exponentially.

Until the late 1990s, the knowledge required to practice records management could remain relatively stagnant. With the installation of email, document management, imaging, workflow, and PDA technologies, among others, copies of documents were being created and unintentionally being hidden in very creative places. Employees became comfortable with computer technology and began to use email for the same purposes to which they made use of the telephone or the office break room: telling questionable jokes, gossiping, or accessing pornography—and then sharing it all with friends. Recognizing the scope of this workplace behavior, plaintiff's attorneys began asking for all of these documents—logs, appointment calendars, etc.—documents that in the past would never have been either created or stored. Methods for finding documents and document fragments also arose, such as restoring from the computer "dustbin" that sometimes make finding more complicated than it ever had been previously in even the most disorganized of offices.

Knowledge of technology has become a competency that is increasingly required of employees—such as knowledge of the many different ways a Blackberry can send a message or email, or knowing to ask the information technology department what it needs to store in cache. While the principles of records management are the same, technology has definitely created opportunities for records managers to exercise some of our most little-known tools—tools such as version control and copy control. We are also challenged by the number of media, particularly audio and visual, that have arisen and become extinct within the past 60 years.

The timeline of records management as seen in Figure 1.6, shows that the greatest complexities have been visited upon our profession within only the past 130 years. The rise of modern office equipment dates only from 1874, and the word processor from the mid-1960s. These, together with the invention and subsequent widespread use of carbon paper and the photocopier, are responsible for the beginning of the proliferation of copies within the organizations for which we work. In the figure below, it is quite easy to see that the rise of technology has had the secondary effect of increasing the volume of

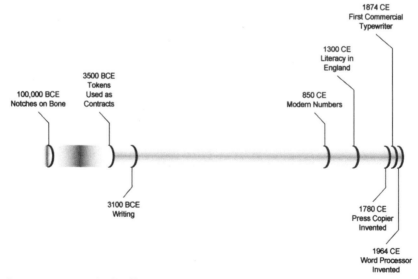

Figure 1.6.   Records Timeline.

what we must manage—although not always with a corresponding expansion of our portfolios within the organization.

The past century has held two transformative eras for records management. The development of "filing and indexing" in the early twentieth century was one of the effects of the geographic spread and increase in size and complexity of the firm. In this period, basic techniques were developed for active records. As the U.S. government grew in the second half of the twentieth century, government employees worked to develop a framework for "records management." Unfortunately, the work of the government, particularly the Hoover Commission reports authored by Emmett Leahy, created the impression that records management was concerned primarily with the semiactive and inactive stages of the records life cycle. We are now undergoing another great transformation, in which the proliferation of electronic records and the use (and abuse) of messaging technology may well restore the first half of the life cycle—i.e., the period from creation through active use—to our portfolio.

NOTES

1. Denise Schmandt-Besserat, *Before Writing: Volume I, From Counting to Cuneiform* (Austin: University of Texas Press, 1992), 158.

2. Georges Ifrah, *The Universal History of Numbers: From Prehistory to the Invention of the Computer* (New York: John Wiley & Sons, 2000), 401.

3. Ifrah, 420–421.

4. Ifrah, 578.

5. Ifrah, 588.

6. Schmandt-Besserat, 163.

7. Schmandt-Besserat, 165.

8. Maria Brosius, "Ancient Archives and Concepts of Record-Keeping: An Introduction," 1–16, in *Ancient Archives and Archival Traditions: Concepts of Record-Keeping in the Ancient World,* edited by Maria Brosius (Oxford: Oxford University Press, 2003), 12.

9. Karel Van Lerberghe, "Private and Public: The Ur-Utu Archive at Sippar-Amnanum (Tell ed-Der)," 59–77, in *Ancient Archives and Archival Traditions: Concepts of Record-Keeping in the Ancient World,* edited by Maria Brosius (Oxford: Oxford University Press, 2003), 74–75.

10. Brosius, 13–15; Piotr Steinkeller, "Archival Practices at Babylonia in the Third Millenium," 37–58, in *Ancient Archives and Archival Traditions: Concepts of Record-Keeping in the Ancient World,* edited by Maria Brosius (Oxford: Oxford University Press, 2003), 39; and Van Lerberghe, 68.

11. Alfonso Archi, "Archival Record-Keeping at Ebla 2400–2350 BC," 17–36, in *Ancient Archives and Archival Traditions: Concepts of Record-Keeping in the Ancient World,* edited by Maria Brosius (Oxford: Oxford University Press, 2003).

12. I am indebted to my husband for this observation.

13. M. T. Clanchy, *From Memory to Written Record: England 1066–1307,* 2nd ed. (Oxford: Blackwell Publishers, 1993).

14. Clanchy, 76–77.

15. Clanchy, 87.

16. Clanchy, 88.

17. Daniel R. Headrick, *When Information Came of Age: Technologies of Knowledge in the Age of Reason and Revolution, 1700–1850* (Oxford: Oxford University Press, 2000), particularly chapter 4, "Displaying Information;" see also Edward R. Tufte, *The Visual Display of Quantitative Information,* 2nd ed. (Cheshire, CT: Graphics Press, 2001), particularly chapter 1, "Graphical Excellence."

18. Georges Ifrah, *The Universal History of Computing: From the Abacus to the Quantum Computer* (New York: John Wiley & Sons, 2001).

19. The first "computers" were women who worked to calculate large or complex formulae.

20. James W. Cortada, *Before the Computer: IBM, NCR, Burroughs and Remington Rand and the Industry They Created, 1865–1956* (Princeton, NJ: Princeton University Press, 1993), 44, italics original.

21. Alfred D. Chandler, Jr., *The Visible Hand: The Managerial Revolution in American Business* (Cambridge, MA: Belknap Press, 1977), 39.

22. Peter L. Bernstein, *Against the Gods: The Remarkable Story of Risk* (New York: John Wiley & Sons, 1998), 90.

23. Joseph A. Litterer, "Systematic Management: The Search for Order and Integration," *Business History Review (pre-1986)* 35, no. 4 (Winter 1961): 461–476.

24. Alfred D. Chandler, Jr., *Strategy and Structure: Chapters in the History of the American Industrial Enterprise* (Cambridge, MA: MIT Press, 1962), 14.

25. Litterer, 470–471.

26. JoAnne Yates, *Control through Communication: The Rise of System in American Management* (Baltimore: Johns Hopkins University Press, 1989), 5.

27. Yates, 12.

28. Yates, 13.

29. Chandler, *The Visible Hand,* 95.

30. Max Weber, *Economy and Society: An Outline of Interpretive Sociology, vol. I,* edited by Guenther Roth and Claus Wittich (Berkeley: University of California Press, 1978), 223.

31. Litterer, 465–468.

32. Litterer, 468.

33. Litterer, 470–471.

34. James R. Beniger, *The Control Revolution: Technological and Economic Origins of the Information Society* (Cambridge, MA: Harvard University Press, 1986), 292.

35. Chandler, *Strategy and Structure,* 76–77.

36. 45th Congress, 2nd Session House of Representatives Ex. Doc. No. 10, *Message from the President of the United States, Transmitting Report of the Commission Appointed to Examine the Security of the Public Buildings in the City of Washington against Fire*. December 10, 1877, Rutherford B. Hayes. Commission appointed 9/27/1877, 1.

37. Hayes Commission report, 7.

38. Hayes Commission report, 9.

39. 50th Congress, 1st Session, Senate Report No. 507, *Report of the Select Committee of the United States Senate, Appointed under Senate Resolution of March 3, 1887 to In-*

quire into and Examine the Methods of Business and Work in the Executive Departments, etc., and the Causes of Delays in Transacting the Public Business, etc. March 8, 1888.

40. 50th Congress, 1st Session, Senate Report no. 507, Part 1, 106.

41. 50th Congress, 1st Session, Senate Report no. 507, Part 1, 112.

42. 50th Congress, 1st Session, Senate Report no. 507, Part 1, 115.

43. 50th Congress, 1st Session, Senate Report no. 507, Part 1, 175.

44. 50th Congress, 1st Session, Senate Report no. 507, Part 1, 175.

45. 50th Congress, 1st Session, Senate Report no. 507, Part 2, 51–52.

46. 50th Congress, 1st Session, Senate Report no. 507, Part 3, 12.

47. 50th Congress, 1st Session, Senate Report no. 507, Part 3, 19.

48. 50th Congress, 1st Session, Senate Report no. 507, Part 1, 239.

49. 62nd Congress, 3rd Session, House of Representatives Document No. 1252, *Message of the President of the United States Transmitting the Reports of the Commission on Economy and Efficiency.* January 8, 1913, 50.

50. 62nd Congress, 3rd Session, House of Representatives Document No. 1252, 163.

51. 62nd Congress, 3rd Session, House of Representatives Document No. 1252, 755–798.

52. 62nd Congress, 3rd Session, House of Representatives Document No. 1252, 83.

53. 62nd Congress, 3rd Session, House of Representatives Document No. 1252, 85.

54. 62nd Congress, 3rd Session, House of Representatives Document No. 1252, 90.

55. 62nd Congress, 3rd Session, House of Representatives Document No. 1252, 104.

56. 62nd Congress, 3rd Session, House of Representatives Document No. 1252, 99. See also Appendix III for a legal brief, 476–480.

57. Chester L. Guthrie, "Federal Contributions to the Management of Records," 126–152, in *Federal Contributions to Management: Effects on the Public and Private Sectors,* edited by David S. Brown (New York: Praeger Publishers, 1971).

58. Chandler, *Strategy and Structure*, 76–77.

59. OCLC listing dated 6/10/2004.

60. United States Department of Agriculture, Office of Plant and Operations, *Procedure Manual for Records Management* (Washington, D.C., U.S. Government Printing Office 1942). OCLC listing dated 6/10/2004.

61. J. William Schulze, *The American Office: Its Organization, Management and Records* (New York: Key Publishing Company, 1913).

62. Schulze, 237–248.

63. Schulze, 224–225.

64. Schulze, 226–227.

65. Schulze, 230–231.

66. Schulze, 235.

67. E. R. Hudders, *Indexing and Filing: A Manual of Standard Practice* (New York: Ronald Press, 1916).

68. W. H. Leffingwell, *Scientific Office Management* (Chicago: A. W. Shaw Company, 1917).

69. W. H. Leffingwell, 165–178.

70. It is useful to recall that Emmett Leahy, a pioneer in the development of modern records management theory and practices, used a representative of Westinghouse Electric, Frank M. Root, in his first Hoover Commission report.

71. William David Wigent, *Modern Filing and How to File: A Textbook on Office System* (Rochester, NY: Yawman and Erbe Mfg. Co., 1920).

72. Shannon must have been the creator of these products.

73. Wigent, 75–77.

74. Wigent, 75–77.

75. Wigent's use of the term "document" is in sharp contrast to the way the term "document" is used by the French to refer to both sets and items within the sets of separate importance. We will explore this in later chapters.

76. James N. McCord, *A Textbook of Filing* (New York: D. Appleton and Company, 1920).

77. McCord, 100.

78. Ethel E. Scholfield, *Filing Department Operation and Control: From the Standpoint of the Management* (New York: Ronald Press, 1923).

79. Scholfield, 65.

80. Scholfield, 157.

81. Scholfield, 157.

82. Eugenia Wallace, *Filing Methods* (New York: Ronald Press, 1923).

83. Wallace, xv.

84. Library Bureau, *Progressive Indexing and Filing for Schools* (Tonawanda, NY: Rand Kardex Service, 1927).

85. Charles W. Gerstenberg, *Principles of Business* (New York: Prentice-Hall, 1918).

86. Frank C. McClelland, *Office Training and Standards* (Chicago: A. W. Shaw, 1919). See also, for example, Ernest H. Crabbe and Clay D. Slinker, *General Business,* 3rd ed. (Cincinnati: South-Western Publishing, 1936) and William R. Odell, Harold F. Clark, Guy D. Miller, Oscar B. Paulsen, Dorothy L. Travis, and Ruth M. Twiss, *Business: Its Organization and Operation* (Boston: Ginn and Company, 1937).

87. Margaret K. Odell and Earl P. Strong, *Records Management and Filing Operations* (New York: McGraw-Hill Book Company, 1947).

88. Helen L. Chatfield, "The Problem of Records From the Standpoint of Management," *American Archivist* 3, no. 2 (April 1940): 93–101.

89. Chatfield, 101.

90. H. G. Jones, *The Records of a Nation: Their Management, Preservation, and Use* (New York: Atheneum, 1969), 18–19.

91. Archivist of the United States, *Seventh Annual Report of the Archivist of the United States for the Year Ending June 30, 1941* (Washington, D.C., 1941), 1–5.

92. Interdepartmental Committee on Records Administration, *Preliminary Reports of Subcommittees on Records Administration*, National Archives Miscellaneous Processed Document No. 43–5 (Washington, D.C., October 1942), i.

93. Odell and Strong, 264.

94. Odell and Strong, 4, 270.

95. Odell and Strong, 4, 270.

96. Odell and Strong, 2.

97. Odell and Strong, 4.

98. Odell and Strong, 339.

99. Odell and Strong, 113–119.

100. Commission on Organization of the Executive Branch of the Government, *Records Management in the United States Government: A Report with Recommendations* (Washington, D.C.: U.S. Government Printing Office, 1948).

101. Commission on Organization of the Executive Branch of the Government, 1949, 11–12.

102. Commission on Organization of the Executive Branch of the Government, 1949, 13.

103. Commission on Organization of the Executive Branch of the Government, *Paperwork Management: Part I, In the U.S. Government* (Washington, D.C.: U.S. Government Printing Office, 1955); Commission on Organization of the Executive Branch of the Government, *Paperwork Management: Part II, The Nation's Paperwork for the Government: An Experiment* (Washington, D.C.: U.S. Government Printing Office, 1955).

104. Commission on Organization of the Executive Branch of the Government, *Part I*, 1955, 1–2.

105. Commission on Organization of the Executive Branch of the Government, *Part I*, 1955, 3.

106. T. R. Schellenberg, *Modern Archives: Principles and Techniques* (Chicago: University of Chicago Press, 1956), 47.

107. Roy C. Turnbaugh, "What Is an Electronic Record?" 23–34 in *Effective Approaches for Managing Electronic Records and Archives*, edited by Bruce W. Dearstyne, (Lanham, MD: Scarecrow Press, 2002).

108. Interviews with IT managers in various corporations.

Chapter Two

The Context of Records

Context plays a key role in dictating our subject matter. Records are defined by context, not by description or example. Information, when it is captured, must be captured in context. Thus records managers are faced with the need to provide and preserve not just the content, but also the context of an organization's records. A critical challenge that today's records managers face is that the various channels through which organizations now present information require increasingly robust context for the documents and records that each business produces.

Context is inherent in our ideas about what makes a document or record whole. We have an enormous challenge in just defining what a document is because of the "disruptions" of technology to the notion of wholeness inherent in hard-copy documents. Those same disruptions affect our understanding and ability to grasp context. Consider, for example, the corporate portal. Many different types of organizations—corporations, non-profits, and government organizations—have portals for both internal and external users. Within the U.S., each of these types of organization is subject to different regulations. All, however, are subject to litigation and the requirements of discovery subpoenas. Everything that is displayed on the portal must be managed as carefully as contracts and intellectual property. What the end user has seen must be available to opposing counsel and, potentially, to a jury.

The on-line trading portal is perhaps the most disruptive extant example of the increasingly complex context requirements that technologies such as portals now impose, in large part because these sites enable broker/dealer communications with customers. According to industry regulations, broker/dealer communications must be maintained for three years on write-once, read many (WORM) media. The end user of a broker/dealer web site does not ultimately perform the trade; he or she only communicates the order preference through a website. Because the website constitutes broker/dealer communication with the customer, it must be maintained for three years.

What, specifically, makes this three-year rule so onerous in the case of the on-line trading portal? The answer lies within the technology that is required to convey rapidly changing information to the user in close to real time. Taking a closer look at this technology, what we see on a computer screen when we visit a website is called a page. Many web pages we visit are formatted as single electronic objects with HTML code. However, with the introduction of Active Server Pages (.asp) and Java Server Pages (.jsp), we find that the flat screen we are looking at more closely resembles a television set than it does a document. Consider an on-line equities trading portal such as e-Trade, with its numerous tracking, analyzing, and activity screens on a single "page." This page gives access to an entire office. In comparison to our off-line computer screens, we view an "office-top," not a "desktop."[1]

The screen view is called a "portal" created by a Java Server Page or an Active Server Page; the areas on the screen represent a number of different Java and HTML devices that are essentially cells in a table. Each cell points at a different "feed." One section may provide the latest industry news, with links to popular Internet web news sites such as CNN.com or ABC.com. These sections are fed by application software products called "content management software" that permits the on-line trading company to send snippets of HTML (each its own electronic object requiring management) to the appropriate cell through a simple approval process in a timely way. The interface may provide a tabbed bar that permits the end user to travel to different rooms within the office; for example, the user's own account information that includes recommended trades for the day, a current market valuation, and a history of recent trades. There may also be a banner with several different stock tickers the end user has chosen: the NYSE, London gold, or Singapore oil futures. Those tickers are not fed directly through the on-line trading company's servers to the end user. They are picked up closer to the end user from the website of another company that does nothing but feed stock tickers to on-line trading company server pages. Those are called "edge-side includes," and are used to reduce the size of the feed from the host to each recipient.

Clearly, a single web page on such a website presents a tremendous amount of rapidly changing information that must be captured in context. Moreover, each page is "personalized" for each end user, which only adds to the complexity of what must be captured. But the complexity does not end there. For a portal to work well, each active cell on the page ordinarily has its own server. Not only is the end user looking at numerous electronic objects, he or she is looking at numerous object sources. Some sources can be clicked on to access an application such as calendaring, or to activate a business process. While the former might be considered a document, the latter may be a database view, with a decision box to be checked. A database may be considered a document, but the end user is usually not interested in an entire database or application—only with his small set of data or the most recent data. The purpose of viewing the data does not necessarily lead to the creation of another document; it may lead to a phone call stating a decision or participation in another business process.

As the reader can well imagine, we are dealing now not just with dynamic web pages with flickering .GIFs; these are active screens, with many objects from many different sources passing by and being acted upon. Imagine a situation where each object contributes to the decision-making activity. No single cell carries more weight than any other; it is a collective and fleeting set of information—perhaps best compared to watching several TV channels simultaneously. To makes matters even more complicated, the server page itself may have logic imbedded in it. For example, it may have coding to represent bidirectional languages such as Farsi (Persian) or Arabic. It may have coding to translate miles per hour into knots per hour or kilometers per hour. It may access a web service that reaches out to an application sitting on a server in another country, that gathers currency exchange prices at a particular moment and on a particular exchange in a third country, translates all quantities and prices to the viewer's currency, and then totals this together.

How could the content flashing across the screen possibly be stored and maintained over time? A video camera would be needed to record what the end user is actually seeing to ensure that both the information and its context are maintained. It may be possible to record what the individual sees on the screen using a number of recording devices and applications installed on the end user's machine, a spyware server placed elsewhere, or through a feed directly back to the on-line trading company's servers. However, any of these solutions creates additional problems, including bandwidth and storage requirements, scalability issues, and privacy concerns. Yet how is a business that is producing such an ever-changing, "fruit salad" web page to protect itself from the end users that are depending upon information provided at a specific time, in a specific way, and with a specific context from that on-line trading site?

But businesses are not the sole sources of this capture challenge for records managers. Government portals now exist which provide as much dynamic information to government officials who must also use this information to make decisions and participate in business processes. Substantiating decision-making is one of the key responsibilities of any government. How can substantiation occur when it cannot be captured without great effort? Similarly, many government portals now provide information to the public, and are accountable for the accuracy and currency of that information—which must also be maintained in context.

This venture into the technological underpinnings of today's dynamic websites raises yet another question: if the information and its context were captured, how would we preserve it with its entire context intact? We would need to preserve the content, the server page, the actions of the user, and the web services accessed by the server page. To put this in the language of HTML, we need to save the content, the formatting, and the click-stream, as well as the logic, if we are to appropriately manage what appears on an organization's portal and meet the requirements of discovery subpoenas.

Certainly the on-line trading portal is an extreme example of what we deal with daily. But other technologies are proving equally troublesome. Email and instant messaging have replaced conversations and gossip. With these vehicles of communication, a document equals an utterance within a conversation, not a complete thought. We can easily question the relevance of these "disruptions" to our conventional understanding of the document. For example, we rarely publish a single piece of correspondence. We generally publish a series of correspondence by an author, between an author and another person, or by several authors. We regard correspondence as an utterance among other utterances for which we either attempt to reconstruct the proximate conversation or put it in relation to a grander conversation we wish to explore. Email and instant messaging are only more extreme examples of this.

Links confound us because of the ephemeral nature of the World Wide Web. We are limited in our ability to preserve the document because the links to which it points are unlikely to exist for more than a few years. Because those links are so easy to follow, they "disrupt" the narrative. We believe we have found the same disruption in web blogs and wikis.[2] In contrast, TiVo creates narrativity we previously never had in the broadcast medium by eliminating commercial, station, and public service breaks.

Narrativity has never existed in a consistent form, and the web does not change the shifting nature of narrativity through history. Certainly, the ability to create one's own universe through a web search raises questions of the discourse between the reader and the author, mediated through the document. Yet footnotes and references are also a way to reach beyond the limits of the "page." Indeed, a great essay consists of two documents: the argument going on in the body of the text and the argument going on in the footnotes. By reaching beyond the page, the footnote disrupts the narrative. By making personal references, the poem reaches beyond the reader's ability to reach the poet's understanding. Mirzoeff suggests that our current understanding of narrativity is impoverished by our narrow perspective. He uses the examples of television soap operas and picaresque novels that have never depended upon traditional Western devices of narrative to bring interest to the characters.[3] Narrativity is about wholeness—about a beginning, a middle, and an end. As noted in these examples, the Internet provides a fertile field for disruptions in our understanding of what is the document or record and what is its context. Those disruptions are not new; think of comic books, the introduction of instrumental-only music, or the role of the Greek chorus as examples of disruptions we embrace.

This concept of completeness is evident in the way many users approach search engines. A web search using, for example, Google, is regarded by many a searcher as a compendium of all possible sources on the World Wide Web for search terms; i.e., the end user often regards the search results as a "complete" document. When failure occurs, the searcher tends to believe that the answer does not exist at all—or, at least, that it does not exist on the Internet. When the search provides spurious results, such as when websites request children's emails in exchange for the answer to a question about Pokemon, the searcher may be thoroughly convinced the results are complete and corrupt, even though a category search may quickly produce correct results.[4] The reader makes an assumption of wholeness that extends to the context of the original question.

Within an organization, the management of project or case files produces similar problems. Each project is designed to define a miniature universe within the organization. Each separate document must be placed in the appropriate category for finding again, otherwise the sheer volume of documents will make finding individual documents impossible. The project file is made up of documents from every possible source that contributed to the completion of the project. It is not really a narrative, but rather a representation of the effort put forth to execute or manage the project. The user of the project file ordinarily believes it is complete. When a document does not appear in its expected location, the user is likely to conclude that it is lost or that it does not exist. Strategies for searching at this point are often truncated because of the user's belief that the "system" is correct and produces complete results.

Another common problem facing departments of information technology in any organization is the decommissioning of a system that holds data or documents. As products are decommissioned, one of the questions we ask is whether we still want a proprietary format for the data or documents as many products from the 1980s and 1990s had proprietary formats. The answer is invariably no; we want to use nonproprietary formats so we can make future conversions and migrations easier and make our archived media readable. Yet, no data or document conversion is 100%, something gets left behind in the old system. We keep the old system around for a few years to access what might have been left behind. We cannot just keep the old data or documents on their media because the entire system—output devices, hard drives, operating systems, software, applications, etc.—is necessary to read the document again. With a proprietary document format "the document" is the entire system. With a nonproprietary format "the document" is more difficult to define.[5]

The obvious issue here is context. What is context? From the perspective of records management, the traditional/conventional focus on the document both overstates and understates the problem. Robek, Brown, and Maedke define a document as "the smallest unit of filing."[6] Records management is concerned with concepts rather than artifacts, another difference between records management and library and information science. Records management is focused on the organization—corporate, non-profit, or government—not its heritage. Records management is concerned with government in that government comprises a set of business processes with information requiring management. Culture and human memory are records management issues only when they are business requirements. Records management does not focus on the way in which a document or record communicates or relates an author with a reader, unless this is a business requirement.

If records are "recorded information of any kind and in any form,"[7] the plaster cast of a footprint is a record; the footprint may be a record as well. A note scribbled on a piece of paper is a record. Anything that might be requested in the discovery phase of litigation produced within the organization, not necessarily in the course of business and irrespective of archival notions of authenticity and trustworthiness, is a record. Recorded information is whatever has been memorialized or captured in a form other than in a person's brain.

Signification, the intentional act of memorializing, makes something a document or information. Animals can perceive signification in a scent (information), but only humans memorialize the signification (for example, by applying a verbal label to the source of the scent or subjecting it to chemical analysis). Information is captured to make a document or record. Why the information was memorialized is irrelevant. I have personally managed broken chunks of concrete and pairs of glasses. The glasses were in a probate file. Even the attorneys using the file holding the glasses did not know why the glasses were there. The attorneys said not to remove the glasses because someone put them there intentionally.[8] Intentionality is a shifting chimera dealt with in-depth by the courts and religion. I can only point in a direction of understanding. The human mind seeks out patterns with abandon and delight. Patterns are meaningful; they signify. Humans create meaning in action, word, and through the physical capture of patterns in art and writing. Humans see patterns in nature just as animals do, but humans create fixed patterns as a means of communication. The patterns are fixed according to social convention.[9] We meant to fix those patterns—i.e., we intended to fix them to create meaning, to signify.

The current French understanding of "document" carries the cultural burden of being intentionally created by an author for reading by a reader. The French term also indicates a solitary artifact. Wholeness is, then, only in the form of a single artifact, not a set of artifacts. A document in English is usually a solitary artifact and does not require a reader, and the author may be a computer, not a human. The French have no equivalent to "record." A "record" in English refers to a complete set of documents encompassing an activity. A single record could be a project file filling many shelves in several rooms, or it could refer to a single-paged contract. To overcome this problem, the French refer to a multiple-document set as a *document pour l'action*. In English, we would call this a project file, a case file, etc., to indicate wholeness a set of documents makes together. This problem of wholeness is why the French have adopted the English term "records management" to describe records management, because they have no equivalent: "En France, l'existence d'un mot unique—'archives'—pour désigner le document depuis le moment de sa création ou réception, en pendant toute la période de sa conservation qui peut être illimitée, constitue un obstacle pour l'analyse, complexité encore accrue par la polysémie du terme 'archives' qui désigne également des bâtiments ou des institutions. Ainsi il nous a paru préférable de conserver l'expression anglo-saxonne Records Management pour insister sur la spécificité de cette gestion du document qui n'est pas seulement du papier mais aussi un document électronique ou un fichier (littéralement, *record* signifie enregistrement)."[10]

The concept of record is expanded for purposes of managing similar sets of individual records called a records series. Records series are sets of documents that are created the same, used the same, and have the same retention—i.e., they have the same records life cycle. Anything that belongs together, irrespective of medium, is kept together at least conceptually and managed similarly. There exist records series that have a total retention of zero. Those are groupings of information proscribed by the organization by policy, such as harassment, pornography, spam, viruses, very large email attachments, or suggestions that information be destroyed when it is required in a lawsuit. Should those types of records enter the organization, they are also subject to discovery. These documents may not be admissible as evidence in a court of law, but they can still be subpoenaed in the discovery phase of litigation. Existence is the only requirement for legal action, hence for management.

The records need not belong to the same business process to be part of a records series. There are many different business processes within an organization with similar records series. Most manufacturing processes will have engineering change orders. Conceptually, all the engineering change orders within an organization belong to the same records series. Conversely, the documents making up a record in a records series need not be similar. Case files or project files are made up of many different types of documents from many different sources.[11] When we speak of a document in records management, this is primarily what we are speaking of: all of the individual, separate objects that belong together in a single record that belongs to a records series. In documentation, that same object is called a fragment. In records management, we regard a record not as a single object, but as an object potentially made up of other objects. In this sense, records management resembles object-oriented programming more than it does documentation. Each object in records management is the input, result, or by-product of a business process that must be tracked separately as well as together.

Content and medium are irrelevant. There are no limitations for defining a group of artifacts as a records series other than that they be created similarly, used similarly, and disposited similarly. Context for records management is equally conceptual, but is the most important because it provides "handles" for management. Context can be as mundane as the letterhead on paper correspondence or the header of an email. Metadata is defined solely with regard to the organization's business requirements for a particular records series, not according to a checklist such as Dublin Core.[12] For example, Dublin Core requires "author" as a required metadata field. For most computer reports, this is a peculiar notion, but should be considered. For complex records, the metadata may require an entire database because it must clearly define the structure of the record by defining the overall structure of the record, which can have many layers, and by relating all the documents to each other. Whatever is being contextualized, organizations are interested in creating the "least-common-denominator" context. As we have seen, defining context costs money and time. That effort must balance both the costs and the risks required. In contrast, document control is the focus within records management on the creation of a specific, individual object. Many business processes focus on the creation or capture and processing of an individual document such as a contract, an environmental report, or an engineering drawing. Among the issues involved in document control are change control, signature control, version control, draft control, and copy control. Each business process will have different requirements for each of these.

For records management, the original problem of the on-line trading site is a technical problem of how to capture the experience to satisfy a court of law.[13] The captured information may end up being called a record, if it stands alone; or a document, if different types of objects are required to make up our understanding of what was seen. Within records management, this is an issue only insofar as we must ensure completeness. For the records manager, it is a concept required to ensure completeness.

Why should we care if we defined the on-line trading site visit as a document, a set of documents, or as an experience that symbolically resembles a document? The answer is that we must worry about what to preserve to ensure that another "reader" can interact with the "author" via the medium—the *support*, as the French put it. Having spent so many years in the pragmatic world of records management, I have come to notice that when we keep preservation in mind from the earliest phases of the life cycle, we can do whatever needs to be done later. That means extending the life cycle before creation to include policy-making. This is the "family-planning" phase of the life cycle. When preservation is not kept in mind, as has been the case for nearly every computer application dealing with documents, we find ourselves in a quandary.

Indeed, one of the more confusing curiosities within records management is the distance that the vendors of document management (now "enterprise content management," or ECM) application software put between themselves and records management. Many industry analysts are unaware that most of content management or document management is a subset within the portfolio of records management.[14] There has arisen an illusion of distance between "content," "documents," and "records," in part because, early on, the ECM vendors bit off the easiest part of the portfolio (document control), never recognizing it as a subset within the purview of records management. The difficulty of venturing beyond the control of active documents is what is behind the "illusion of distance" that the ECM vendors created—that and the fact that developing and packaging the records management functionality separately and then selling it as an "optional" add-on allows them to make more money.

None of this serves to mitigate the problem, however. The document management vendors have created a process whereby a document is "declared" a record. The reason for this is to pass control of the document over to the records management application. In the past, this meant transferring the electronic document over to an electronic records repository. This gave the impression to many information technology professionals that the two—document management and records management—were somehow different. The net result is that when a litigation, tax, or audit hold is required within a repository, only those documents that are registered with the records management application can be secured. Any document that has not been "declared" cannot be secured for the hold. When confronted with this, product managers of records management software solutions change the subject.

Yet finding a preservation method for electronic records has not been difficult so long as preservation is listed as a requirement for the life cycle. For example, ECM products that write off documents in groups to near-line storage such as optical disks and can then track the document on the disk, have performed a large part of the task. Most ECM products do not perform this activity, making migration quite complex. What has been much more difficult is providing a sufficiently robust context. The problem exemplified by the on-line trading site, as well as the problems of disrupted narrativity, is the problem of measuring how robust the context is and then providing as well as preserving both the context and the content. Putting this issue in proportion, when we preserve a scholarly book with footnotes, we do not think about preserving all the books and other documents in the footnotes and references. When we preserve correspondence, however, we work hard to preserve as much related, and sometimes unrelated, correspondence as we are able. This is the role of context: to ensure "wholeness" despite the disruptions of technology.

Because records management is focused on business requirements, we are in many instances at the mercy of our organization's methods of risk management. Some organizations preserve records only after they have been fined for not doing so. In 2003, five large Wall Street trading firms were fined US$8,000,000 for not keeping their email correspondence with customers. Only now is the financial services industry taking this seriously, and organizations are spending millions of dollars to achieve compliance. Depending upon the industry and the circumstances, it appears that organizations may be willing to tolerate a high level of risk—i.e., they are willing to take the chance of being fined not only for not maintaining the context, but also for not maintaining the content.

The notion of records is defined by a very particular business, legal, and governmental history. Having a clear and precise definition for documents has not been very helpful in managing electronic information. We prefer to err on the part of the purpose it serves within the organization rather than between the author and the reader or society. Within records management, the document is a concept, a symbol. We cannot afford to focus on a particular definition of a document because we will then be limiting our ability to manage documents in the method required by our organization. If we focus on only one aspect of records, such as the cultural or scientific purposes, litigation purposes, regulatory purposes, or the business process or knowledge management purposes, we miss a business or governmental requirement. Even if we focus on one aspect of a document, such as authenticity (such as that represented by the International Research on Permanent Authentic Records in Electronic Systems [InterPARES][15]), we will miss other important aspects of authenticity required by courts of law, security, or regulatory measures. In this respect, the approach to records must be multivalent—capable of encompassing multiple aspects.

This multivalence required of records is reflected in what we see constituting records: documents. Documents also have a multivalence. The only universal requirement of a document or a record is that it be complete. A symbol is a conceptual representation with multiple meanings that requires completeness and that can be interpreted only by context. Records and documents are symbols par excellence. As concepts, they organize our world; as reality, they contain indices pointing back to their concepts.[16] A document or record signifies to someone; it embodies information. Most discussions of documents or records tend to assume a document or record that has writing on it; however, we also manage documents or records that are not writing, such as the bloody glove in the O. J. Simpson trial. The discussion of the glove in the administrative phase of the trial was a discussion concerning whether the glove was "evidence" or "nonevidence."[17] Once the bloody glove was identified by an officer as potential evidence in the case, it became a document and remains so until it is destroyed. Whether the glove was distinguished as evidenceor nonevidence does not change its nature as a document.

Not all records managers have a portfolio covering the entire life cycle. Many of us manage records in boxes or a file room. This is how our organizations regard us: as managers of dead records or of collections of pieces of paper. Yet even managing those items requires us to have the skills to understand complex relationships among objects, as well as managerial skills that meet or exceed most other roles found in management.

Our primary products are systems analysis for content-related technology applications; legal, statutory, regulatory, and standards analysis with regard to records media, policies, and maintenance; and content- and document-related policies and procedures, filing systems, and records retention schedules. Retention schedules are our most well-known product, but policies and procedures are the most widespread product. The systems analysis we perform is primarily in the area of requirements gathering. We gather business requirements, such as the need to comply more fully with regulations; functional requirements, such as the need to ensure copy control; and technical requirements, such as the need to manage content on so-called smart phones and personal digital assistants (PDAs). We also remind the primary analysts that information exists as documents and that even forms may need to be retained despite their design as data-entry mechanisms for databases.

Research of statutes, regulations, agency rules, agency orders, bulletins, and standards-making body rules such as ISO 9002 requires a very different type of research technique from ordinary legal research. The product searched for is very specific and does not require legal interpretation. We look for how long different types of records are to be maintained, in what format they may be maintained, and whether any special policies apply (such as where the records are kept, if an index is required, or if they must be retrievable fairly promptly). Unfortunately, the mechanized search tools currently available are not very effective because the content being searched has been written and rewritten by thousands of different people, using very different terminology. The statutes and the agency regulations are a matrix of all the different requirements, the records affected, and what is required.

Policies and procedures address everything from who owns the information that has been created on behalf of an organization, to how to handle an email attachment. The breadth found within these policies and procedures reflects the problems found within specific organizations. In most organizations, however, one of the most increasingly critical requirements is for policies and procedures for managing the minutiae of email and instant messaging.

Filing systems reflect how people use information every day. We create categories for documents that assist people in the ways they do their work and help them to find those same documents, some of which requires creating index fields. Archivists would call these index fields "metadata"; librarians would call them "facets." We examine each document, each subfile, each file, to find out what is the least amount of information we can associate with each document to ensure that the documents will go to the correct location and can be retrieved with the least effort. Sometimes this is easy, as with a life insurance policy that already has a database with information from the policy—the only index necessary is the policy number. Sometimes this is very difficult, as with any type of correspondence or memoranda, and particularly so with email. The difficulty lies in the fact that not every piece of correspondence is self-identifying; hence optical character recognition (OCR) and full-text indexing will not help. The employee sending or receiving the correspondence or memoranda must clearly identify the classification. In the case of email, this is a task that may take as much time as the original creation and routing of the document.

Retention schedules address the life cycle of each document set within the organization. We inventory information materials within an organization that could be conceived of as documents or records. We group these into functional sets that have the same life cycle, called records series. We create a hierarchical, functional classification for all workflows within the organization and associate each set with a workflow. We define the periods of time records series are kept in the office and in off-line storage. We also indicate the workgroup that has been given responsibility for tracking each records series, the medium in which it is to be kept, and whether the document is required for business continuity.

A curious side-effect of each of these activities is the creation of business intelligence. The organization of information creates more information—*actionable* information. Management can now ask, for example, how many pieces of correspondence and memoranda are required to manage the average exception, or how many contracts of this particular type were created this year. Records management does not fill a clear niche within either organizations or the academy. It concerns legal issues, but also operational issues. It is a part of information science, yet it belongs in business. It is part of informatics, yet it belongs with archiving. The speed with which records management programs are cut during a recession and the paucity of records management programs in universities is evidence of how records management is regarded as a cost center in one instance, and a "backwater" profession in the other. The high profile that records management currently enjoys is the result of many recent and spectacular corporate fines and litigation cases. When these issues fade, interest in records management will fade as well.

NOTES

1. Part of this chapter was a paper, "The Symbolic Document," presented at the Document Academy annual meeting, *DOCAM '04,* at the University of California, Berkeley, October 24, 2004. I am profoundly grateful to Niels Windfeld Lund for permitting me to present my offering to the Document Academy.

2. A web blog is a series of utterances on a single web page, usually on a particular subject, but not necessarily by the same person. Blogs are used by reporters, and pseudo-reporters, as chat rooms, and also by help desks to keep track of problems. A wiki is a web document created by committee (in the same sense that the moose is an animal created by committee). Some wikis, such as the Wikipedia (http://www.wikipedia.com), permit anyone to contribute or edit. Some are created by an assigned group.

3. Nicholas Mirzoeff, *An Introduction to Visual Culture* (London: Routledge, 1999).

4. This example comes from my own experience as a mother and wife.

5. I am indebted to Gregory A. Vance, Vice President of Infrastructure Architecture at OneAmerica Financial Partners, Inc., for this observation.

6. Mary F. Robek, Wilmer O. Maedke, and Gerald F. Brown, *Information and Records Management,* 3rd ed. (Lake Forest, IL: Glencoe, 1987), 565.

7. Robek, Maedke, and Brown, 568.

8. Determining intentionality can sometimes be a challenge. One of my favorite stories is from Patrick Cunningham, who worked for the Archdiocese of Chicago. He once found a forty-year-old sandwich in a file. He knew it could not be a document because the files he was looking through should not have sandwiches as contents. While humorous, this is an excellent example of the concept's edge.

9. Nelson Goodman, *Languages of Art* (Indianapolis, IN: Hackett Publishing Company, 1976); and W. J. T. Mitchell, *Iconology: Image, Text, Ideology* (Chicago: University of Chicago Press, 1986).

10. G. Drouhet, G. Deslassy, and E. Morineau, *Records Management: mode d'emploi* (Paris: ADBS, 2000), 9.

11. Manuel Zacklad, "Processus de documentarisation dans les Documents pour l'Action (DopA): statut des annotations et technologies de la coóperation associées," paper presented at *Le numérique: impact sur le cycle de vie du document,* Québec, Canada, October 2004.

12. Simon Cox, "A Guide to the Dublin Core Datamodel with Some Notations for Recording Dublin Core Metadata," paper on the Dublin Core Metadata Initiative website, 1999. http://www.agcrc.csiro.au/projects/3018CO/metadta/dc-guide/ (22 July 2004).

13. Katarzyna Wegrzyn-Wolska, "Le document numérique dynamique: une«étoile filante»dans l'espace documentaire," paper presented at *Le numérique: impact sur le cycle de vie du document,* Québec, Canada, October 2004. This paper discusses what was captured on a dynamic website, how long the page stayed static, how it was captured, and how long it was held. Some pages at Slashdot.org (a subscription-based website with the stated mission of providing "News for Nerds") are kept static for only ten seconds. The on-line trading site considered in this chapter is constantly changing because of the updates in the feeds from the stock ticker and analysis tools.

14. And yet oddly enough, the historical evolution of Records Management (RM) products by Enterprise Content Management (ECM) vendors has tended to treat RM as a subset of Document Management (DM).

15. The purpose of the InterPARES project is to define authenticity for all documents for all time.

16. Charles S. Peirce, "Logic as Semiotic: The Theory of Signs," in *Philosophical Writings of Peirce,* ed. Justus Buchler (New York: Dover Publications, 1955), 112.

17. This was part of the discussion after my presentation to the Document Academy in October, 2004. The bloody glove is my example, but the observation that the glove could be declared "nonevidence" was Michael Buckland's.

Chapter Three

What Is a Record?

The arrival of the Spanish in North America brought domesticated horses—small Arabian horses we now call mustangs. Horses had not been seen in the Western Hemisphere in millennia. When those Arabian horses escaped, the aboriginal Americans captured them. The reaction of each group to the horse was different. The Shoshone captured the horses and ate them. The Arapahoe used them to pull their travois, replacing their dogs. The Apache learned how to perform tricks of riding and shooting bareback that would make them one of the most formidable enemies of the European settlers. Records, like the escaped Spanish mustangs, are defined and managed differently by every organization, leading to many competing definitions, all correct within their industry contexts, and all incorrect as ultimate definitions.

This chapter compares the prevailing definitions of a record, as well as ideas determining the existential nature of records—reliability and authenticity. Some of the definitions of records primarily define content. Some take account of contexts, yet do not provide sufficiently broad contexts to account for business requirements. Most definitions leave no door open for interdisciplinary discussions with economics, management, or information technology (IT). As records are exclusively an object of interest for an organization, any definition must include room for business requirements and for interdisciplinary discussion. This discussion is particularly important and urgent between those who manage information, the records managers, and those who transfer, extract, and transform information, the managers of IT. Accordingly, this chapter proposes a new definition of a record, one that reflects what we actually have to manage.

The first topic covered in this chapter is the set of requirements archives defines for records—primarily authenticity and reliability—in comparison to how those requirements affect records management. Then we will examine the constraints records management places on the concepts of authenticity and reliability from the perspective of litigation. We will also look at several definitions of records, along with the deficiencies inherent in those definitions. Finally, we will examine what it is that records managers are required to manage, and, working backward from that description, find an accurate definition of records in the workplace.

ARCHIVES AND DEFINITIONS OF RECORDS

The international standard ISO 15489 "Information and documentation— Records management" defines records as "information created, received, and maintained as evidence and information by an organization or person, in pursuance of legal obligations or in the transaction of business." The primary source of this definition is archivists and museum curators, both academic and practical, not the records management community. We will examine this definition and the sources from which it came, as well as other primary requirements of a faithful record, such as authenticity and reliability. We will find that the ISO definition, and in fact any definition that stems from the archival community, generally does not stand up to the workaday tests required of records management. The solution is to look at the business requirements that define records for us and decide on a provisional definition of records that can be imported into any work environment.

The main problem with the ISO 15489 definition is that it is a poorly formulated definition—it defines itself by reference to itself, thereby resulting in a tautology. Records are "information . . . maintained as . . . information." Nor does this definition limit the type of information. It does not exclude information maintained in a person's head, for instance, which is maintained as information, but is not managed as a record until it is written down—for example, in the form of a report, a procedure, or a deposition. In other words, the information must be in a fixed form. This also has inherent problems, including use of reserved terminology such as "evidence, "business," and "transaction," but it does at least limit what records managers might manage.

The ISO 15489 definition has two additional problems, best exemplified by email. The first concerns the creation and management policies about information that we may want to forbid within an organization. Employees' emails have been known to contain information about coworkers that has been very useful in litigation.[1] One of the activities many records managers are called upon to perform today is to participate in the creation of email policies recommending that employees think about what they are writing before they send the missive. This a problem for the definition because people are now using their companies' business tools for inappropriate, nonbusiness communications, as opposed to "business transactions," and because anything on the server is now open to subpoena as evidence.

Another problem this definition does not address is the profound volume of documents created by employees that are used simply for human logistics, such as the scheduling of meetings and lunch dates and passing on reading material that may or may not be very interesting. The issue in this instance is the lack of classification, retention, and destruction procedures for email. This is also a problem for the definition because most organizations have yet to realize that all of these emails out on the server, in the absence of retention policies, are being "maintained as evidence." Such documents present a very large nuisance because they must be sorted through every time the organization receives a litigation subpoena. In one recent instance, an organization received a third-party subpoena for all documents related to Enron. The organization had never had any dealings either with Enron or with deals regarding Enron, yet it consumed one thousand attorney hours just to demonstrate this. Those one thousand attorney hours were used to sort through emails and copies of emails with jokes and news reports about Enron. When does this problem rise to the level of needing management—which is to say, when do document problems become records problems? Currently, many companies are purchasing software applications and services to install email management products precisely to relieve themselves of the voluminous burden of short-term emails. By defining "legal obligations" and "transaction of business" so narrowly, the ISO 15489 definition, if carefully followed, would damn any organization that simply wanted to find something, much less organize it and present it for a litigation subpoena.

Much is written in the archival literature about how electronic records differ from hard-copy records. As we shall see below, the methods by which records are managed well in an electronic environment are no different from the methods used to manage records well in a hard-copy environment. The key phrase here is "managed well." In many instances, the digital world is being held to an impossibly high standard that even the hard-copy world could not attain. For example, all media is expected to last for hundreds of years; reading tools, such as different versions of software, are being expected to substitute for every other type of reading tool. The reason these extremely high standards cannot be attained is not some qualitative difference between the two environments; rather, it has to do with how people relate to information generally and how they relate to electronic information particularly. Understanding how people actually create and use information within the work environment is one of the areas of records management that distinguishes it from other areas within information science where information is managed, such as libraries, archives, and museums. That understanding encompasses aspects of informatics, such as how people create and handle documents within the electronic environment.

Because records management is so focused on the work environment, it is also focused on processes. Organizations require well-designed and audited processes to ensure that the right information is delivered to the right person at the right time, and it is the process, not the technology, that ensures this. This situation is in stark contrast to current archives thinking, wherein "the right information" is entrusted to technology, the "trustworthy record-keeping system," rather than to a trustworthy process.

Generally speaking, archivists do not need to have records-handling knowledge to perform their work. Indeed, one of their goals is to be "use-agnostic." Archivists want to ensure that records are available to whatever purpose the citizenry or scholars might choose to put archival information. This requirement pushes archival work in the direction of description and preservation not only of the artifacts, but of the context, the provenance, of each artifact or set of artifacts. Indeed, archives and museums are defined by the role that these respective institutions serve within a culture. Their primary role is the preservation and presentation of information that has been deemed to be of value to the culture as a whole, as well as having value to individuals and groups within a culture.

The demands of such preservation and presentation are onerous. From the archaeological dig to its arrival at the Field Museum of Natural History, an artifact and its surrounding environment must be thoroughly described, or its value is limited, if not questioned. The artifact and its descriptions must be preserved. Its presentation to the culture, group, or individual must reflect or even enhance its value. The portfolio of archives and museums does not include managing the living environment that created the artifact, nor the artifact as it made its way through its living environment, even when it was sitting in a trunk or buried in rubble. The archivist's portfolio begins when the living environment has no more need to work on or with the artifact, or when the artifact is resurrected from its resting place. To put this in the language of the business world, archivists play no role in records business processes. Even the business processes of records management, called the life cycle, have two termini: destruction and archives. Records are sent to the archives when the business processes within the organization, either in a corporation or a government, have no more use for them.

Because archivists are not involved in records business processes, they must simply accept whatever comes out of the workplace pipeline. Archivists must then clearly define what is required to ensure that what they have has real value and faithfully reflects their portfolio. Among these requirements, reliability and authenticity are some of the characteristics most discussed by archivists with regard to documents and records. Because archivists obtain artifacts after creation and processing is complete, reliability and authenticity play an important and clearly defined role. The record must be reliable and authentic for the archivist to perform his or her work on it successfully. The archivist is not responsible for making the records reliable or authentic or even necessarily for determining whether the records are reliable or authentic; rather, the archivist is responsible for preserving the record so that it retains these characteristics throughout its useful life—i.e., a "custodial" relationship to the record. In the archive, that life is unpredictable only in the way in which the record may be used by various constituencies. What is predictable from the archivist's perspective is the length of time a record is required. In many instances, that requirement is permanent.

In contrast, within the business world, the longest anything is kept is for the life of the corporation—a length of time that may be as brief as a year or as long as 200 years. Despite the longevity of names such as Krupps or Rothschild, the corporation itself may be purchased or reorganized. Thus we see that, compared to the archivist's portfolio, the burden of preservation in records management is not so onerous. Whereas archives face the constant threat of extinction if the artifact itself or the means to extract meaning from the artifact disappears, companies face fines or interrupted business—vastly different fates.

WHAT RELIABILITY AND AUTHENTICITY ARE NOT

Reliability and authenticity are related to the notion of trust. Economists study trust in relation to markets. John McMillan states that trust is one of the five elements for a workable market platform.[2] Scholars studying developing countries find that trust is a very large element in the creation of any trading relationship.[3] One of the most important jobs academic librarians have taken upon themselves is the teaching of information literacy to undergraduates—a subject that now includes assessment of how well to trust an Internet source. Authorship is one of the perennial issues in literary studies: how do we trust an anonymous document or one written by fraud or proxy? Anthropologists question the authenticity of myths, as well as the conclusions drawn about various versions of myths leading to quite different conclusions about the nature of being human.[4] These types of studies tell us that trust is extraordinarily complex and cannot be created or destroyed according to a menu of forms, processes, and transmissions. Trust is contextually established and may be reestablished or destroyed at each exchange.

Authenticity, in contrast, is not a measure of trust, but a measure of appropriation. Authenticity is an intellectually troubling Western tradition. As a property of an artifact, authenticity carries with it the burden of defining what is really real. Only the rulers, not the ruled;[5] the purchasers, not the creators;[6] the colonists, not the colonized[7] determine what is authentic. As Stephen Pritchard observes, "This has a strange resonance in defining Indigenous 'cultural property,' since European-derived names, concepts, and categories have overwritten and effaced Indigenous ones. Here the question of who names, and thereby authorises, is inseparably tied to questions of self-determination. Two issues of great importance are who defines the relationship as 'belonging' or 'proper,' and to what extent such a definition would be compatible with creative and dynamic aspects of culture."[8] As I shall demonstrate below, U.S. law, to which we are responsible in the United States of America, defines "authenticity" clearly as something the custodian of the document or record declares in a court of law. Authenticity is not a property to be defined or maintained, but a claim made by the owner. That claim may be challenged and defeated according to any one of a number of methods, not by a set of properties established by archivists.

The lack of attention paid by archivists to this aspect of authenticity in their many studies and funded projects is troubling, particularly with respect to the International Research on Permanent Authentic Records in Electronic Systems (InterPARES) project,[9] with its goal of developing the tools and methodology for preserving digital records. Persons responsible for maintaining our record of the past have not studied the history of their own work.[10]

RECORDS MANAGERS AND AUTHENTICITY

Records managers do not concern themselves with authenticity per se. Records managers are concerned with every aspect of the creation, distribution, use, maintenance, transfer, storage, and disposition of records—insofar as his or her portfolio permits. For the records manager, authenticity is a requirement demanded by the organization for which the records manager works and by the courts through the rules of evidence. The records manager does not define, determine, protect, or preserve authenticity; rather, the records manager helps to make it happen, according to the demands and restrictions of the environment. For the records manager, authenticity is an outcome defined by others.

What does it mean for the organization to define authenticity? Authenticity can be an aspect of information within an organization, between organizations, between organizations and individuals, or between individuals and individuals.

Within an organization, the most common form of communication is still the memorandum.[11] Within the world of paper, some departments required that the author sign his or her initials adjacent to the "to" line of memoranda, to attest to the authenticity of the document. In fact, in many workplaces, employees do not read memoranda that do not have the author's initials; such documents are not considered reliable within the corporate culture of the organization. Such corporate cultures do not inquire into, reflect, or refer to the "socio-juridical system in which the record is created."[12] In contrast, within the electronic world of email, there are no signatures. Emails from people we know are considered authentic until proven otherwise. Before we began to suspect emails, even from close associates, we gladly opened them, as well as any associated attachments—thereby spreading many computer viruses. When many employees realized that this form of "human engineering" was affecting them, they became wary of all emails.[13]

Between organizations, authenticity is relative to the exchange taking place. For example, among organizations exchanging documents, the transmittal attending the document is as important as the document itself. A transmittal may be in the form of a letter, a memorandum, or an email; it lists the documents it attends, as well as the date sent. The transmittal is the proof used by the sending organization that the documents were sent according to an agreement between the two organizations. In this way, the transmittal can be as important as the document it attends, because it constitutes proof of contractual compliance. Another example of information between organizations is the envelope in which a document may be sent. More often than not in the hard-copy world, the envelope is discarded. Some occasions, however, require keeping the envelope with the documents inside, such as occasions requiring comparison of the dates of receipt, the metered frank, the postal cancellation, and/or the date of the documents inside the envelope. The envelope was ordinarily retained under those circumstances to demonstrate that the receiving organization was not tardy in its actions—i.e., that a formal or tacit agreement had not been breached.

Digital signatures are one of the hopes the archival community holds out for ensuring the authenticity of a document.[14] The world of business is not so stringent or hopeful. The Electronic Signatures in Global and National Commerce Act of 2000, also known as the E-Sign Act,[15] allows any electronic signature with which the parties to an exchange are comfortable. Electronic signatures include digital signatures, those that are created using cryptography, and public key infrastructure (PKI).[16] An electronic signature can also be something as simple as verification by a blank return email—as when we sign up for a listserv—or as complex as a three-party PKI.

What the E-Sign Act does is to leave the level of authenticity and authentication up to the parties involved.[17] Essentially, the E-Sign Act assumes that each organization manages its own level of risk—its own level of authenticity, reliability, and trustworthiness. The problem with this assumption is that, considering what we know about the range of common business practices today, all of the elements that go into making what an archivist would consider an authentic record are up for grabs within any organization, including the very existence of a vital record. For example, when Enron created complex accounting documents in order to make "nontransactions" look like profitable ventures, the company's board of directors and executive officers knew what they were doing. They deemed the risk of getting caught versus the risk of continuing to receive compensation an acceptable risk. Likewise, Enron's auditor, Arthur Andersen, determined that the destruction of Enron records in the face of a potential investigation by the Securities and Exchange Commission was an acceptable risk. These decisions may appear foolish in hindsight, but such behavior represents only the extreme side of risk management—and as such underscores the basic problem with the assumptions of the E-Sign Act.

Authenticity is as much an issue of trust as it is of chain of custody and verification. Trust is difficult to establish among individuals. The online marketplace eBay has done an extraordinary job creating a trust environment in which the authenticity of every item for sale and the success or failure of consummating that transaction can be judged by each buyer. It does this by offering the buyer an opportunity to rate the seller and then posts those ratings in each of the seller's offerings. eBay endorses no one. The process creates trust. Not every buyer will be comfortable with every product or seller, but eBay's very success is indicative of a high level of trust among a large population willing to spend its money.

Most organizations regard records management as an element of risk management. For example, organizations choose not to have or not to enforce a records retention and disposition schedule (RRS). Having and enforcing an RRS lowers the costs of document discovery during litigation and may even lower the cost of any settlement or fine imposed. Organizations, both government agencies and corporations, that have not been served with lawsuits are less likely to see the value of such a program. For any organization, public or private, the level of authenticity is established by the business environment as well as the judgment of high-level managers concerning levels of acceptable risk. In short, the level of reliability and authenticity are business requirements which are determined, in part, by managers. In records management, we are well aware that the level of reliability and authenticity is in many instances determined by inaction. Events such as the passage of the Sarbanes-Oxley Act of 2002[18] have the effect of bringing records management to the forefront, but, more often than not, organizations continue to regard records management as only an afterthought.

As we have seen, authenticity, reliability, and trustworthiness of records are not absolutes. The quality of each varies according to an organization's tolerance for risk.

AUTHENTICITY IN THE COURTROOM

Authenticity is defined by the courts in civil as well as criminal cases. Records managers have an intimate relationship with the rules of evidence because they handle records and in many instances are involved in responding to subpoenas during the discovery phase of litigation. Rules of evidence provide a checklist of requirements for determining whether recorded materials can be presented to a court as evidence.

Evidence in records management is what is acceptable as information in a trial. Whether information is accepted as evidence is determined by the negotiations among the judge, the attorneys, and the relevant laws concerning evidence. A good example is the 1995 trial of O. J. Simpson and the questions that surrounded the authenticity of the "bloody glove." The glove's authenticity was in question because of unclear chain of custody. The glove had been placed in a police officer's back pocket, and the integrity of the handler was questioned. Was the "bloody glove" authentic? The glove's handlers, the police, are required to preserve the authenticity of the glove through a specific ritual or sequence of actions. Where the ritual is absent, authenticity must be established by the party who would have the artifact submitted as evidence. The judge has final authority to accept or deny information as evidence—i.e., he judges the artifact's authenticity. Should the judge decide the artifact is not admissible as "evidence," it becomes "nonevidence" and then

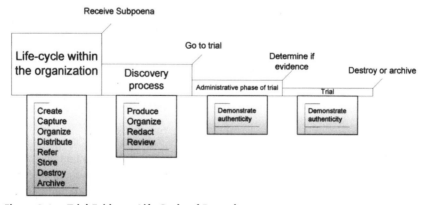

Figure 3.1.   Trial Evidence Life Cycle of Records.

enters into an alternate business process (see figure 3.1, for a schematic of the evidence life cycle of records). Note that these processes have no bearing on whether an artifact is a document or a record. All items presented to the trial process are documents because they signify something and are records because they must be managed.

RELIABILITY AND AUTHENTICITY NEEDS FOR RECORDS AS TRIAL EVIDENCE

The rules of evidence of any state or nation are clear about what information captured in the course of business can be submitted as evidence. The rules are fairly consistent even for different types of legal systems. Those rules and laws also declare what is "authentic" and what is not. Records managers are held to the standard required by their organization and any litigation that may occur. Generally speaking, evidence in criminal cases must be much tighter than evidence presented for a civil case. Most of the cases for which a records manager will respond are civil cases. For example, the Civil Evidence (Scotland) Act 1988 states:

> **5.**—(1) Unless the court otherwise directs, a document may in any civil proceedings be taken to form part of the records of a business or undertaking if it is certified as such by a docquet purporting to be signed by an officer of the business or undertaking to which the records belong; and a statement contained in any document certified as aforesaid may be received in evidence without being spoken to by a witness. (2) For the purposes of this section, a facsimile of a signature shall be treated as a signature.

Any document for which the company claims reliability and authenticity is reliable and authentic as long as an officer of the corporation will sign that it is. No further test or proof is required.

> **6.**—(1) For the purposes of any civil proceedings, a copy of a document, purporting to be authenticated by a person responsible for the making of the copy, shall, unless the court otherwise directs, be—(a) deemed a true copy; and (b) treated for evidential purposes as if it were the document itself. (2) In subsection (1) above, "copy" includes a transcript or reproduction.[19]

Any copy an appropriate employee claims is a true copy is a true copy. No further test or proof is required. What this means is that the substitution is a reliable and authentic record.

The standard of documentary authenticity for civil cases is not very high in general. The content of the documents are trustworthy because the company says they are trustworthy, and they are trustworthy as records because the company says they are trustworthy. Hence, the documents are reliable because the company says so, and the documents are authentic because the company says so. No questions are asked about modes, forms, states of transmission, or manner of preservation and custody. In addition, no distinction is made between hard-copy and electronic records. In addition, the process and life cycle by which the record is produced is not questioned.

Turning to records that may be used in criminal actions (as well as civil), business records generally fall within the hearsay clause of the rules of evidence. Hearsay is a complex legal term, but for our purposes it is generally information that is not provided by a person who is a witness or the defendant. Rephrasing, hearsay is secondhand information. Let us look closely at the U.S. Federal Rules of Evidence current as of this book's publication hearsay rule for its direction on authenticity and reliability, "Rule 803. Hearsay Exceptions; Availability of Declarant Immaterial":

The following are not excluded by the hearsay rule, even though the declarant is available as a witness:

(1) Present sense impression.—A statement describing or explaining an event or condition made while the declarant was perceiving the event or condition, or immediately thereafter.

(2) Excited utterance.—A statement relating to a startling event or condition made while the declarant was under the stress of excitement caused by the event or condition.

(3) Then existing mental, emotional, or physical condition.—A statement of the declarant's then existing state of mind, emotion, sensation, or physical condition (such as intent, plan, motive, design, mental feeling, pain, and bodily health), but not including a statement of memory or belief to prove the fact remembered or believed unless it relates to the execution, revocation, identification, or terms of declarant's will.

(4) Statements for purposes of medical diagnosis or treatment.—Statements made for purposes of medical diagnosis or treatment and describing medical history, or past or present symptoms, pain, or sensations, or the inception or general character of the cause or external source thereof insofar as reasonably pertinent to diagnosis or treatment.

(5) Recorded recollection.—A memorandum or record concerning a matter about which a witness once had knowledge but now has insufficient recollection to enable the witness to testify fully and accurately, shown to have been made or adopted by the witness when the matter was fresh in the witness's memory and to reflect that knowledge correctly. If admitted, the memorandum or record may be read into evidence but may not itself be received as an exhibit unless offered by an adverse party.

(6) Records of regularly conducted activity.—A memorandum, report, record, or data compilation, in any form, of acts, events, conditions, opinions, or diag-

noses, made at or near the time by, or from information transmitted by, a person with knowledge, if kept in the course of a regularly conducted business activity, and if it was the regular practice of that business activity to make the memorandum, report, record or data compilation, all as shown by the testimony of the custodian or other qualified witness, or by certification that complies with Rule 902(11), Rule 902(12), or a statute permitting certification, unless the source of information or the method or circumstances of preparation indicate lack of trustworthiness.[20] The term "business" as used in this paragraph includes business, institution, association, profession, occupation, and calling of every kind, whether or not conducted for profit.

(7) Absence of entry in records kept in accordance with the provisions of paragraph (6).—Evidence that a matter is not included in the memoranda reports, records, or data compilations, in any form, kept in accordance with the provisions of paragraph (6), to prove the nonoccurrence or nonexistence of the matter, if the matter was of a kind of which a memorandum, report, record, or data compilation was regularly made and preserved, unless the sources of information or other circumstances indicate lack of trustworthiness.

(8) Public records and reports.—Records, reports, statements, or data compilations, in any form, of public offices or agencies, setting forth (A) the activities of the office or agency, or (B) matters observed pursuant to duty imposed by law as to which matters there was a duty to report, excluding, however, in criminal cases matters observed by police officers and other law enforcement personnel, or (C) in civil actions and proceedings and against the Government in criminal cases, factual findings resulting from an investigation made pursuant to authority granted by law, unless the sources of information or other circumstances indicate lack of trustworthiness.

(9) Records of vital statistics.—Records or data compilations, in any form, of births, fetal deaths, deaths, or marriages, if the report thereof was made to a public office pursuant to requirements of law.

(10) Absence of public record or entry.—To prove the absence of a record, report, statement, or data compilation, in any form, or the nonoccurrence or nonexistence of a matter of which a record, report, statement, or data compilation, in any form, was regularly made and preserved by a public office or agency, evidence in the form of a certification in accordance with rule 902, or testimony, that diligent search failed to disclose the record, report, statement, or data compilation, or entry.

(11) Records of religious organizations.—Statements of births, marriages, divorces, deaths, legitimacy, ancestry, relationship by blood or marriage, or other similar facts of personal or family history, contained in a regularly kept record of a religious organization.

(12) Marriage, baptismal, and similar certificates.—Statements of fact contained in a certificate that the maker performed a marriage or other ceremony or administered a sacrament, made by a clergyman, public official, or other person authorized by the rules or practices of a religious organization or by law to perform the act certified, and purporting to have been issued at the time of the act or within a reasonable time thereafter.

(13) Family records.—Statements of fact concerning personal or family history contained in family Bibles, genealogies, charts, engravings on rings, inscriptions on family portraits, engravings on urns, crypts, or tombstones, or the like.

(14) Records of documents affecting an interest in property.—The record of a document purporting to establish or affect an interest in property, as proof of the content of the original recorded document and its execution and delivery by each person by whom it purports to have been executed, if the record is a record of a public office and an applicable statute authorizes the recording of documents of that kind in that office.

(15) Statements in documents affecting an interest in property.—A statement contained in a document purporting to establish or affect an interest in property if the matter stated was relevant to the purpose of the document, unless dealings with the property since the document was made have been inconsistent with the truth of the statement or the purport of the document.

(16) Statements in ancient documents.—Statements in a document in existence twenty years or more the authenticity of which is established.

(17) Market reports, commercial publications.—Market quotations, tabulations, lists, directories, or other published compilations, generally used and relied upon by the public or by persons in particular occupations.

(18) Learned treatises.—To the extent called to the attention of an expert witness upon cross-examination or relied upon by the expert witness in direct examination, statements contained in published treatises, periodicals, or pamphlets on a subject of history, medicine, or other science or art, established as a reliable authority by the testimony or admission of the witness or by other expert testimony or by judicial notice. If admitted, the statements may be read into evidence but may not be received as exhibits.

(19) Reputation concerning personal or family history.—Reputation among members of a person's family by blood, adoption, or marriage, or among a person's associates, or in the community, concerning a person's birth, adoption, marriage, divorce, death, legitimacy, relationship by blood, adoption, or marriage, ancestry, or other similar fact of personal or family history.

(20) Reputation concerning boundaries or general history.—Reputation in a community, arising before the controversy, as to boundaries of or customs affecting lands in the community, and reputation as to events of general history important to the community or State or nation in which located.

(21) Reputation as to character.—Reputation of a person's character among associates or in the community.

(22) Judgment of previous conviction.—Evidence of a final judgment, entered after a trial or upon a plea of guilty (but not upon a plea of nolo contendere), adjudging a person guilty of a crime punishable by death or imprisonment in excess of one year, to prove any fact essential to sustain the judgment, but not including, when offered by the Government in a criminal prosecution for purposes other than impeachment, judgments against persons other than the accused. The pendency of an appeal may be shown but does not affect admissibility.

(23) Judgment as to personal, family, or general history, or boundaries.— Judgments as proof of matters of personal, family or general history, or boundaries, essential to the judgment, if the same would be provable by evidence of reputation.[21]

Sections 6, 7, 8, 9, 10, and 16 are documents that can be admitted into evidence. Sections 1, 2, 3, 4, 5, 15, 16, and 18 are statements heard by others or require statements to be read from a document (with the exception of sections 5 "recorded recollections" and 18 "learned treatises" that can be offered as documents by an adverse party). Each of the above sections describes some type of document, or a statement from that document, that is a candidate for evidence in a criminal (or civil) trial.[22] Only sections 6 (records of regularly conducted activities), 7 (the absence of an entry in records), and 8 (public records and reports), permit tests of trustworthiness—i.e., determinations of authenticity. Section 6 describes business records as "Records of regularly conducted activity," section 7 describes the absence of business records described in section 6, and section 8 describes public records and reports. Only section 16, statements in ancient documents, requires demonstration/test of authenticity, but it describes "ancient documents"—i.e., those that have been in existence for 20 years or more. Sections 6 and 10 (absence of public entry) require authentication by reference to Rule 902. Section 10 describes the absence of a public record as described in section 8 or section 9 (compilations of vital statistics such as births, deaths, marriages, etc.).

Of the 23 categories of hearsay, five have a requirement of tests for reliability or authenticity: sections 6, 7, 8, 10 and 16. Section 6 describes those tests:

> if kept in the course of a regularly conducted business activity, and if it was the regular practice of that business activity to make the memorandum, report, record or data compilation, all as shown by the testimony of the custodian or other qualified witness, or by certification that complies with Rule 902(11), Rule 902(12), or a statute permitting certification, unless the source of information or the method or circumstances of preparation indicate lack of trustworthiness.

The section presents two reliability requirements and three authenticity tests. The two reliability requirements are that the record has been created in the regular course of business, and that it has been the regular practice of the organization to create such records. Reliability here is the result of a business process that is not extraordinary and a document created in the process that is not extraordinary. As for authenticity, the first authenticity test is that someone with intimate knowledge, "as shown by the testimony of the custodian or other qualified witness," be able to assure that the two reliability requirements are the case with a particular document or set of documents.[23] In other words, if someone with a link to a document will speak for it, the document is both reliable and authentic.

The second authenticity test is that the document or set of documents have a certification conforming with sections 11 and 12 of Rule 902, the rule on self-authentication. Rule 902 describes sets of documents wherein "Extrinsic evidence of authenticity as a condition precedent to admissibility is not required. . . . " Business records must have something akin to an affidavit similar to that required above in the Scottish Civil Law of Evidence, "accompanied by a written declaration of its custodian or other qualified person." The Scottish law affidavit has four strict requirements: "(A) was made at or near the time of the occurrence of the matters set forth by, or from information transmitted by, a person with knowledge of those matters; (B) was kept in the course of the regularly conducted activity; and (C) was made by the regularly conducted activity as a regular practice."[24] Requirements (B) and (C) are the same as those described in Rule 803 (6) concerning creation. The document is part of normal business processes and was created by a worker associated with the business process. Requirement (A) requires proximity in time or a source, "a person with knowledge of these matters," or a custodian.[25] A document is not what it appears to be; it is what the environment and its shepherd says it is.

The reader will note that Rule 803 (6) and Rule 902 (11) both apply to "The original or a duplicate of a domestic record." None of these requirements of reliability or tests of authenticity are onerous for the organization involved unless the organization does not manage its records. The tests are the same for hard-copy as for computer records: "The courts generally have admitted computer records upon a showing that the records fall within the business records exception, Fed. R. Evid. 803(6). . . . See, e.g., *United States v. Cestnik*, 36 F.3d 904, 909–10 (10th Cir. 1994); *United States v. Moore*, 923 F.2d 910, 914 (1st Cir. 1991); *United States v. Briscoe*, 896 F.2d 1476, 1494 (7th Cir. 1990); *United States v. Catabran*, 836 F.2d 453, 457 (9th Cir. 1988); *Capital Marine Supply v. M/V Roland Thomas II*, 719 F.2d 104, 106 (5th Cir. 1983). Applying this test, the courts have indicated that computer records generally can be admitted as business records if they were kept pursuant to a routine procedure for motives that tend to assure their accuracy."[26] The courts will also permit hard-copy versions of computer records following certain procedures, *Public Citizen v. John Carlin, Archivist of the United States*, 184 F.3d 900 (D.C. Cir, 1999).[27] In short, "The procedure of creation of a record is the body of rules according to which acts or portions of them are recorded,"[28] is a good definition of reliable records. What is missing from this definition, however, is an understanding that the rules themselves are quite minimal. Just as the E-Sign Act leaves the level of authentication up to the parties in the exchange, the Rules of Evidence leave up to the creators of the records how detailed, time-consuming, and exacting the "procedure of creation of a record" will be.[29]

The third authenticity requirement is "a statute permitting certification." Corporations maintain numerous documents that must have some form of official public seal, notary mark, or signature of the corporate secretary. Those documents, such as articles of incorporation, bylaws, or minutes, are sometimes filed with the state, as with articles of incorporation. These are usually called documents.

The court defines reliable and authentic records that may be used for evidence. The rules for creating and maintaining reliable and authentic records within an organization are quite minimal, ordinarily requiring solely that the custodian will attest to such.

EVIDENCE AND TRANSACTIONS IN RECORDS MANAGEMENT

To define what makes a record reliable or authentic means defining a particular organization's business requirements. Those business requirements may emphasize speed over accuracy or budget issues over recordkeeping. Statutes and regulations concerning records are a part of business requirements. The business requirements imposed by archivists often take an extreme view of both reliability and authenticity.[30] Reliability and authenticity do not define what a record is. They are variable qualities that are either part of an organization's risk management program, or they are not. We have described some requirements and tests that are not very onerous and do not disqualify substitutes so long as someone with apparent authority is willing to attest to the document's reliability and authenticity.

There are even organizations, primarily government agencies, that have a classification of documents created in the regular course of business called "nonrecords." Either directly or indirectly, business functions within government address the needs of citizens, but even within government, there is a division between "program" functions and "administrative" functions. For example, in the discussion above about Rule 803, section 7 describes the categories of activities producing "records:" "(A) the activities of the office or agency, or (B) matters observed pursuant to duty imposed by law as to which matters there was a duty to report, excluding, however, in criminal cases matters observed by police officers and other law enforcement personnel, or (C) in civil actions and proceedings and against the Government in criminal cases, factual findings resulting from an investigation made pursuant to authority granted by law . . . " (A) and the first part of (B) are "program"-related and the second half of (B) regarding criminal cases and (C) regards the results of civil and criminal investigations. Only the information produced as a result of the activities described in (A), (B), and (C) in Rule 803 are considered "records," as they are part of the portfolio assigned to an agency. The purpose of "program" functions, then, is to serve citizens directly. The product of the processes defined as "program" is called "records."

In contrast, the purpose of "administrative" functions is to manage the day-to-day operations of the government, such as housekeeping, computer operations, and mail delivery, and to provide human resources support to the public employees—indirectly serving the citizen through good management of public funds. The product of the processes defined as "administrative" are called "nonrecords." Public funds are used for both program and administrative functions, but administrative functions directly serve the public employee and serve citizens only indirectly, whereas program functions directly serve citizens. Administrative information may reside in a public archive for some brief period of time, but it will eventually be destroyed. Program information, however, will eventually reside in an archive for a very long time. The management method used to get both types of information safely through the varied processes toward achieving that end is records management.

The distinction that government agencies make between a record and a nonrecord is important because it helps to explain some of the definitions of records that have been created by archivists. However, both program and administrative information, and hence records and nonrecords, are subject to criminal or civil litigation and can be subpoenaed—which means that both must be managed as records.

There is no such thing as a nonrecord within records management. Any information-containing object that must be managed is a record—any object, ranging from an adhesive note, to a phone message, to the minutes from the meetings of a corporation's board of directors. The object is defined by the need for management rather than by its function as an artifact. Rule 803 (7), quoted above, describes as records "(C) in civil actions and proceedings and against the Government in criminal cases, factual findings resulting from an investigation made pursuant to authority granted by law." Those factual findings could include drafts, adhesive notes, and voice mail messages. As part of an investigation, each of those nonrecords would then become a record, according to the U.S. Federal Rules of Evidence. The fact that the documents could become evidence is sufficient proof that all information artifacts within an organization, including government agencies, must be managed. All information artifacts have the potential to be records, even within government. Essentially, any captured information that can get an organization into trouble is a record—and this definition applies whether the organization in question is public or private, government agency or corporation.

HOW ARCHIVISTS DEFINE RECORDS

One of the most common popularly accepted definitions of records is offered by David Bearman: "evidence of a business transaction."[31] As demonstrated above, this definition cannot stand within records management. Indeed, were this definition to be adopted, very little information within an organization would ever be managed. Bearman's definition uses the nonlegal notion of "evidence" as a simple demonstration. The term "evidence" stems from the Indo-European *weid*, "to see," and Latin *videre*, "to see, look," and Greek *eidos*, "appearance or form," from which we get the word "idol."[32] As we saw above, the legal concept of evidence is quite complex, but there is only one thing the records manager needs to know: evidence is what is presented to a judge or a jury during a trial—not what happens in the regular course of business. What becomes evidence has undergone a testing process, some of which we examined above with Rules 803 and 902.

Records management is both liberated and constrained by its relationship with risk management and with litigation. For records managers, the term "evidence" used in the Bearman definition and the ISO definition ("information created, received, and maintained as evidence and information by an organization or person, in pursuance of legal obligations or in the transaction of business") misleads us. Within records management, evidence is what is admitted and presented in the trial phase of litigation. Not all records can be evidence. Not all litigation goes to trial.

Records that become evidence are a subset of a part of litigation called "discovery." Within discovery, the parties to a suit are required to exchange any documents that may be pertinent to the situation, an exchange that is called "document production." It should be noted that the documents produced may never rise to the level of evidence. The fear in document production is that opposing counsel may find a path of information that may lead to further document production that will inevitably lead to evidence and either a trial or a settlement. Until the mid-1990s, many defendants' attorneys earned their pay by keeping a suit in document production and making it so expensive and time consuming that the plaintiff eventually called off the suit. Recognizing that wealthy defendants could make prosecution too costly for aggrieved plaintiffs, the government leveled the playing field and the rules were changed so that all parties had to produce documents voluntarily, thoroughly, and quickly, without numerous court orders.[33]

Because document production or "discovery" does not necessarily become evidence, any artifact that appears relevant to a case may be requested. If an employee used instant messaging to harass coworkers, the relevant instant messages are requested. If cartoons with questionable content were posted on the company bulleting board, those cartoons are requested. Any captured information, whether it captures an "act" or even "business," is subject to discovery. The only criterion required in discovery is relevance to the case, not whether the artifact is called a record or document.

The advent of requests for computer records, a separate development from the "rules change" referred to above, reversed the trend to play out discovery to an unacceptably high dollar amount, again making document production expensive and onerous—depending upon an organization's level of records management. It has also led to the creation of a new field, computer forensics, in which computer investigation and analysis techniques are used gather evidence to find out what happened on a computer and who was responsible for it. The objective is to perform a structured investigation of computer activity while maintaining a documented chain of evidence, such that the resultant evidence is suitable for presentation in a court of law.

Computer forensics has produced a spate of examples of how a record custodian's ignorance of how a computer, a computer system, or an application works can produce embarrassment and adverse results within a legal system. One recent example is the destruction of Enron-related emails at Arthur Andersen and the subsequent revival of most of those same emails through backup tapes. This is a fairly common example of copy control—well known in records management, but poorly known or managed by information technology. Another example of a problem that organizations under litigation face is when computer hard drives are seized and the contents reconstructed. Most companies are unaware that when a document is deleted, the document itself remains for up to a month until it has been overwritten. What is in fact deleted at the time of deletion is the pointer to the document, which "tells" the various software that the document exists. The document itself can be exhumed and read again, until such time as it has been overwritten by documents subsequently stored on that hard drive. This is an example of poor destruction practices that is well known in records management. Experts in electronic document production and evidence have worked long and hard to describe the differences between electronic and hard-copy records.[34] They point to ease of alteration, ease of copying, the ephemeral nature of the media on which electronic records are written, etc. However, the primary difference appears to be that the electronic world does not force filing practices on workers in the same way that the physical world does. Everyone is a pile maker in virtual reality. You may disagree and ask whether each of us has to set up *some* organizational scheme on our own hard drives, just in the interest of being able to find things again. Is it not more an issue of basic, widespread ignorance among the majority of computer users, concerning the capabilities of the technology—back-up capabilities in one instance, and what actually happens in deletion, in the other? I would argue that it is more an issue of out of sight, out of mind, whereby the documents are not physically sitting on the desk or in boxes on the floor and therefore in our way.

Any one of the above-mentioned examples can be produced during discovery and could either be used as evidence, or point to further information that could be used as evidence, or point to behavior suggesting that the organization believes it is guilty. This means that the use of the term "evidence" must be reserved solely for that information that has passed all the tests and is being submitted for a trial. Hence, the profession of records management must reject the term "evidence" for use in any general definition of records or information.

Roy C. Turnbaugh makes a reasoned argument why the government archivist must also deal with a different definition of records, saying that a government archivist is responsible to government laws and court cases involving the government, not to definitions created by other archivists: "These statutory definitions, fleshed out by case law and regulations, make up the setting within which government records programs must function. For this reason, it serves no useful purpose when electronic records projects try to formulate new definitions of record, such as: 'The complete set of documentation required to provide evidence of a business transaction' or 'A document made or received and set aside in the course of a practical activity.' Since these definitions are outside the law, they are without effect for government records programs, which must function inside the law. In fact they only confuse matters even more."[35] Just as records managers must define evidence according to the rules of evidence, government archivists must define records according to the relevant government records statutes, regulations, and case law. By different reasoning, we arrive at the same conclusion: that records cannot simply be "evidence."

The following table 3.1 shows the most elementary requirements demanded by different parts of the legal life cycle for records to be considered as evidence. To enter the legal system, a document must exist physically and be subject to subpoena. The document is not yet evidence, but is beginning the long process for consideration to be accepted as evidence or rejected as nonevidence. To be useful to an organization, the document must exist outside someone's head, be complete, and have its context maintained. Some

Table 3.1.   **Features Required by Different Parts of the Life Cycle**

Feature Required	Must-have for Legal Action	Must-have for Organization	Must-have for Archivists
Exists outside someone's head	X	X	X
Can be subpoenaed	X		
Complete		X	X
Context maintained through life cycle		X	X
Authentic			X

organizations worry about whether documents can be subpoenaed, but this is not normally one of the requirements for a successful life cycle. Only archivists require that documents be authentic. Like organizations, archivists do not normally worry whether documents can be subpoenaed. Organizations do not worry per se about authenticity, but about costs and benefits. For example, organizations do need context to ensure something can be found again and placed within its context, yet few have or follow procedures for when an employee leaves. Those records are tossed in a box and sent to off-site storage with a cryptic description of "Joe's desk files." Joe is no longer with the firm and no one may even remember who Joe is. Most likely, there was nothing interesting or important in his desk, but even a subpoena could require another employee to go through that box.

Similar strictures are placed on the term "transaction." Transactions are a very particular type of record. Transaction documents instantiate an exchange of service or product for consideration. For example, in the U.S., sales tax in each state must be recorded for each transaction and then submitted to the state tax service. The tax service wants only records of each transaction—i.e., each exchange of consideration for a product or service. Transactions are a specific business activity that is exclusive of many other activities. Transactions do not include the meeting minutes of boards of directors, for instance, or the documents associated with quality programs or health and safety programs.

The term "business" has similar strictures. For example, records are created "in the regular course of business," according to Rule 803(6). So far, no court has arrived at a definition of "the regular course of business," but this use does suggest that there are activities done in business that are not in the regular course of business—forgery, for example. Forged documents are presentable as evidence, but they are not a part of a "business." Rule 803(6) goes further in describing what a business is: "The term 'business' as used in this paragraph includes business, institution, association, profession, occupation, and calling of every kind, whether or not conducted for profit." While the term "business" does not have as many strictures on its use as the terms "evidence" and "transaction," it does have strictures that exclude it as a potential candidate for any general definition of information or records.

The terms "transactions" and "business" are subject to the same limitations pointed out above by Turnbaugh: they are not part of the legal definitions to which government archivists are subject. Records in any context cannot be defined as "evidence of a business transaction," either because the terms used within it are so fraught with restrictions that they cannot be usefully employed in a definition, or because the context requires a specific definition and interpretation of a definition that excludes innovation such as the one proposed.

The ISO 15489 definition, "information created, received, and maintained as evidence and information by an organization or person, in pursuance of legal obligations or in the transaction of business," has the same limitation because it depends upon "evidence," "business," and "transaction." The ISO definition as a representation of best practices misleads all organizations in the elements of what records managers must manage (in addition to which it is formulated as a tautology, as noted previously).

Having found the official as well as the most commonly used definitions lacking, let us examine other proffered definitions of records. The best known definition is from Robek, Maedke, and Brown's *Information and Records Management,* a classic in the field of records management: "Recorded information of any kind and in any form."[36] This definition begs the question of how "recorded" is defined, and, even more importantly, how "information" is defined. Neither term is further clarified within any edition of this classic. Nor do the authors describe the relationship of a document to a record. As we shall see below, this is one of the greatest differences between records management and archives.

Penn, Pennix, and Coulson, in their *Records Management Handbook,* define records as "any information captured in reproducible form that is required for conducting business."[37] This definition requires that information be "reproducible." Yet not all information is reproducible, as we shall see below. This definition also begs the question of the term "information," and limits information to "conducting business"—the same problem as with the Bearman definition.

In any definition of records, the context must be very carefully considered. The ISO and Bearman definitions use terms that would narrow the focus to a tiny proportion of captured information in any nongovernment context and cannot replace the legal definitions required by the government context. While definitions created by records managers do take context into consideration, they fail by not pointing to content. The strength of the ISO and Bearman definitions is the recognition that a record is a holder of content and it is the content that must be managed. The weakness of these same definitions is in not recognizing that organizations, just like humans, use information, not evidence. The strength of the records management definitions is in recognizing the primacy of information, but the weakness is in not clearly defining what that content might be.

DOCUMENTS AND RECORDS

We have begged the question of whether a record is a document. Let us remove ourselves from the world of common law to the world of statutory law and review Peru's definition of a document. Peru has a statutory system: "Public or private writings, printed matter, photocopies, facsimiles or faxes, plans, tables, drawings, photographs, x-rays, films, microforms of any type or representing any type of electronic support, other audio or video reproductions, voicemail in general, *other things that compile, contain or represent a fact, a human activity or its result is a document*" (Peru Law No. 26612, 5/21/96, art. 5; italics are mine). A document in Peru could be the plaster cast of a footprint, the metadata for an email, the post-it note on a report, the pencil markings on a financial report, precisely what we defined as a record above—the broad-ranging inclusiveness that we have seen to be necessary based on the preceding discussions.

What is most important about this definition is that it legally defines content—"a fact or human activity or its result"—represented as "compile, contain or represent a fact, a human activity or its result," that must be managed. This definition of a document could also serve as a definition of a record. As definitions go, it is an excellent one for our particular purposes because it does not limit types of format or content. A human activity or its result can be a record or document. Documents, however, play a different role within records management. The individual document within records management is best exemplified by Robek, Maedke, and Brown's definition of a document as the "smallest unit of filing."[38] This definition does not relate a document to a record. We will explore below why this must be the case, but let us first examine a current mantra concerning documents: content, context, and structure, and their relation to particular information artifacts.

The phrase "content, context, and structure" appears to have no clear starting point, although I have spoken with several persons, each of whom claims to have originated it. The migration path appears to have begun with, for example, the *Report of the Task Force on Archiving of Digital Information* from 1996: "In the digital environment, as we have seen, ideas are typically embedded in particular formats and structures that are dependent on hardware and software technologies subject to rapid change. Conceived at this higher level of abstraction—that is, in terms of format and structure—the definition of content poses considerable difficulties for managing information integrity in an archival context, and we are just beginning to come to terms with the expression of these problems in the digital environment."[39] In the hard-copy environment, the same issue holds—i.e., content and structure are difficult to tease apart.

Correspondence is an excellent example of this problem. A letter is typically typed (or printed) on letterhead. Letterhead ordinarily has three characteristics attesting to its authenticity: the weight of the paper, the watermark, and the name and address of the organization in a particular font and color. There may also be a seal. Not all organizations are so careful as to consistently include all of these components/elements. Because the return address is part of the paper, not typed, do we conclude that it is a part of the structure of the document? Could we conclude that it is contextual metadata? What about the envelope? As discussed previously, the envelope would probably not be retained unless the individual opening it noticed a significant discrepancy in some of the dates, and only if it meant the recipient would appear to be unresponsive. Would the recipient necessarily date-stamp the letter when it was received? In my experience, this latter eventuality is unlikely. What are we to make of the signature? It is added after the letter is approved for format and content, yet the content it provides is often illegible. I have heard and participated in several discussions that the signature on outgoing correspondence should be written in blue ballpoint pen to ensure that the recipient can verify its authenticity. In this view, the signature appears to be part of the structure of the letter. What constitutes the content, then, and what the structure?

As we can see, this is unclear even for hard-copy records; it is just as complex in the electronic world. Consider, for instance, the PROFS case,[40] a 1993 Federal District and Circuit Court case that galvanized the archival community. It raised the issue of authenticity and reliability via what archivists call "metadata"—formerly restricted to the definition of a field in a database. From the perspective of records management, the problem in the PROFS case was that a poorly designed email product, known as PROFS, was being used for internal correspondence in the Executive Office of the President, and that further records management was not being performed on the documents. The email system did not have a method for capturing an unambiguous sender and recipient in the content of the email messages.

As defined by the court in the PROFS case, the minimum set of information required to be captured is:

1) An intelligent representation of name of sender.
2) An intelligent representation of name of all recipients, including on distribution list of carbon copies.
3) The date of transmission.
4) The date/time of an acknowledgement of receipt, only where requested by sender.[41]

The first three items are standard content for any memorandum. The third is never in the content of the message but is used for what is called "nonrefutability"—an assurance that a person cannot deny he or she received a document by blaming the unreliability of the email system or the computer system on which the email was sent and received. The last item is ordinarily not part of the normal course of business and reflects a lack of trust by the sender for the recipient.

From a records management standpoint, the PROFS case is a reflection of how poorly White House IT managers of the time understood the business requirements of any office, but is also a reflection of a behavioral change occurring at that time in offices worldwide. One of the greatest peculiarities of email is that managers and knowledge workers read and write their own internal and external correspondence rather than allow a personal or departmental secretary to do so. In the hard-copy world, secretaries did not simply type the documents; they were also responsible for implementing policies concerning the content, format, and audit trail information for the executive or department. Every administrative assistant job I had in graduate school came with a secretarial manual as well as arguments with supervisors about how many spaces to leave or the correct form of salutation. In the world of email, the manager or knowledge worker who never learned how to type, who would never have been caught using a typewriter, who had no training in the proper format of a memorandum, was creating and sending his or her own correspondence. Email was, and still is, regarded as a toy—not a formal piece of the office, much less something that requires management.

To this day, email products are not designed in such a way as to facilitate the management of email. Indeed, they foil our best attempts to corral and brand these missives. The definition must extend to the records series to which the document belongs and all the requirements to which that set belongs, including folder structure, document order, user access, privacy, security, and nondisclosure. Content, context, and structure are a poor mantra because they draw our attention away from the reality of what we have, to an abstract description that has changed dramatically within the past fifteen years and will continue to change dramatically as new technological devices enter common usage in the workplace. Consider, for example, the complexities that arise when one's PDA, mobile phone, and iPod are combined in a single device. How will we then define structure, context, or content? The content will be different, depending upon what device one uses to read with.

DEFINING RECORDS

While we may never get a better definition of records than that each document is an instantiation of information determined by context, we must persevere to get down to the smallest common denominator, because ultimately, that is what we must move around, compare, and manage. Within programming, a notion has developed over the past twenty-five years that may be of assistance: the object. Recent work on digital libraries has begun to use the term "digital objects" consistently. However, it is unclear whether those objects are defined in the same manner as programming objects. "An object is a real or abstract item that contains information (the attributes that describe it) and methods that allow it to be manipulated. Any object can be comprised of [sic] other objects, which can be comprised of [sic] other objects, and so on until the most basic objects of the system have been discovered."[42] An object is a type, hence it does not have to exist. It is both a holder with handles and a base of activity. It is also recursive, in that it can contain other things that are also objects.

This is a much better definition for the world of things that we manage than any definition of a record or a document thus far discussed. It overcomes the problems we have stated above, in addition to a few more (such as that it does not need to represent anything real). An object is a whole that can be moved around without losing its context, because it has clearly defined content, attributes, and methods. An object can hold or be automatically associated with other things, including information about its context—something a document cannot do.

For the management of records, the idea of an object is a better source of understanding what it is, precisely, that we manage. When we examine a part of records management called document control, we get a better idea of the least common denominator. Document control is a set of policies and procedures designed to ensure the quality, integrity, and accountability of an object, even if the object is a draft. However, it is also a set of policies and procedures designed to ensure the quality, integrity, and accountability of a record. Like objects, a record may be made of many objects, and it may take decades to create, like a trust file. The record, in this case, is a concept, not a thing— just as an object is a concept, not a thing. We can point to the record once it is completed—as a file folder on a screen or as a set of paper on a shelf—and say that that is the record. We know the record is complete and whole because it has followed the path, the policies, and procedures, required by that class of records. A particular record is a token of a type.

This is where records management parts ways entirely with archives and documentation. One of the reasons a single document has so little importance as an item to be defined within records management is that records management deals with classes of objects. Records management concerns itself with defining and enforcing types and accepts as a fact of life the forces creating tokens that instantiate types.

Another useful concept from the world of programming is the concept of the class: "The descriptor for a set of objects that share the same attributes, operations, methods, relationships, and behavior."[43] To translate this into the language of business, classes are created in the same or similar processes, used in the same or similar business processes, have the same best practices or risk management restrictions, and are disposited the same way.[44] A good example of this is the engineering change order in manufacturing. The company may have a number of different factories producing different objects. Each product has a different set of engineers who create the design and change the design through the use of change orders. Every change order has the same method of creation, use, and destruction. All of the change orders from every factory belong to the same type or class, called "change orders."

An excellent example of a single record that can be enormous is the set of documents required for the purchase of a complex asset such as a building or a piece of property—closing documents. Anyone who has undergone the mortgage process will have sat through a "closing," at which interminable documents, each serving some small purpose, must be explained, signed or initialed, and dated. Each individual document serves a separate and exclusive purpose—the larger and more complex the asset, the larger the number of documents. Without every single document, the transaction is not consummated. The resulting "file" is the record of the transaction; the individual documents are meaningless outside the closing. Every closing of a particular type of asset—a house mortgage, an airplane sale and leaseback, a corporate acquisition—has a different dance to establish the sets of closing documents required. The closings themselves have a nearly identical dance, but may require more or fewer documents and people attending. The subsequent dances are similar, but differ vastly according whether one is the purchaser or the seller. The class of asset (the content) and one's activity concerning the asset (the behavior) determines to what class the transaction belongs.

A class in records management is what is traditionally termed a "records series." Each records series is related to a business process as an input, an output, or a decision tool, even in document control, where the production of an individual document is managed carefully through policies and procedures, it is the class of document, the "document type," that is managed via a determined process.

Unfortunately, the term "document type" became confused within the area of technology called "document management." This confusion stemmed from the need for a template and the purpose of a document. Within records management, a template is called a template and the purpose for the design of a particular document is called a "document type." A "document type" in records management is a template that includes policies and procedures for creating it. Where this confusion is best illustrated is in the template for a memorandum. Even before email, a memorandum was an all-purpose template that served many purposes. Those purposes could include memo of law, transmittal memo, policy announcement, major procedural change, company picnic notification. As the reader can see, the purposes of a memo range from the sublime to the trivial, but always internal to the organization. The purposes, however, must be kept separate, as well as the handling. This is the same problem we now have with email: it could be one of many things, in addition to which it is also used for communication outside the organization—something that was previously reserved for correspondence.

Use of the terms "object" and "class," however, begs the question of databases, as these are the original source for the idea of object-oriented programming. Most records managers believe databases do not contain records in the sense that we manage.[45] To refer once again to the previously cited definition from Peru: "other things that compile, contain or represent a fact, a human activity or its result is a document," we know that a database is a compilation. We can unequivocally say, however, that a database is a record. Most databases have retention built into them. The replacement of a phone number or an address is a retention rule: until superseded. Most accounting programs dump the general ledger of one year onto a tape or other storage device so that the new year can be populated. The retention rule for the database is: current; and for the tapes, whatever the company decides it should be. Many databases are designed not to have supersession, but to be historical. Some databases were not so much designed to be historical as that they got that way through poor planning or accident of design. These latter are a problem for any organization and require the same type of weeding that any paper file does—a very expensive but often necessary activity.

The output of databases is another important product requiring management. Called "reports," these output products play a very important role—in financial audits, for example. Special software products, called Enterprise Reports Management (ERM) products, have been developed to handle reports that cannot be stored on a single optical disk. These products are used by large financial organizations, such as banks, to give managers a look at their pieces of the data. These are also "dumps" from Enterprise Resource Planning (ERP) software products that require retention, generally for financial reasons. One section of records management is called "reports management," but concerns itself more with the inventory, design, and distribution of reports than with the retention rules of database outputs and the databases themselves.

To summarize, a record is domesticated information—information captured on an external storage device within the context of a particular institution and instantiating a particular type. This definition is not the prevailing definition, but it is the one that most clearly defines what we manage in records management. This definition does not indicate whether the record itself is managed. Just as herds of mustangs, the descendants of horses owned by the Spanish, run wild in the western part of the U.S., so records lie unmanaged within particular institutions. Bill Gates's now infamous Netscape email and the deletion and shredding of emails concerning Enron within Arthur Andersen are recent examples of records that were not managed or managed properly. A record is a piece of domesticated information that should be managed. Whether a record is or is not managed is the decision of the institution—one of the business requirements determined by the executive leadership of the institution.

NOTES

1. *Zubulake v. UBS Warburg LLC.* 217 F.R.D. 309, 312 (S.D.N.Y. 2003); No. 02 Civ. 1243, 2003 WL 21087136 (S.D.N.Y. May 13, 2003); 216 F.R.D. 280 (S.D.N.Y. 2003); 220 F.R.D. 212 (S.D.N.Y. 2003); No. 02 Civ. 1243 (S.D.N.Y July 20, 2004).

2. John McMillan, *Reinventing the Bazaar: A Natural History of Markets* (New York: W. W. Norton, 2002), 135.

3. John Humphrey, Robin Mansell, Daniel Paré, and Hubert Schmitz, *The Reality of E-commerce with Developing Countries*, http://www.gapresearch.org/production/ecom -merce.html section 6 (2003 June 16).

4. Jonathan Z. Smith, *Imaging Religion: From Babylon to Jonestown* (Chicago: University of Chicago Press, 1978), 90–101.

5. Bernard S. Cohn, "Representing Authority in Victorian India," 165–210 in *The Invention of Tradition,* ed. Eric Hobsbawm and Terence Ranger (Cambridge: Cambridge University Press, 1983).

6. Nelson H. H. Graburn, editor, *Ethnic and Tourist Arts: Cultural Expressions from the Fourth World* (Berkeley: University of California Press, 1976).

7. Homi Bhabha, "Signs Taken for Wonders: Questions of Ambivalence and Authority under a Tree in New Delhi, May 1817," in *Europe and Its Others,* ed. Frank Barker (Colchester: University of Essex Press, 1985), 156.

8. Stephen Pritchard, "The Artifice of Culture: Contemporary Indigenous Art and the Work of Peter Robinson," *Third Text* 19, no. 1 (January 2005): 67–80, 71.

9. The InterPARES project is an international attempt by governments and archivists to define the baseline for authentic electronic records for all time, http://www .interpares.org/ (13 April 2005).

10. To be associated with racism, imperialism, and the seamier side of Western tradition without differentiation is at best shoddy scholarship.

11. This is why emails are formatted as memoranda with four basic lines: to, from, date, and subject. Email systems began as intraorganizational communication methods, hence the format as a memorandum.

12. Luciana Duranti, "Reliability and Authenticity: The Concepts and Their Implications," *Archivaria* 39 (Spring 1995): 5–10. Indeed, anyone who has tried to decide which version of a memorandum, even in paper form, is the original will understand this. The "tissue" carbon is the only copy the originator would have kept, *sans* initials, not a complete version of the original that would have been sent out. This is further exacerbated by the problem of "back carbon copies" (bcc). A bcc is created when a person other than those listed on the "to" and carbon copy (cc) lines is notified. The bcc may or may not have initials on it, as it is still a carbon copy. The original with the initials is therefore also lacking part of its complete form.

13. For example, I know that emails from unknown persons with no subject line are suspect, as are all emails from financial institutions with which I do not do business.

14. The InterPARES project kicked off with a workshop on authenticity 2000 January 22 called "Authenticity in a Digital Environment" presented by the Council on Library and Information Resources. In particular, Luciana Duranti notes Clifford Lynch's paper, "Authenticity and Integrity in the Digital Environment: An Exploratory Analysis of the Central Role of Trust," http://www.clir.org/pubs/reports/pub92/lynch.html (16 June 2003), cf. Duranti "Concepts, Principles, and Methods."

15. Electronic Signatures in Global and National Commerce Act of 2000 made signatures other than ink signatures on paper legal for business purposes. This made legal the pressing of "I Accept" buttons and return receipt emails. This does not extend to specific family law documents such as adoption papers and wills.

16. Public Key Infrastructure is an asymmetric method of encryption that permits an individual to "sign" an electronic document using a private key and have that signature "read" by a selected person using a public key. For an excellent explanation of PKI, see Steven Levy, *Crypto: How the Code Rebels Beat the Government—Saving Privacy in the Digital Age* (New York: Penguin Books, 2002).

17. James K. Watson, Jr. and Carol Choksy, "Digital Signatures Seal Web Deals," *InformationWeek* 804 (2000): RB26–RB28. Also at http://informationweek.com/804/rbdi-gital.htm (2003 June 16). In addition, see Nicholas Bohm, "Authentication, Reliability, and Risks," http://www.mcg.org.br/auth_b1.htm 16 June 2003 for a discussion concerning authentication and varieties of risk.

18. U.S. Congress, House of Representatives, *Sarbanes-Oxley Act of 2002,* H.R. 3763, 23 January 2002.

19. Civil Evidence (Scotland) Act 1988. 1988 chapter c. 32.

20. 28 U.S.C. section 902.

21. 28 U.S.C. section 803; at http://www.access.gpo.gov/uscode/title28a/28a_5_8_.html (17 June 2003).

22. Note that for a family, those statements can be on rings, gravestones, urns, and the like; compare Suzanne Briet, *Qu'est-ce que la documentation?* (Paris: EDIT, 1951), 8.

23. Records managers attend seminars, such as the Managing Electronic Records (MER) Conference held annually in Chicago, to see demonstrations concerning how to be such a "custodian or other qualified witness" when his or her company is in litigation and the litigation goes to court.

24. Civil Evidence (Scotland) Act 1988. 1988 chapter c. 32.

25. The author responded to Rule 803 (7) (absence of records) in the course of work by writing a memorandum as per 902 (11) describing the method by which a legal file is set up when a new matter is established. The memorandum described why certain file folders were empty. The general practice of the firm was to create a file with a standard set of empty folders so that lawyers had places to put documents. This saved the attorneys time in that they did not need to request a folder be made or make one on the fly. If a folder was not used, it was considered less of a waste of firm assets than having the attorneys create folders themselves. This was a solution to both an efficiency issue and a behavior problem. Attorneys were creating folders by themselves and then blaming everyone but themselves when the documents were lost, yet no record of either the documents or the folders existed.

26. Orin S., Kerr, "Computer Records and the Federal Rules of Evidence." *USA Bulletin* 49, no. 2 (2001), http://www.usdoj.gov/criminal/cybercrime/usamarch2001_4.htm (17 June 2003).

27. Contra Duranti, "Concepts, Principles, and Methods," 271.

28. Duranti "Reliability and Authenticity." (1995).

29. The work of, for example, the InterPARES project does not address the requirements of the workaday world and the role of managers, international or otherwise.

30. There are moments in the literature when this appears not to be the case. For example, Anne J. Gilliland-Swetland writes concerning the case studies performed by the InterPARES

Authentication Task Force: "Each case is highly sensitive to its own national, juridical, institutional, and technological contexts." Anne J. Gilliland-Swetland, "Testing Our Truths: Delineating the Parameters of the Authentic Archival Electronic Record," *The American Archivist* 65, no. 2 (Fall/Winter 2002): 196–215. Yet the observation that records have a context broader than a creation process and metadata gets lost. The questions used to discover the case study do not address business requirements; they only rise to the level of business process. Indeed, the Authenticity Task Force Requirements for Assessing and Maintaining the Authenticity of Electronic Records begins with a description of archivists requirements and then jumps to metadata and other requirements; see Heather MacNeil, "Providing Grounds for Trust II: The Findings of the Authenticity Task Force of InterPARES," *Archivaria* 54 (Fall 2002): 24–59.

31. David Bearman, *Electronic Evidence: Strategies for Managing Records in Contemporary Organizations* (Pittsburgh, PA: Archives & Museum Informatics, 1994).

32. Calvert Watkins, editor. *The American Heritage Dictionary of Indo-European Roots,* 2nd ed. (Boston: Houghton Mifflin, 2000).

33. 28A U.S.C. Rule 26 "(a) Required Disclosures; Methods to Discover Additional Matter. (1) Initial Disclosures. Except in categories of proceedings specified in Rule 26(a)(1)(E), or to the extent otherwise stipulated or directed by order, a party must, without awaiting a discovery request, provide to other parties: . . . These disclosures must be made at or within 14 days after the Rule 26(f) conference unless a different time is set by stipulation or court order, or unless a party objects during the conference that initial disclosures are not appropriate in the circumstances of the action and states the objection in the Rule 26(f) discovery plan."

34. Kenneth J. Withers, "Computer-based Discovery in Federal Civil Litigation," *5th Annual Electronic Discovery and Records Management Seminar* (Little Falls, NJ: Glasser LegalWorks, 2002). Also at http://www.fclr.org/2000fedctslrev2.htm (17 June 2003).

35. Roy C. Turnbaugh, "What Is an Electronic Record?" 23–34 in *Effective Approaches for Managing Electronic Records and Archives,* ed. Bruce W. Dearstyne (Lanham, MD: Scarecrow Press, 2002), 32. Within the passage quoted, the first quotation is from the Pittsburgh Project and the second is from InterPARES.

36. Mary F. Robek, Wilmer O. Maedke, and Gerald F. Brown, *Information and Records Management,* 3rd ed. (Lake Forest, IL: Glencoe, 1987), 568.

37. Ira A. Penn, Gail Pennix, and Jim Coulson, *Records Management Handbook,* 2nd ed. (Aldershot: Gower Publishing, 1994), 3.

38. Robek, Maedke, and Brown, 565.

39. *Report of the Task Force on Archiving of Digital Information,* commissioned by the Commission on Preservation and Access and the Research Libraries Group, Inc., May 1, 1996, at http://www.rlg.org/ArchTF/tfadi.index.htm (18 June 2003).

40. *Armstrong v. Bush,* 721 F. Supp. 343, 345 n.1 (D.D.C. 1989); *Armstrong v. Bush,* 139 F.R.D. 547, 553 (D.D.C. 1991); *Armstrong v. Executive Office of the President,* 807 F. Supp. 816 (D.D.C. 1992); *Armstrong v. Executive Office of the President,* 810 F. Supp. 335 (D.D.C. 1993); *Armstrong v. Executive Office of the President,* 1 F.3d 1274 (D.C. Cir. 1993); *Armstrong v. Executive Office of the President,* 877 F2d 690, 715 (D.D.C. 1995).

41. *Armstrong v. Executive Office of the President,* 810 F. Supp. 335 (D.D.C. 1993) at 341.

42. Andrew Haigh, *Object-oriented Analysis & Design* (New York: Osborne, 2001), 12.

43. James Jacobson, Ivar Rumbaugh, and Grady Booch, *The Unified Modeling Language Reference Manual* (Reading, MA: Addison-Wesley, 1999), 185.

44. The term "disposited" is used as in the sense of "disposition," not as in "disposed" or thrown away.

45. Conversations and listserv conversations on this topic.

Chapter Four

What Records Do We Manage?

Discussions with records managers reveal that most of them believe they are actually managing very few of the records within their respective organizations. The reason is that their current portfolios define paper or microforms as the sole media assigned to their care. These records managers will point to the email system and the documents created by desktop productivity software that remain in electronic form as evidence of their foreshortened domain.

While the professional association representing records managers, ARMA International, Inc., has made efforts to cover the body of knowledge of what the archivists term "electronic records," these efforts have been stymied by several different forces. The first such force is the definition given to "electronic records" as declared by the archivists, which excludes precisely the documents that are getting most organizations into trouble: emails with a temporary retention. However, as we saw in chapter 3, some of the more prominent ideas in current archives thinking are inadequate to the work of records managers. The records management community has not carefully reflected long enough upon that definition of electronic records and the attendant discussion of metadata and preservation to recognize that the archivists' meditations are of small value to us. The second force is that the work done by the archivists on "electronic records" is uninformed by an understanding of the common usage and capabilities of modern technology as well as by basic records management principles—principles of document control, for example. None of the studies funded under National Historic Preservation and Records Commission (NHPRC) grants examine what leading ECM products can do, nor do they look at the literature describing and testing these products. Instead, most of these studies buy and program freeware or inexpensive applications that have very limited functionality. Nor do these studies examine the effects of document control on the outcome of the "authenticity" of documents. The third force preventing ARMA from thoroughly addressing electronic records is that records managers who do learn how to manage records in multiple formats are so busy doing so, that they have little time left to share information. This also translates into a lack of financial incentive to share information freely, because so much money can be made writing books and presenting paid seminars on electronic records. The fourth force is that while records managers have a desire to learn about records in different formats, their hard-copy ghetto presents barriers of prejudice, both from the records manager and information technology and upper-level executives concerning records management principles. For example, a university expressed surprise at discovering the records manager had the best knowledge of which parts of the university had credit card numbers. An insurance company implementing an ECM system was surprised to discover that the records manager had better knowledge of the document types kept within the policy files than the underwriting department. Both of these records managers work in hard-copy ghettos. Records managers themselves have not aggressively pursued knowledge of electronic content and business processes. Why else would ARMA still exist and be playing catch-up?

As we noted in Chapter 3, the definition of records given by archivists does not cover the information that is actually managed in paper by records managers. Records managers are bound by judicial issues of discovery and evidence, legislative issues, and regulatory issues that force us to manage every document as a record. Public records laws cover only a tiny portion of the information managed by records managers. In Chapter 3 we also examined the U.S. Federal law of evidence in part to demonstrate why the term "evidence" is a reserved term and to address in part the problem of "authenticity" in records. In this chapter we will look at a more onerous judicial issue: discovery of records, or "document production."

DOCUMENT PRODUCTION

In civil law, when one party sues another, each party is required to produce documents and persons for examination by the other party. This exchange of information is called "discovery." The document-sharing in this process is called "document production." Whereas documents must satisfy the courts' rigorous requirements for being used within the trial, document production is simply an exchange of every type of information regarding the issue at hand. Imagine having to search every single C-drive in a fifty-thousand-person company for email regarding a particular topic. You have to search every C-drive because your IT department has limited the size of each person's email in-box, and everyone has begun saving email to their personal computer's hard drive. Perhaps you must restore ten thousand backup tapes to find an email that had been deleted, but you don't know just when.

Paper document production is onerous because it is labor intensive. However, the labor is cheap. Electronic document production is very expensive because the labor is costly. In addition, the volume of electronic documents, in comparison to paper documents, is greater by at least an order of magnitude.

Let us examine the U.S. Federal rules (as of this book's writing) regarding this matter. The rules we must examine are Rule 26(b) and Rule 34 in 28 USC Appendix, Federal Rules of Civil Procedure.[1] The laws of civil procedure, unlike other types of laws, are created and revised by the courts and recommended to the legislature for passage as statutes. These rules describe what may be obtained through discovery, hence they describe what records managers must manage; they describe what are records.

> Rule 26(b) Discovery Scope and Limits. Unless otherwise limited by order of the court in accordance with these rules, the scope of discovery is as follows:
>
> (1) *In General.* Parties may obtain discovery regarding any matter, not privileged, that is relevant to the claim or defense of any party, including the existence, description, nature, custody, condition, and location of any books, documents, or other tangible things and the identity and location of persons having knowledge of any discoverable matter. For good cause, the court may order discovery of any matter relevant to the subject matter involved in the action. Relevant information need not be admissible at the trial if the discovery appears reasonably calculated to lead to the discovery of admissible evidence. All discovery is subject to the limitations imposed by Rule 26(b)(2)(i), (ii), and (iii).

What may be discovered are "any books, documents, or other tangible things." The rule does not limit production to "declared" records, official records, programmatic records, or even written records (this is clarified in the upcoming rules). What may be gathered includes what Samuel Johnson in *A Dictionary of the English Language* called "intelligence given," his definition of information.[2] This statement does not in any way explicitly exclude adhesive notes, voicemails, drafts, phone logs, cartoons posted on a bulletin board, or any of the other items that do not demonstrate "evidence of a business transaction." Nor are any of these required to be created "in the normal course of business." No definition can whittle away what must be produced. Any and every object containing some form of information must be managed. In the event this is not clear enough, Rule 34 goes into even more detail:

> (a) Scope. Any party may serve on any other party a request (1) to produce and permit the party making the request, or someone acting on the requestor's

behalf, to inspect and copy, any designated documents (including writings, drawings, graphs, charts, photographs, phonorecords, and other data compilations from which information can be obtained, translated, if necessary, by the respondent through detection devices into reasonably usable form), or to inspect and copy, test, or sample any tangible things which constitute or contain matters within the scope of Rule 26(b) and which are in the possession, custody or control of the party upon whom the request is served; or (2) to permit entry upon designated land or other property in the possession or control of the party upon whom the request is served for the purpose of inspection and measuring, surveying, photographing, testing, or sampling the property or any designated object or operation thereon, within the scope of Rule 26(b).

(b) Procedure. . . . A party who produces documents for inspection shall produce them as they are kept in the usual course of business or shall organize and label them to correspond with the categories in the request.

(c) Persons Not Parties. A person not a party to the action may be compelled to produce documents and things or to submit to an inspection as provided in Rule 45.

Rule 34 defines what may be gathered as: any designated documents (including writings, drawings, graphs, charts, photographs, phonorecords, and other data compilations from which information can be obtained, translated, if necessary, by the respondent through detection devices into reasonably usable form), or to inspect and copy, test, or sample any tangible things. Lest this list leave the reader in doubt, Rule 34 again lists "any tangible things." Again, there can be no question that this list is expansive, not limiting. This rule adds, however, a further burden: a party who produces documents for inspection shall produce them as they are kept in the usual course of business or shall organize and label them to correspond with the categories in the request. This means that the documents cannot be copied and tossed into garbage bags and dropped at the opposing party's loading dock. The order must be maintained or the documents must be carefully ordered to correspond to the request.

Finally, lest an organization believe it is off the hook because it is not a direct party to the dispute, Rule 34(c) permits everyone vaguely associated with the suit to be subpoenaed. Continuing the discussion of "evidence" from Chapter 3, defining what we must manage as "evidence of a business transaction" is dangerous to the continued existence of any organization, because the definition is not expansive enough; it does not define what we must manage.

DOCUMENT SCIENCE VERSUS RECORDS MANAGEMENT

We have begged the question of how we are to describe the objects we manage. The legal systems of the continent of Europe describe what they manage as "documents." There they have a long and illustrious history of two practices: one called "Document Science" and the other called "diplomatics." These two methods are difficult for the Anglophone world to study because very little has been translated into English. As noted in chapter 1, records management has its own history in the U.S. that began with the rise of management studies in the late nineteenth century. Only after World War II were records management and archives officially introduced through the National Archives and Records Administration via the two Hoover Commissions. Records management in the U.S. has never been formally introduced to "Document Science" and was not formally introduced to "diplomatics" until the publication of Luciana Duranti's book *Diplomatics: New Uses for an Old Science.*[3]

According to Duranti, diplomatics is "the discipline which studies the genesis, forms, and transmission of archival documents, and their relationship with the facts represented in them and with their creator, in order to identify, evaluate, and communicate their true nature."[4] The reader will recognize this as the study and proof of archival documentary authenticity. Diplomatics is not interested in all documents or records. It is certainly not interested in adhesive notes and phone logs. More importantly, diplomatics is not concerned with the management of records. Schellenberg notes that modern records management's study of the file room and its techniques was comparable to the study of diplomatics.[5] However true that may be, studying the file room is a far cry from managing the life cycle and ensuring that records intersect with their business process appropriately, in addition to managing all the documents we could never have created in the Middle Ages, such as phone logs and personal email.

Our purpose is to help organizations reach business objectives regarding the management of their unstructured content. We may testify in court about the "true nature" of a document, but only because we were instrumental in the creation, formatting, and distribution of those documents, not because we studied it. Duranti's study is peripherally interesting to records management, but is ultimately of no consequence to it because it is entirely and unquestioningly focused on the idea of authenticity. For many records managers, that is a luxury that we can afford to contemplate only in the abstract. Furthermore, Duranti confuses legal terms that we as records managers cannot afford within our practice to confuse. Duranti confounds statutory Continental legal terms such as *personne morale* or *personne juridique* with the common law term "artificial person." She says herself that the two are not equivalent, yet persists in equating them.[6] Further, she uses common law to define one of the most important terms in diplomatics: authentic.[7] Knowing that diplomatics is a Continental practice, she continuously mixes incommensurate legal systems: Continental statutory law and common law. As noted above, the U.S. practice of records management is defined by our common law legal system.

As discussed above and in Chapter 3, records are broadly defined within the U.S. legal and business systems. That broad definition is commensurate with European scholarship on "documents."[8] The concept of record as a single or multiple set of documents with a particular life cycle intersecting with one or several business processes is not entirely foreign to European principles of Document Science, but it is sufficiently foreign that English terms are used by Europeans to refer to what we do. For example, the term "records management" is incorporated into French without translation.[9] The difference between the two is well described by the French: "Nous nous attacherons à montrer que la valeur informationnelle, si elle est nécessaire, n'est pas suffisante pour documenter les activités d'un organisme, et qu'il importe de prendre en compte la dimension de l'archive. La fonction archivistique a, en effet, élaboré des stratégies qu'il convient d'appliquer aux dossiers électroniques pour préserver leur intégrité, leur authenticité, leur conservation au fil du temps, et leur accessibilité. Concrètement, un stockage électronique réalise sans une gestion responsable est une solution totalement insatisfaisante qui met en péril la gestion et l'exploitation des informations en tant que ressources professionnelles. Par ailleurs, nous souhaitons insiste sur le document papier qui doit être considère, traite et pris en compte comme système d'information, exactement au même titre que les archives électroniques."[10] Studying the value of information is insufficient; studying how information can be managed responsibly assists us in understanding how to document the activities of an organization.

One of the fundamental differences between Document Science and records management is that the European practices manage physical objects—documents—with a very long historical tradition, and the U.S. practice manages concepts—records—with a relatively short tradition. This fundamental difference between managing real things and managing concepts also belies the origin of the document scientist and the records manager. The document scientist deals with how things *must* be; a document must be authentic, trustworthy, and reliable. In contrast, a records manager deals with balancing how things *should* be, using the policies created by governing bodies and the reality of the here and now. In this way, a records manager is much more like a librarian in a pubic library. Another difference between the document scientist and the records manager is that the tradition of the document scientist stems from an environment where access to information was restricted. The environment that records management stems from is one in which information must be shared to be of value. Compare the tradition of diplomatics as described by Duranti and our understanding of the history of English literacy. By 1300, even English serfs were learning to read and to use the services of public notaries to ensure their debts and entitlements were public. Contrast this with the history of the continent, where entitlements were still being kept in monasteries that had landed nobility as patrons. In the English example, even serfs were learning that public information—information to which they have access—protects them. In the Continental example, information is not public; it is under the control of the most powerful person around, making him even more powerful.

Self-conscious access to information is the difference that Alfred Chandler finds in differentiating the rise of modern U.S. business as a very different sort of institution from all those institutions that have gone before. Chandler has his own interest in differentiating the environment of the bureaucrat studied by the documentation scientist and the business enterprise: "Actually the management of a private business enterprise and that of a public civil or military organization are fundamentally different. They are, of course, all bureaucracies in Max Weber's sense of the word—hierarchies manned by professional officers—and so have features common to that social form. But the business enterprise has different objectives and functions and far more clear-cut criteria for failure and success. The primary objective of an enterprise is to show a return on investment by the production and sale of goods and services. The continuing profit-and-loss record of a firm provides a fairly precise and objective criterion of its performance and that of its operating divisions and departments. Except in time of war, such impersonal, clear-cut standards for the performance of managers of a military corps or a government bureau are hard to find. Performance in these enterprises, and with it promotion and changes in personnel, must be judged by more subjective standards. Moreover, since these public units do not usually generate the capital to finance their existing and future activities, the legislature provides the funds and appoints the top personnel. Their managers depend far more on the legislature than the executives of an industrial enterprise depend on the board of directors, which theoretically has the same sort of control. The greatest concern of legislators and their advisors has normally been to keep costs as low as possible. . . . They tend to care not so much for what the unit's staff can do, but rather how little it can do and still meet minimum requirements."[11]

Context affects use, both freedom of use and how something is used. The differences between diplomatics and records management and the differences between Weberian bureaucracies and U.S. companies leads to widely differing definitions of the document or record. The documents and records of a U.S. corporation are primarily meant to be transparent to the users, whereas the documents of a medieval fief are meant to be known primarily to the ruler, i.e., no transparency. One of the definitions given by Sylvie Leleu-Merviel is illustrative of the ontologically prescriptive nature of many French definitions: "Le document se définit alors comme un ensemble de données matérialisant l'inscription d'une trace pérenne sur un support, conformément a un code convenu."[12] The document has content, duration, a medium, and is readable according to a socially agreed-upon method. The French are also the inventors of the semaphore, a method of transmitting commands and information using flags. The semaphore itself was a fleeting trace of information passed from post to post.[13] The semaphore had to be "read" by someone with access to a codebook.

Documents are defined differently in Continental Europe than they are in the U.S., and conceptually they function differently. To clarify this, let us examine the history of the idea of documents.

DOCUMENTS AND TABULA

To better understand where documents fit into records management, particularly as documents are mentioned by the statutes that define what we manage, let us examine what they are. "Document" derives from the Indo-European *Dek* "to take, accept or be fitting," and from the Greek, "to cause to accept."[14] Archivists trace "document" to the Latin *docere* "to teach or cause to accept," hence *documentum* "an official publication, edict or directive."[15]

The reader can see from these definitions that the idea of a document has a force behind it—a force of command and control. Some parts of a corporation or the world of business require command and control, as with contracts and manuals. However, corporations function as much by communication and coordination. Good examples of communication and coordination within a corporation are the intelligence function and intangibles management, such as the creation of social capital for the promotion of innovation.[16] The information produced by these functions does not have traditional "document" force behind it. The E-Sign Act of 2000 gave force to return-receipt emails and HTML buttons marked "I Accept" as methods of creating contracts thereby giving these electronic documents the same degree of force as their previous paper versions.

Susan Briet defines a document as "all concrete or symbolic token, preserved or recorded toward the ends of representing, of reconstituting, or of proving a physical or intellectual phenomenon."[17] Her most famous example is the antelope in the zoo. For Briet, a document is a token of a type, an instantiation of a human constructed category. The antelope in the zoo is a token of the type "antelope." She is not incorrect. Such an exhibit is meant to be a

Figure 4.1. Roman Tabularium (Large Building in the Back).
Courtesy of ArtRes

token of the animal representing a type for the public.[18] Briet's definition of a "document" is more extreme than the ones those of us in records management already accept. The "any tangible things" mentioned in Rules 26 and 34 of the Rules of Civil Procedure (above) do not exclude plaster casts of muddy footprints or sulfur casts of snowy footprints. Those of us who have had to manage "evidence rooms" with the endless chunks of concrete, presentation boards with blown-up pictures of documents, shoes, and anything else that could be preserved at standard temperature and pressure, recognize Briet's definition not as a logical extreme, but as the dead center of the issue. The document is whatever the environment requires it to be—not what an archivist or an information scientist defines it to be. Just as with the definition of a record, the definition of a document is determined entirely by context. More importantly, a document, like a record, is a concept, not a real thing. We point to instantiations of documents and records. We point to tokens of the type "document" in the same way we would point to tokens of the type "table."

The term "table" points us to another "documentary" tradition much older than that of the term "document." The Roman *tabularium* was a records room where business accounts were kept. *Tabula* (from which we get the words "table" and "tabulate") were stored there (see figure 4.1). Dictionaries are mute concerning the root of these words, but I posit they come from Sumerian *dub* and Assyrian *tuppum,* general terms for any clay tablet.[19] Letters could be *tuppu*; so could accounts and contracts. These terms are no longer part of the derivation of the main term we use, "document," but they are more descriptive of what records managers manage than the main term because it points to a business tradition rather than a governmental one.

DOCUMENTS WITHIN THE ORGANIZATION

Inside an organization, what is a document? Within records management, the definitions are as simple and profound as those of Susan Briet. Consider this definition offered by John W. Gross: "A document may consist of one sheet or many sheets but has a beginning and end determined by content."[20] While this definition is paper-based, it points out something we often take for granted in any communication: it has a beginning (a middle) and an end. Robek, Maedke, and Brown state that a document is "the smallest unit of filing."[21]

With the advent of "text management" or "content management," however, a document as traditionally understood is no longer the smallest unit of filing. SGML was invented for the purpose of managing sections of manuals or paragraphs in documents that were produced electronically. The reason it was necessary was to provide the ability to manage individual blocks or elements of text within a larger document—as, for instance, paragraphs within aircraft maintenance manuals. When Boeing manufactures a plane, each aircraft may be unique. Each plane must have a different manual, so paragraphs are selected to correspond to the plane being built and are then inserted in the appropriate place in the individualized manual. Similarly, for purposes of publishing a document to the web, we may be filing the header and footer separately from the parts that comprise the main body of a human-perceived document. Indeed, moving on to portals, we may be filing the logic of the Java Server Page separately from the presentation and the content.

We have, however, avoided the question of Internet content as record or document. Most persons with passing familiarity with the web know how HTML works—that it separates presentation from content. HTML was based on SGML, so that having created a template, the user can plug the content in at any point. The so-called content management systems are aids in performing this function. At their most elemental level, these are actually "layout management" systems. Other products also perform this function for the publishing industry, although not until recently could that content be fed easily to the Internet. These software products have teamed up with the capabilities of document management and workflow products with the result that they actually add a level of records management to layout management. This is also what electronic forms management products[22] are about, albeit on a much grander scale. The template and the content are separate, even in a triplicate carbon form. One individual designs a page with labeled baskets, in which another well-defined individual will put well-defined data. The only real difference between content management and forms management is that content management is intended to be a layout for a final presentation, whereas a form is meant to be a set of "buckets" for data that will begin, continue, or end a workflow. A content management system is a method for creating documents that may be used within the context of a process.[23]

One of the differences between content and forms management, besides their relationship to a process, is whether the content can be dynamic. Content put in a form—either as a template or as data filled into one of the baskets—must remain static. A web page, however, can be as dynamic as the potential reader can tolerate. Content management products have assumed that the filler content will be provided by a local server. There are other products, such as stock feeds, that provide real-time, or slightly delayed-time, content. Unfortunately, these can be so costly in terms of time to load that their cost outweighs any potential benefit. This is where "edge-side includes" are effective—remote feeds of information that begin feeding only when the page is called. The most common example is a live stock ticker. Like other forms of content, this is a separate module, but like all modules, the more active it is required to be, the more it will slow down all other feeds, so it must be included judiciously, rather than as an "always-on" feature.

Another type of Internet document is a portal server page. Any useful portal product has a complex architecture: a separate server must be provided for every feed other than static news views such as weather or sports. In a way, a single page-view of a portal could be the viewing of six, ten, even twelve separate "pages" using content pulled from twelve separate servers, content that might each be understood as a separate document. Even though each page in the view has separate presentation and content and potentially separate logic (converting knots/hour to miles/ or kilometers/hour, for example), it is still a single "view," a single document.

We may believe we understand what the "document" is in the portal example; it is the individual cell being viewed. Yet in the modern organization, the purpose of the portal is to produce a single view of our office, rather than a single view of our desk (an "office-top" rather than a "desktop"). Push comes to shove when we try to manage these "office-tops" as documents of discovery. Relying on what is viewed on the portal, the question must be asked: what caused the individual to make a decision that later leads to some form of litigation? The answer may be one of the cells, or it may be the entire page-view. Consider an example drawn from the on-line trading website (familiar to us from Chapter 2). An investor checks her broker's online investment portal. While checking the wheat futures market cell, the investor notices the weather cell is predicting that a snowstorm will hit Kansas the next day—a storm that could destroy the wheat harvest and the entire crop. The investor takes action and buys wheat futures at what she believes to be a rock-bottom price, only to discover the next day that the weather cell was acting up and that no such storm is predicted. She loses a substantial sum of money and sues the broker who, in turn, sues the portal maker. During discovery, what is produced is a series of re-creations of the portal page at the time the investor viewed the page. Separately, the wheat futures ticker and the weather ticker are produced. What is the document? Whatever the context defines as an indivisible object is the document. In some instances that could be a snippet of HTML; in other instances, it could be an entire web page.

Another extreme side of the document as a plaster cast. The plaster cast is the result of two human activities: one that could be with or without signification, the footprint; and one with clear signification, the plaster cast. In the broker's website, there is no question of writing, but the question of a beginning, middle, and end is unclear.

Grappling with this thorny electronic problem, David Bearman says an electronic document is "composed of data objects in the form of text, image, and sound that are linked by pathways defined by the author."[24] This definition identifies the problem that not all documents exist as a single blob of digital signals—there are pointers creating virtual documents. However, it does not mention the problem of metadata, presentation filters, or of logic being a part of the document itself, as with a Java Server Page or even a web portal; nor does it address the issue of whether the reader perceives a document. Michael Sutton describes documents as "a record of a business transaction or decision that can be viewed as a single, organized, contextual unit; in a document management system, a document is a grouping of formatted information objects that can be accessed and used by a person," and "a grouping of formatted information objects that can be accessed and used by a person."[25]

These definitions have certain strengths and weaknesses that we have already seen in other definitions. We cannot use the term "business transaction or decision" because it does not reflect everything that must be managed. A "formatted information object" begs the question of what is meant by "formatted" and what is "information." The use of the term "object" is laudable, as we shall see below, but—as we shall also see below—it actually begs the question of "class."

Sutton's strength is in his description of a document as "a single, organized, contextual unit . . . that can be accessed and used by a person," as this comes close to what is meant in common business parlance when we refer to a document. As a contextual definition, this more accurately describes what we experience as a document on the Internet. Links made only by the author, as Bearman suggests, raise the question of how we are to regard multiple author weblogs, wikis, as well as the result of a web search. One of the criteria that Google uses to produce the hierarchy in its search results is how many other authors link to a page. Unfortunately, both of these definitions could refer as much to an entire website or a folder full of documents as it could to a single document.

Perception and use by a person are the defining characteristics. Authenticity and reliability are problems of particular tokens—particular instantiations of documents. "Content, context, and structure" as a mantra is an attempt to tease apart the experience of a token by a person who might be judging authenticity and reliability. Records managers manage tokens as types and ensure that the business requirements for each type are fulfilled within the limitations of the organization. A token is the instantiation of a type with its own particular circumstances of creation. Records managers can no more be responsible for each token than they can be responsible for each utterance made within an organization. Unlike the traditional treatment of a document by the *documentation scientist* or diplomatics as a force, a document within records management is just the "smallest unit of filing," as Robek, Brown, and Maedke have declared. Sometimes the smallest unit looks like a traditional document, a contract; and sometimes it is the furthest thing from it—a clause from a contract stored for later re-use or an adhesive note.

Even within archives, the definition of what constitutes a document is not entirely agreed upon. Patrick Cadell describes one of the large differences separating France's and Scotland's respective understandings of the document and the information that creates the document. In Scotland, any information that is registered is immediately available. In France, registered information, other than the final document, is unavailable for 100 years.[26] This difference is reflected in the current archives definition that separates what they would consider ephemera from a final version that will be used by society. Another crucial difference is that diplomatics examines the authenticity of artifacts that are real. Records and documents are always concepts— always tokens of types for records management. Archives and diplomatics manage and analyze a small subset of all of the documents that are actually created within an organization. The documents are managed and analyzed as human artifacts.

THE RELATIONSHIP OF DOCUMENTS TO RECORDS

What is the relationship of documents to records? Documents make up records. More important, however, is our understanding that records managers manage concepts to ensure that the instantiations, the tokens, have the characteristics necessary to perform business. To illustrate this difference, let us examine the most complex type of record, the project file or case file, which is a type of file commonly found within at least some departments in many business organizations and in fact reflects the way many companies do business. The file itself is a concept relating to all the information created by work performed on a particular person, place, or thing. A file may comprise thousands of documents of every variety listed above, yet be considered a single unit for purposes of handling. Conversely, the information within the file may be subdivided by function: agreements, permits, environmental documents, budget, actuals, previous versions, drafts, outside correspondence, internal memoranda, etc. When retention is applied to a file, it is applied either to the file as a whole or to subdivided functions. For example, the drafts may be thrown away when the project is completed, but all remaining documents are kept for twenty years. We must conclude that the entire file is a record that may be made up of different types of documents and other information sources, such as calculations, financial information within a financial application, and databases. The file itself is a concept that may include links or references to documents that do not fit within the folder. The following figure shows what I call the natural history of records, as demonstrated by the various sources of documents that may comprise a record within a fictitious law firm, Barton & Patrick.

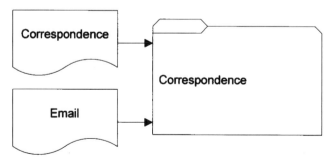

Figure 4.2.   Single Records: Discrete Individual Units Created from Single Electronic Files.

The simplest type of record is where there is only one document type such as correspondence, each created separately. Letters and many emails fall into this category. Figure 4.2 illustrates this type of record. The second simplest I call "simplex" because each is different, but each is created in assembly line fashion by a database and form template. Invoices are a good example of this type of record. As in figure 4.3, the database must also be considered as a record, most particularly when the database is decommissioned and worries arise over how long the entire hardware, software, application, and data system must be maintained and then destroyed. The third type of record is more complex because these documents have multiple sources. The portals discussed in chapter 2 at their simplest are this type of dynamic, compound record. As illustrated in figure 4.4, these may have multiple sources and multiple outputs reflecting the activity that is performed in and through the portal.

A brief review of the literature shows that project files are not mentioned in most of the textbooks even as glossary items.[27] Only a few journal articles have been devoted to this topic, despite the fact that, as noted above, such files are common in American business organizations.[28] In Robek, project files are a "Type of Record." They are "Correspondence, notes, and other data related to a specific project, such as product development, or system documentation." Other "Types of Records" are correspondence, transactional records, case files, and specialty files.[29] Case files are similar to project files: "Medical and other personnel records, claims, lawsuits, contracts, insurance and similar files. Usually refer to a specific person or property item." The difference between case files and project files in Robek appears to be that case files refer to property or persons, and project files refer to anything else.[30] Both case files and project files are recommended to be maintained as a whole.

Penn, Pennix, and Coulsen also separate case files and project files. They define case files as "files that pertain to particular sets of circumstances. They often document a specific transaction or are related to a particular person or

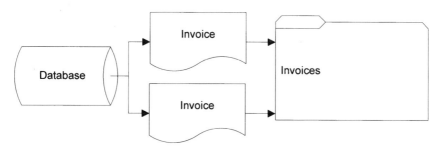

Figure 4.3.   Simplex Records: Individual Units Created from Databases.

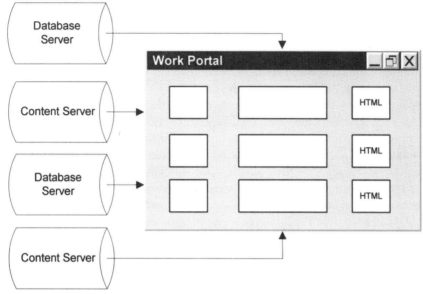

Figure 4.4. Dynamic, Compound Records: Represented as Single Units Created from Several Electronic Files or Databases.

organization. Good examples of case files would be mortgage files, medical records, personnel records, insurance policy files, workers' compensation files, and income tax files. These types of files can be filed in a series, are usually unitized, and have a common denominator for arrangement such as the name of an individual or organization or a specially assigned number."[31] This description is broader but is also a trifle confusing because of the primacy given in the description to the word "transaction." The Penn, et al. "case file" transactions are more complicated than what we ordinarily encounter in accounts payable or accounts receivable records. Their "case file" transactions require a greater degree of documentation by one or all parties (credit information for a mortgage or tax records for an income tax file). Penn, Pennix, and Coulson go on to define project files as "a special type of file because they usually relate to a fixed time frame, bracketed by the start and end of the project. Though project records can be in the form of individual documents, most are unitized by subject." They go on to describe project files by saying they are a subset of subject files. They differentiate project files from subject files by retention: "they are generally filed physically separate from subject files and grouped as projects."[32] For Penn, Pennix, and Coulson, project files memorialize a period of time regarding a specific subject; case files memorialize a circumstance, such as a person or an organization. Penn, Pennix, and Coulson believe project files should be kept together: "when a project is com-

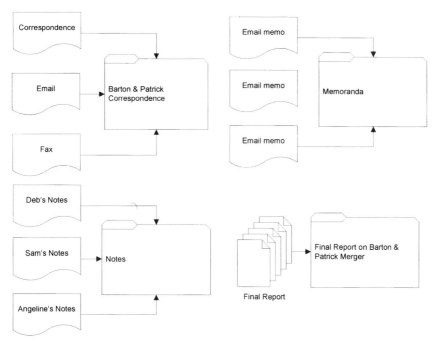

Figure 4.5.   Static, Compound Records: Single Units Created from Several Single Electronic Files and Databases, but Ever-growing until Closure.

plete they can be evaluated as a unit for retention purposes."[33] They use the term "unitization" to describe the need to keep a project file intact for retention scheduling purposes. Although the authors do not elaborate further, they should be applauded for this excellent contribution to our tool chest. What they describe is not the consideration of an entire records series, but the defining of one unit of any records series (see figure 4.5).

Robert L. Sanders's definition of project files is that they are a subset of case files: "Information managers are familiar with project files as a subcategory of a type of office records usually called case files. While all case files are associated with specific persons, things, instances, or activities, project files document activities with discrete objectives, starting dates, and completion dates."[34] Sanders' definitions differ from those of Robek, et al. and also from Penn, et al. by suggesting that project files are subsumed under case files in a hierarchical relationship. Sanders's stance on unitization is that fragmentation is a disaster waiting to happen: "File fragmentation is the major problem confronting the maintenance of a healthy project file . . . the problems are more severe for project files."[35] He goes on to describe the problems created by the fragmentation of the L.A. Metro Rail project file which included litigation.[36]

A fourth set of authorities concerning project or case files are records management applications, which should be considered owing to their impact on our everyday practice. Most records management applications characterize records as either "case" or "subject" files. Case files are those with nonpredictable retention events. Subject files have predictable, calendar-based retention events. Case files can be scheduled together for disposition as hardcopy, electronic, or a combination of hard-copy and electronic records.

What does this mean for the files? A file represents a particular project performed for a client, but not necessarily a single transaction. Returning to Penn, Pennix, and Coulson's description of a project file: "Project files are a special type of file because they usually relate to a fixed time frame, bracketed by the start and end of the project. Though project records can be in the form of individual documents, most are unitized by subject. In fact, they resemble subject files enough to be appropriately called a subset of subject files. However, they are generally filed physically separate from subject files and grouped as projects so that when a project is complete they can be evaluated as a unit for retention purposes."[37] This is a pretty good description of the files that attorneys create and maintain for a client's project. The project has a beginning, a middle, and an end; the attorney is paid for the work performed on the project. When the file is in hard-copy format, the file is sent to storage in one piece—i.e., it is unitized. The file may fill several storage cabinets, indeed, several rooms, depending upon the size and complexity of the problem.

Within most organizations today, a project file in electronic form is currently a jigsaw puzzle. Emails are kept in the email system, sometimes with attachments and sometimes without. Documents are kept on C-drives, G-drives, or document management systems; sometimes with index information, and sometimes without. Paper documents are kept in folders in various locations. The emails, electronic documents, and papers may or may not have sufficient index information to associate them with the project. Certainly, there is no picture of the complete file or project represented on the computer screen, with folders indicating collections of similarly functioning documents. A project file, then, is the complete set of information corresponding to a single process performed by an organization to accomplish a task requiring a period of time to accomplish.

All "originals" are placed in the file. This ensures that the file is complete and accurate. There are a variety of tricks in the hard-copy world for ensuring that this takes place—such as stamping one internal copy the "file copy," or reproducing it on colored paper. The purpose of worrying about this is that documents can get scattered to the four winds when many people are working on a project. Filing piles up, but one needs to be able to determine whether a pile contains just copies kept in a working file, or whether it belongs in the "official" file. This practice also facilitates business resumption should there be a disruption of some kind. For example, an environmental consulting firm had the problem that the key person working on a project might leave the company before the completion of the project, making it difficult for someone else to pick up the thread of what was going on in the project because there was no single, official source for all documents. The idea here is that the work exists independent of an individual, and everyone should have access to what they need.

The file, defined as the work done on the project, is what Penn, Pennix, and Coulson mean when they use the term "unitized." Defining the unit that will be placed on the shelf together, or that will be indicated as a single file folder on the computer screen, is the first problem to be overcome. As the above discussion suggests, for project files, this is not the same as pointing to a cabinet and saying, "Those are invoices." Different types of projects may be placed on the shelf together for retrieval purposes, but, for retention scheduling purposes, may be counted as separate records series. The most efficient manner of storing active project files in a large, centralized file room is on the shelf in numeric order without regard to the contents.

The tabbed folders, as mentioned above, usually hold a particular type of document: correspondence, memoranda, attorney notes, research, court papers, drafts, settlement agreements, contracts, and many other types too specialized to mention here. In some instances, projects are sufficiently large to require several tabbed folders holding the same type of document, such as several volumes of correspondence in chronological order, or research on multiple topics. This is specifically a hard-copy problem, as an electronic folder can virtually handle an unlimited number of documents. The hard-copy file is easier to work with when all the correspondence is adjacent within the file and all the court papers are adjacent within the file—i.e., for a large file, one need look only in expandable pockets numbered 1 and 2 for the correspondence, not somewhere within pockets 1 and 12. While this sounds rather simple, it is worth noting that good, off-the-shelf software capable of handling this particular hard-copy problem has been available only since 1997.

Similarly, electronic documents create an additional problem for management of project files. Even though the paper record may be the "official record" for these project files, many electronic documents do not get printed and placed in the file. Records management applications that handle both hard-copy and electronic records can make this appear seamless to the end user (even if it is not seamless to the records manager) by classifying both together within the same virtual folder. By clicking on the folder, the end user can either request the paper document or view the electronic document without needing to know the medium of that document.

Basically, a project file should be the complete diary of what the project was about and how the work proceeded. Twenty years after the file has been retired and the architects who worked on the project are either dead or working for other firms, the company must be able to figure out what was done and when, and how to respond to questions from the client. The file must be complete for business continuity purposes, but also as a quick reference for any purpose the project team has. The lack of documentation can lead to business decisions to pay a settlement or make good on a problem that is ultimately not the fault of the firm. Although the contents of the file may be copies of records found in other records series within the company, the needs of the organization are more important than the need to expunge copies.

One problem we currently find in many business organizations is that electronic folders are created on a "share drive" or "G-drive" for a project file, but no subdivisions are made. The employee who seeks to retrieve a particular document is faced with many different types of documents with inadequate, sometimes even inscrutable, titles. Within such electronic folders, contracts sit alongside thank-you notes. This is the prevailing situation in all too many organizations, where corresponding paper files may be exquisitely well managed, while the electronic file is an incomplete mess.

THE ROLE OF DATABASES IN RECORDS AND RECORDS MANAGEMENT

Other than double-entry accounting books, companies did not have much written information other than correspondence until the mid- to late nineteenth century. The nineteenth century saw an enormous rise in the type of documents created by companies, beginning with manuals of operations and reports.[38] With the advent of computers, whatever information required a calculation or could be parsed into small bits and placed in tabular form, was— and then became the content of databases. What was left were documents. The difference between tabular information and business documents is not that one is highly structured and one is unstructured; anyone who must handle forms can see the similarity between a data-entry screen and the slots on the form to be completed. The difference is that information that goes into tabular form is data and what remains in a business document is persuasion or legal language.

The most elementary form of business document is correspondence. From Paul's letters in the New Testament to the modern paper letter, these are highly stylized and formalized. Statutes such as the E-Sign Act of 2000 recognize that the stylization and formalization of some business intercourse is so extreme that a paper document is truly only a formality in many types of commercial transactions. If two parties wish to do away with paper in order to consummate an agreement, they may do so. For example, when software is installed onto a computer, most often a screen with the actual licensing agreement appears in a dialog box requiring either acceptance or denial of the agreement through the "pressing" of a button; no document is created or received on either end. Ordering products using Internet websites requires entering credit card information, but no signature is required, unlike the procedure for the same transaction in a "brick-and-mortar" shop. The purchaser will receive an email confirmation of the purchase that serves as a receipt. Some shops use an electronic representation of a signature created using a signature pad, but only the store receives a document with that representation. When withdrawing money from an automatic teller machine (ATM), only a personal identification number (PIN) is required. In other instances, such as supply chain management, electronic inventory, and supply information is passed between business partners and uploaded into the databases of each as part of a larger contractual agreement. The electronic data interchange (EDI) or extended markup language (XML) information can then be reassembled into invoices or packing slips when necessary, but are held in electronic form for every purpose, including audits. Each part of this activity—receipt of data, reassembly into an invoice, the packing slip, etc.—is a document; each is a separate record.

We use databases to perform all of these transactions for which a document can be created, but for which we require an act—much like a handshake—rather than a signature upon a piece of paper. What can be put in a database is limited only by our imaginations and technology. A great deal of the work now being done by the library, archives, museum, and records management community is this type of work: addressing the question of how to divide a document into appropriate parts and then label the parts so a single search will present a unified and meaningful results set.

What we put in a database are called data. The Indo-European root for datum is *dō-* meaning "give."[39] A datum is a given, something upon which we all agree. Data are facts upon which we all agree or would agree, given the same position of observation. A datum is accessible to all parties. Unlike information, a single datum will not change us in some fundamental way because its signification is unclear without a context.

The output of a collection of data manipulated in some new way, however, is information. Consider, for instance, the weekly report for widget production that indicates a loss of production because of machine malfunction in Manufacturing Facility X. That new configuration of information can tell us what we need to know to diagnose or decide. The output is a report, whether in graphical or tabular form. The output of a database is persuasive — i.e., it is data given a context. That output constitutes a document. Contracts enforce, court papers plead, invoices remind, packing slips confirm. In and of themselves, documents do nothing, but within the context of daily business activity, each tells the organization what is required or provides information to diagnose or decide. Documents help us to act.

Records are the reminder that documents have a context. Records management is to documents what pragmatics is to linguistics: it is the context for meaning. Just as the past tense of a verb requires knowledge of both the past and present reflected in the utterance, records management maintains the past and present reflected within the document.[40] The utterance still has meaning in the semantic sense, but it can no longer persuade. A document can be persuasive, but a record persuades. Documents in and of themselves perform important acts within an organization, but their part in the business process is assured only when they are managed as records. A single record may include many documents; whatever the context requires. A database that may be used to create documents is a set of facts with relationships that can be persuasive, but cannot persuade without manipulation and context. The manipulation is output. The output is a document that is a record or part of a record. The input of a database is also a document that is also a record or part of a record.

Because the purpose of a record is to preserve the document with its entire relevant context, and that context may include a database, a record changes the rhetorical nature of a document into a fact — a given, not a piece of persuasion. A record is a given that is different from a datum. The Indo-European root of the term "record" is *kerd*[41] that means "heart" — the same root as is found in "accord," "cardiac," and "credible." The noun and the verb have the same root, hence no definition of the noun "record" can have the verb "record" used in the definition. When we learn something by heart or copy it, we have "recorded" it.[42] The other root of "record" is *rē-* that means to bestow or endow.[43] The word "record" could prosaically be defined as "bestowing the heart." This may strike one as poetic, but put within the context of a business or political relationship based upon trust, it makes perfect sense. In the English tradition from which this term comes to us (pre-literate England), the information that was considered a given was testimony by five knights who were giving up their memory. This memory was gradually transferred to writing. The writing thus retained the notion of memory through the use of the term "record."[44]

Within the larger context of information, a record is like a datum in that it is dependable, but it is dependable because it has fulfilled certain social requirements that are not required of a datum. Whereas a datum is a fact given by nature, a record is a fact with context given by business or government. Both a datum and a record are present for observation and inspection. The verb "record" means to commit to memory. The use of the term in English is particularly interesting, as it is directly related to the term "recorder"—a person who registers things for later recall. The reader will note that no medium is required or specified for recording, only that it is recorded: remembered. Neither is a specification required to "declare" something a record. Any recorded thing is a record. The Oxford English Dictionary includes many meanings for "record," among them "having been committed to writing as authentic evidence of a matter having legal importance," "The fact or condition of being preserved as knowledge," "attestation or testimony of a fact," "An authentic or official report of the proceedings in any cause coming before a court of record, together with the judgement given thereon," "A copy of the material points, pleadings, and issue between defendant and plaintiff on a matter of law, constituting the case to be decided by the court," "An account of some fact or event preserved in writing or other permanent form."[45]

The Indo-European roots of "inform" are *merph*, meaning "to form or give shape" and *en*, meaning "within" or "among." Thus the word "inform" has a meaning of forming or giving shape within. In a manner of speaking, information is something that will change us in some way by giving form to something inside of us. In this sense, data is not information because a datum is given, hence it will not change us. A document is information because it has a persuasive power; its purpose is to change us. A document that is a record, however, is also given because it is already "given from the heart." In a manner of speaking, neither a datum nor a record is information because they are already given, known; hence they cannot change us. This is only partially true because they are known only to a specific group of persons. Information is given only to its creators and collectors. What gives information its true nature is that it is shared to affect others, to change them in some way, to persuade them, to create revelation, to help them decide or diagnose.

Combining statute and word history, the records we manage will change us. We manage information in the form of records. There is no specification of the subject, nor of whether it directly relates to the organization. We do not manage tacit knowledge and we do not manage just written documents. We manage the form of the documents and ensure that they are serving their function appropriately. We organize documents through classification into records and organize records through classification into records series. We ensure that the metalevel management required by records is being performed from conception to ashes.

A NATURAL HISTORY OF DOCUMENTS

Following on the methods used in biology, we have observed four different types of documents in the above discussion:
1. Single: discrete individual units created from single electronic files, for example, emails;
2. Simplex: individual units created from databases, for example invoices;
3. Static, compound: single units created from several single electronic files with static content (or templates such as quarterly reports), for example reports with text, graphics, and spreadsheets;
4. Dynamic, compound records represented as single units created from several single electronic files with dynamic content: dynamic web pages or portal.

Each of these may be a record or part of a record. Their structure, permissions for user access, and life cycle cannot be determined by describing them as I have done here. As discussed above and in the Introduction, the structure of each of these requires that it be managed differently. We will find in the next chapter on the life cycle that even if these have a similar format, the management of each must be carefully thought out. The key to understanding each is to discover what the employees who use these files throughout the life cycle understand as whole and significant.

NOTES

1. 28 USC Appendix. Federal Rules of Civil Procedure, V. Depositions and Discovery, Rule 26. General Provisions Governing Discovery; Duty of Disclosure and Rule 34. Production of Documents and Things and Entry Upon Land for Inspection and Other Purposes. http://www.access.gpo.gov/uscode/title28a/28a_4_5_.html (10 May 2004).

2. Samuel Johnson, *A Dictionary of the English Language* (London: W. Strathams, 1755). See Trevor Livelton's delightful and careful treatment of the definition of "records" and "information," including Johnson's definition in his *Archival Theory, Records, and the Public* (Lanham, MD: Society of American Archivists and Scarecrow Press, 1996).

3. Luciana Duranti, *Diplomatics: New Uses for an Old Science* (Lanham, MD: Society of American Archivists, Association of Canadian Archivists, and Scarecrow Press, 1998).

4. Duranti, *Diplomatics,* 45.

5. T. R. Schellenberg, *Modern Archives: Principles and Techniques* (Chicago: University of Chicago Press, 1956), 27.

6. Duranti, *Diplomatics,* "In France and Quebec, the term equivalent to juridical person is *personne morale* or *juridique.* In England, the United States, and English-speaking Canada, there is a legal distinction between 'natural' and 'artificial' persons that is close to the distinction between physical and juridical persons, but the jurists in those countries do not agree on a definition of the two terms. Moreover, diplomatics has developed in France, Germany, Spain, and Italy, that is, in countries where the concept of juridical, as

opposed to physical, person is deep-rooted in the minds of all citizens, and diplomatic doctrine is built on it," 42, fn. 20.

7. Duranti, *Diplomatics,* 45, fn. 29. As noted above, authenticity in records management is a hoped-for outcome, not something that we create or guarantee.

8. See, for example, Niels Windfeld Lund, "Omrids af en dokumentationsvidenskab. [Outline of a Documentation Science]," *Norsk tidsskrift for bibliotekforskning* 4, no. 12 (1999): 24–47; Sylvie Leleu-Merviel, "Effets de la numérisation et de la mise en réseau sur le concept de document," *Information-Interaction-Intelligence* 4, no. 1 (2004): 121–140; also see http://www.rtp-doc.enssib.fr.

9. G. Drouhet, G. Deslassy, and E. Morineau, *Records Management: mode d'emploi* (Paris: ADBS, 2000), Introduction. Joan van Albada, the current President of the International Council of Archives, tells me that the word "record" does not translate into Dutch; personal conversation.

10. Drouhet, Deslassy, and Morineau, 5.

11. Alfred D. Chandler, Jr., *Strategy and Structure: Chapters in the History of the Industrial Enterprise* (Cambridge, MA: MIT Press, 1962), 322.

12. Sylvie Leleu-Merviel, 125.

13. Daniel R. Headrick, *When Information Came of Age: Technologies of Knowledge in the Age of Reason and Revolution, 1700–1850* (Oxford: Oxford University Press, 2000), "Communicating Information," 181–211.

14. Calvert Watkins, editor, *The American Heritage Dictionary of Indo-European Roots,* 2nd ed. (Boston: Houghton Mifflin, 2000); see also John K. Davies's description of the document in the Greek *koinon* in his "Greek Archives: From Record to Monument," 323–343 in *Ancient Archives and Archival Traditions: Concepts of Record-Keeping in the Ancient World,* edited by Maria Brosius (Oxford: Oxford University Press, 2003), especially 338–339.

15. *Oxford English Dictionary: The Compact Edition* (Oxford: Oxford University Press, 1971).

16. Stevan Dedijer and Nicolas Jéquier, *Intelligence for Economic Development* (Oxford: Berg Publishers, 1987).

17. Michael K. Buckland, "What Is a 'Document'?" *Journal of the American Society of Information Science* 48, no. 9 (September 1997): 804–809. See also Ronald E. Day, *The Modern Invention of Information: Discourse, History and Power* (Carbondale: Southern Illinois University Press, 2001), 7–37. Briet's use of the term *"indice"* that is questionably translated to the English as "sign" ("token" may have been a better choice) raises interesting problems. While C. S. Peirce, "Logic as Semiotic: The Theory of Signs," 98–119 in *Philosophical Writings of Peirce,* edited by Justus Buchler (New York: Dover Publications, 1955), classifies an index as a sign along with icons and symbols, there is some question as to whether an index is a sign at all. On this issue see further, Brandt, Per Aage, "Grounding Iconicity," in *Iconicity—A Fundamental Problem in Semiotics,* edited by B. Brogaard, T. D. Johansson, and M. Skov (Aarhus: NSU Press, 1999).

18. While we believe ourselves to be more humane than those creating the sterile zoo animal exhibits of the 1920s that more closely resembled a cabinet of curios, what we do now is to create tokens of the animal's habitat that include the animal, i.e., we now instantiate a mini-African Savannah with zebras and possibly ostriches and other animals in it.

19. J. N. Postgate, "Middle Assyrian Documents in Government," 124–138 in Brosius, 126; and Klaas R. Veenhof, "Archives of Old Assyrian Traders," 78–123 in Brosius, 88.

20. John W. Gross, "Inventory and Scheduling Records," *Records Management Quarterly* 7, no. 1 (January 1973): 28–31.

21. Mary F. Robek, Wilmer O. Maedke, and Gerald F. Brown, *Information and Records Management,* 3rd ed. (Lake Forest, IL: Glencoe, 1987), 565.

22. Electronic forms management products share little resemblance to the "forms management" found in records management. Forms management in records manage concerns itself with the control of the types of forms in use within an organization, as well as maintenance of the history of those forms. Electronic forms management products permit an organization to create a form on the web and then to permit either shallow or deep validation of fields as well as forced user completion of fields.

23. EDI functions more like forms management. XML is meant to work like either content management or EDI.

24. David Bearman, *Electronic Evidence: Strategies for Managing Records in Contemporary Organizations* (Pittsburgh: Archives and Museum Informatics, 1994), 161.

25. Michael J. D. Sutton, *Document Management for the Enterprise: Principles, Techniques, and Applications* (New York: Wiley Computer Publishing, 1996), 342 and 123 respectively.

26. Patrick Cadell, "Access and Information: European Attitudes and Anxieties" *Archives: Journal of the British Records Association* 28, no. 108 (April 2003): 3–13.

27. Mary Claire Griffin, *Records Management: A Modern Tool for Business* (Boston: Allyn and Bacon, 1964); Emmett J. Leahy and Christopher A. Cameron, *Modern Records Management: A Basic Guide to Records Control, Filing, and Information Retrieval* (New York: McGraw-Hill, 1965); William Benedon, *Records Management* (Englewood Cliffs, NJ: Prentice-Hall, 1969); Milburn D. Smith III, *Information and Records Management: A Decision-maker's Guide to Systems Planning and Implementation* (New York: Quorum Books, 1986); Terry D. Lundgren and Carol A. Lundgren, *Records Management in the Computer Age* (Boston: PWS-Kent, 1989); Betty R. Ricks, Ann J. Swafford, and Kay F. Gow, *Information and Image Management: A Records Systems Approach* (Cincinnati: South-Western Publishing Co., 1992); Patricia E. Wallace, Jo Ann Lee, and Dexter R. Schubert, *Records Management: Integrated Information Systems,* 3rd ed. (Upper Saddle River, NJ: Prentice Hall, 1992), Norman F. Kallaus and Mina M. Johnson, *Records Management,* 5th ed. (Cincinnati: South-Western Publishing Co., 1992); Susan Z. Diamond, *Records Management: A Practical Approach* (New York: American Management Association, 1995); Mary F. Robek, Gerald F. Brown, and David O. Stephens, *Information and Records Management: Document-based Information Systems,* 4th ed. (New York: Glencoe/McGraw-Hill, 1995); Jeffrey R. Stewart, *Professional Records Management* (New York: Glencoe/McGraw-Hill, 1995); Mark Langemo, *Winning Strategies for Successful Records Management Programs: Proven Strategies for Developing New Programs and Improving Existing Ones!* (Denver: Information Requirements Clearinghouse, 2002); David O. Stephens, and Roderick C. Wallace, *Electronic Records Retention: New Strategies for Data Life Cycle Management* (Lenexa, KS: ARMA, International, 2003).

28. Ralph Westington, "Case Records Filing System," *Records Management Quarterly* 10, no. 2 (April, 1976); Robert L. Sanders, "The Promise of Project Files: A Case Study," *Information Management Journal* 33, no. 1 (January 1999): 64–67.

29. Robek, Maedke, and Brown, 3rd ed., 158.

30. Robek, Maedke, and Brown, 3rd ed., 159.

31. Penn, Pennix, and Coulson, *Records Management Handbook,* 2nd ed. (Brookfield, VT: Gower, 1994), 215.

32. Penn, Pennix, and Coulson, 226.

33. Penn, Pennix, and Coulson, 226.

34. Robert L. Sanders, 64.

35. Robert L. Sanders, 65.

36. A project file or case file is like a narrative of what happened. Documents are separated into folders by type, but to make sense, one often has to jump among many different folders and documents to make sense of the whole. When these types of files are fragmented, the narrative is interrupted, making it difficult to know what is happening and who is responsible for doing each part of the project.

37. Penn, Pennix, and Coulson, 226.

38. JoAnne Yates, *Control through Communication: The Rise of System in American Management* (Baltimore: Johns Hopkins University Press, 1989), 5.

39. Watkins, *Indo-European Roots.*

40. Michael Silverstein, "Shifters, Linguistic Categories, and Cultural Description," 11–56, in *Meaning in Anthropology,* edited by Keith H. Basso and Henry A. Selby (Albuquerque: University of New Mexico Press, 1976).

41. Watkins, *Indo-European Roots.* The Latin form *recordation,* recollection.

42. Hence the Spanish *recorder,* and French *reconnaitre,* remember.

43. Watkins, *Indo-European Roots.*

44. M. T. Clanchy, *From Memory to Written Record: England 1066–1307,* 2nd ed. (Oxford: Blackwell Publishers, 1993), Introduction.

45. *Oxford English Dictionary: The Compact Edition* (Oxford: Oxford University Press, 1971).

Chapter Five

The Life Cycle: Business Processes in Relation to Records

Information is one of the raw materials of business processes. Without information, the process creates no product, creates products with defects, or creates the wrong product. Information is an input, an output, or a decision tool for every business process. When information is captured in some form it can, depending upon the context as we saw in chapter 3, become a record. Just as supply chain management worries about ensuring just-in-time delivery of the correct materials at the appropriate time and place, a records manager worries about the delivery of the right records to the right people at the right time and place. Both are concerned with how their respective objects arrive. The major difference between the supply chain manager and the records manager is that the records manager has an additional set of worries: how the records are handled after they are used, how they were created, what policies dictate their management, how they are distributed, whether they are to be destroyed or archived, whether appropriate audit trail information is collected and maintained, and whether the records are properly destroyed, among others. What has traditionally differentiated the records manager from the information technology (IT) professional is that the IT professional is more concerned about the methods by which appropriate information arrives electronically, and the records manager is concerned about that and everything else.

In the 1990s, a considerable amount of literature was produced on the subject of "business process re-engineering." These writings were the logical result of the process innovation trend that had taken place in manufacturing in the 1970s and 1980s. This earlier trend in manufacturing process improvements was the concatenation of pressure from several forces: primarily Japanese manufacturers and their innovative quality management methods, but also the coming of age of assembly-line robotics and the introduction of the idea of "just-in-time" deliveries. It was a logical extension to bring the notion of process redesign to business processes that involve primarily information.[1]

Information technology was the tool used to redesign processes in the 1990s. Information technology had been used for decades to create and manipulate grand collections of discrete data chunks—tabular data. Those grand collections belonged to departments within corporations and government agencies that had created the collections using disparate ideas of how the data should be collected and the methods by which it should be stored. This disparity resulted in mutually unintelligible information that could not be shared among departmental data collections and could not be shared across technology platforms, even within the same business. As few business processes reside solely within a single department, using the information collected across departmental and corporate or agency boundaries became the first great IT challenge of the 1990s. The second great IT challenge was automating the business processes themselves and managing documents. For companies with processes that require a great deal of documentation, such as pharmaceutical companies, automation was a way of collecting both the documents and the audit trail information that would help both to ensure quality and to speed the approval of new drugs. Companies with complex but clear processes, such as check clearing in the banking industry, were also targets of these early efforts at process automation.

The one set of business processes that actually managed information, however, was never addressed: those processes that track how information is created, including its policies and procedures, how it is distributed and used, how its currency lapses, how it is stored, and how it is disposited. Parts of those processes may have been automated—those parts that coincide with the mission of the business, that are extremely high volume, or for which a significant savings in time would result in a cost savings or increased revenue. Within records management, those complete business processes that function to move information from conception to the death certificate are called the "records life cycle."

Within any organization, the business processes that perform the work of the organization intersect with the business processes that manage the information within the organization. For convenience, let us call business processes those that the organization identifies with its main work, including both front-office, "offensive" activities, and back-office, "defensive" activities; and let us use the term "records life cycle" for those activities that manage information. Records life cycles are business processes; they are just processes where the focus is solely on information and not on tangible assets, people, or facilities.

The concept of the records life cycle is one of the most important within records management, as it is the perspective that yields the greatest benefit to the organization. It is the perspective of management. The first evidence I have found of the concept of the records life cycle is in a 1940 article by Helen L. Chatfield, "The Problem of Records from the Standpoint of Management."[2] Yet, interestingly, many textbooks on records management do not even mention the life cycle.[3] Some mention it, but do not make use of it as a concept for explaining what records management is.[4] Some have a brief section on the life cycle, but do not explain what it is.[5] Some have a section on the life cycle, explain what it is, but then do not demonstrate how to use the concept for the purposes of management.[6] Some textbooks employ the term, only to muddy it with other concepts that have nothing to do with the life cycle, such as "entity life history" and "records continuum."[7] What these explanations lack is an understanding that the effectiveness of each phase is only as good as every preceding phase, as well as an understanding of how the life cycle as a process integrates with other business processes.

WHAT THE LIFE CYCLE DOES

Observation of any office environment yields the following: people create information, they use it, they distribute it, they put it somewhere or leave it where it can be reached conveniently; then they throw it away, lose it, forget about it, or put it someplace where it is out of the way. If the information has not been forgotten or thrown away after it has been put out of the way, people forget about it again, lose it again, destroy it, save it for the purposes of the organization, or save it for posterity by putting it in an archive. The question of which actions are taken from among the choices above has everything to do with personality and portfolio. Organized people will organize information to the best of their abilities and according to the context they view as important. Disorganized people will either lose or forget about information. Risk takers will throw things away. People who avoid risk will save everything, but will not necessarily be able to find it again, unless they are also organized people.

Just as an organization's various jobs cannot be configured around the personalities of the persons holding them, the management of an organization's information cannot be dependent upon the personality of each individual that comes into contact with it.[8] Nor can the management of an organization's information be dependent upon the personality of each department's manager, or upon the personality of the organization's executive officers. Information must be managed.

One of the methods used by records management to manage all forms of information is to create an idealized records life cycle for each identifiable form of information, also called a "records series." As the reader may have just noted, we use the phrase "the records life cycle" as a singular when there are actually as many life cycles as there are records series. This raises the problem of terminology. Biology studies the life cycles of various living things. Within business, many companies pay close attention to product life cycle management. Project management has a life cycle. Software has a life cycle, as do aircraft structures, brands, cattle, components, computing infrastructures, corporations, customer information, drugs, environments, highway bridges, site remediation, and supplier literature. Each of these life cycles is a process of change, particularly a process of maturation tracked through time.

Records life cycles, product life cycle management, project management, computing infrastructure management—all of these are business processes. Life cycle processes are more difficult to manage than other types of business processes because they are likely to occur over time and thus require a perspective different from most other types of management. Those organizations that are poised for a "quick win" tend to pay less attention to them. Even for an organization that does pay attention to long-term goals, the records life cycle poses the problem of balancing short-term and long-term issues: motivation of managers, the ensuring of maintenance through budgeting shortfalls, and corporate memory for policies, procedures, and training.

Business processes that are more visibly associated with the business, such as purchasing and logistics, usually do not have an owner, but the process itself and the interrelationship of the steps is clearer: a widget is produced and shipped, a court paper is filed producing a response from opposing counsel, an audit report is incorporated into the annual report and the report is published, the patient is treated and gets better or dies. Information life cycles are difficult to recognize because the output—the final destruction or archiving of a document—is not visible, nor is it apparently directly linked to the organization's mission.

Fragments of the life cycle that tend to be managed quite well are those where the creation or capture and distribution of a document set is vital to the core competency of an organization. The pharmaceutical company's assembly of documents into a new drug submission is a good example; so is loan processing within a bank. The result is we have technology applications that perform an outstanding job on a fragment of the document-related activities within all business processes within a specific industry, but then drop the documents like a hot rock at the conclusion of that fragment. Records managers are the owners of the information life cycles, but only insofar as the organizations that employ them recognize complete life cycles and only for as much information or for as many media as the organization recognizes as having a life cycle. Databases are an excellent example of captured information which clearly has an ongoing life cycle, but for which no life cycle is assigned, either for its content or for its output. This is in part because records managers will not address databases.[9] Reports management is certainly concerned with managing the output of databases in the form of reports. Robek, Brown, and Maedke list reports management as a part of records creation, but say nothing about the underlying database itself, from which the reports are generated.[10] While Penn, Pennix, and Coulson list reports management as a "program element," they, too, do not list databases.[11]

Where other business processes have steps, life cycles have phases. The beginning of a business process is the beginning of activity that moves along from step to step until a clearly identifiable endpoint occurs. Most individuals involved in basic business processes understand where their steps fit into the larger process—although in every industry and level of government agency individuals can be found who do not know where the information comes from or where it goes to; so far as they are concerned, the business process begins and ends at their desks.[12] Life cycle processes, unless they are heavily managed and documented, do not have the same clear movement from one step to another; steps are characterized more generally as phases, such as creation or storage. Phases themselves are less easily characterized. For example, in the check-clearing process within a bank, each step of the process is clear: the check is written, it is accepted by the merchant, it is deposited, etc. A contrasting life cycle example will illustrate the difference: active records become inactive records generally when they are not required to be referenced or retrieved more than once per month. At what point do employees reflect upon the fact that the records they use have changed state from active to inactive? Records accessed less than once per month are usually not on anyone's "to do" list unless or until the space occupied by the physical records is needed for something else.

PHASES OF THE LIFE CYCLE

Disagreement also exists as to the number of phases in a records life cycle. Robek, Brown, and Maedke do not specifically discuss the life cycle, but list four progressive sections as the divisions of the records management process: organization and evaluation, active records maintenance, inactive records maintenance, and records creation.[13] Penn, Pennix, and Coulson name three or four: creation, maintenance and use that includes active and semiactive or inactive, and disposition.[14] The U.S. National Archives and Records Administration (NARA) lists three: creation, maintenance, and disposition.[15] The National Archives of Canada lists seven: information management planning; collection, creation, receipt, and capture; organization; use and dissemination; maintenance, protection, and preservation; disposition; and evaluation.[16] The U.K. Parliamentary Archives lists three phases: current, semicurrent, and noncurrent.[17] The International Council of Archives (ICA) lists three: conception, creation, and maintenance.[18] William Saffady notes two stages: active and inactive.[19] Stephens and Wallace do not discuss the life cycle per se, but list several phases under the rubric of "total life cycle control" as an important principle for "electronic records retention scheduling": on-line retention, near-line retention, off-line retention, and total retention.[20] Shepherd and Yeo mention three: creation, capture, storage, use, and disposal; current, semicurrent, and noncurrent; and active, semiactive, and inactive, but these do not play an interesting role within their work.[21] Hare and McLeod mention four: creation, active, semiactive, and inactive.[22] We could go on, but I do not believe doing so would be particularly fruitful. None of these approaches is incorrect; they reflect the experiences and perspectives of the respective authors. Instead, let us look more closely at the idea of a life cycle.

A life cycle describes the aging management that an organization applies to sets of objects. Product life cycle management, for example, is concerned with the creation of new ideas, vetting those ideas into likely winners and others, the development of the idea into a viable product, prototyping and testing the product, approval and marketing of the product, sale of the product while the market is interested in it, revision and reformulation of the product, and, finally, the retirement of the product. These activities span many departments within a company: research and development, testing, and manufacturing; and marketing, advertising, sales, and product managers. The sets of objects being tracked belong to a particular category, and decisions regarding the life cycle are made on those sets.

Decisions could also be made regarding sets of sets. These metadecisions would be practiced by upper-level executives who would be looking at the entire life cycle of all the products. For example, a decision could be made to try to speed up the research and development phase of every product, or a decision could be made to combine the marketing efforts for several products in a specific campaign, and choices would be made concerning the appropriate mix of products. Most important, however, is that rather than simply observing what happens to the products as employees handle them, the companies are aggressively managing those products.

Compared to product management, information management shares some of the same problems with its various stages. Any later stage must be kept in mind when establishing earlier stages. If a product or a document is poorly designed, its "manufacturer" will create a useless product or one full of defects that consumers reject. We can recall automobiles, but we cannot recall a poorly worded email. The purpose of records management is to manage records as aggressively as products are managed. First, each set of records must be aggressively managed to get the records through each phase. Records life cycle phases are not the observation of what happens, but of what *must* happen to each set of records—i.e., what actions the organization must take with respect to those records at each particular phase of the life cycle. Any description of the life cycle that looks like the observation of what happens rather than the management of what happens should be set aside. This would include the descriptions developed by Penn, Pennix, and Coulson (creation, maintenance, and use that includes active and semiactive or inactive, and disposition), NARA (creation, maintenance, and disposition), the U.K. Parliamentary Archives (current, semicurrent, and noncurrent), the ICA (conception, creation, and maintenance), Saffady (active and inactive), and Stephens and Wallace (on-line retention, near-line retention, off-line retention, and total retention), and the last two descriptions provided by Shepherd and Yeo (current, semicurrent, and noncurrent; and active, semiactive, and inactive), and Hare and McLeod (active, semiactive, inactive).

Second, sets of life cycles must be examined together to maximize an organization's utility. Some determination must be made of the relative value of each records series to the organization with regard to intangible accounting and risk management, to determine where effort should be directed. Sets of records series should be compared to determine which could benefit from application of information technology. Sets of records series should be compared to determine whether and when a shared repository could be beneficial and what the nature of that repository could be. Sets of records series can also be compared to determine whether broad user access, privacy, security, and sharing is possible. Should some sets be discontinued? Should others, such as correspondence, be retooled using newer technology?

Records life cycle descriptions that do not include a metalevel of decision-making should also be rejected. Robek, Brown, and Maedke list a phase called "organization and evaluation," but do not specifically discuss the records life cycle in the text. Shepherd and Yeo mention a moderately complete list, but fail to list a planning phase. These same two authors go on to mention a concept from systems analysis, "entity life history;" however, within systems analysis and design, this concept describes obtainable "states" and their relationships for information objects. Their subsequent diagram, "record entity life history," in no way resembles a systems analysis entity life history.[23]

The only description that fits our requirements is that of the National Archives of Canada: information management planning; collection, creation, receipt and capture; organization; use and dissemination; maintenance, protection and preservation; disposition; and evaluation. This description is not perfect. Having sections on "collection" and "evaluation," it is designed for archivists, not for records managers, but has the benefit of being more thorough than the previously reviewed life cycles. It has sections that are not phases, but descriptive of activities that impact the life cycle, such as "use and dissemination" and "maintenance, protection, and preservation." It also lacks a key phase, retirement, that is most often performed poorly, making it impossible to manage anything after that phase. Nor does this definition distinguish disposition as a phase that affects how well a record is managed when it reaches the archives. Finally, we must keep in mind that any document can be subject to a litigation subpoena at any time. Like "use" and "maintenance," this is an activity that can occur at any time during the life cycle, but affects everything we do, as discussed in detail in previous chapters.

Figure 5.1 demonstrates the relationships and interdependencies among the phases of the records life cycle, as they operate within the approach I have outlined above. Note that the Use and Dissemination phase has significant overlap with the phases that precede and follow it; also note that Maintenance, Protection, and Preservation are activities that apply throughout much of the life cycle.

As noted above, the term "collection" is inappropriate because records managers do not collect records; rather, records managers are assigned a portfolio by an organization, and employees either comply or do not comply with the defined policies and procedures. Librarians and museum curators, in contrast, do collect. Archivists may collect if collection is a part of their portfolio. The Canadian Archives description has the virtue, however, of covering

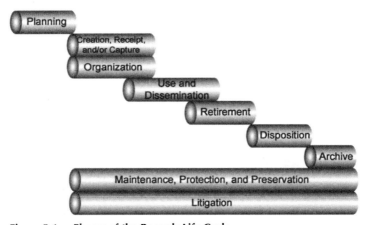

Figure 5.1. Phases of the Records Life Cycle.

all of the possible types of information centers, both organizational and cultural. As our concern here is organizational information, however, we will not examine collection.

Also observe that the Canadians use the term "evaluation" instead of "appraisal." Records managers do not "appraise" records. As noted above, we evaluate records extensively and in many more ways than archivists do, but we do not "appraise" records in the sense of evaluating their role in future culture or government. Again, that is determined by executives in charge of the records program, not by records managers.

The remainder of this chapter examines in detail the activities of each phase of the records life cycle, relying primarily on the phases outlined by the Canadian Archives, with modifications as noted above.

INFORMATION MANAGEMENT PLANNING

It is the metalevel of decision-making described above that concerns sets of records series and that is the subject in discussions of "electronic records," as it dictates everything else that will follow. Where "information" is used in place of "records," it is usually because most people do not know what a record is and the term "information" is so much trendier and has a connotation of being all-inclusive. We witnessed the same phenomenon with "document" management in the late 1990s and now see the same situation with respect to "content" management. The consultants and practitioners in information management, document management, and content management are in many instances either unaware that they are records managers, or they vehemently deny it.[24]

Records management planning begins with determining where records management fits within the mission statement, goals, values, and objectives of the organization. The higher the profile of records management within the organization, the more aggressively information can be managed. As many records managers will testify, within most organizations, records management today has a very low profile and a very low priority. That priority can change, however, when an organization must respond to recognizable threats involving similar organizations. The Arthur Andersen/Enron records scandal and the Sarbanes-Oxley Act of 2002 elevated records management to a very high profile, particularly within publicly held companies in the U.S. Many records managers now report that they are receiving unprecedented cooperation and are even being sought out by CEOs and Chief Corporate Counsel.[25]

How business is conducted changes rapidly. Electronic funds transfer affected how we understand the exchange of funds. The E-Sign Act changed how we view documents needing signatures. The Check Clearing for the 21st Century Act (commonly referred to as "Check 21") changed how we view the authenticity of checks. These are major changes, but factors such as customer expectations and incremental improvements in information technology affect how we manage information. This means that every few years each organization should undertake to ensure that it is capturing all its records in the dragnet, and that records management policies and procedures are up to date to capture any changes that may have taken place in business processes, documents, and information technology; that it may choose to use the services of a records management consultant to get an outside perspective on the organization's existing (or nonexisting) records management policies and procedures. To obtain this information requires interviews with upper-level executives to understand their perspective on strategic objectives and business requirements, as well as intensive interviews with representatives of every part of the organization. This effort should include reviews of where technology is succeeding or failing in the opinions of upper-level executives and employees, as well as the records management consultant; a thorough examination of the life cycle of each records series; a review of changes to retention created by standards, regulations, statutes, and business practices; and a review of how well policies and procedures are working, as well as the enforcement required to ensure compliance. The end result will be—at minimum—a revised set of policies and procedures, a revised retention schedule, suggestions for improvements in information technology, and even the replacement of technologies or introduction of technologies not currently used.

Only with a clear departmental mission, goals, values, and objectives aligned with the organization and a clear mandate to enforce an information management program can the records manager proceed to determine what measures for success can be defined and introduced, as well as how those measures should be monitored and enforced. The measures, monitoring, and enforcement must be determined for the records manager, the records management department, and all other stakeholders in the life cycle. Performance monitoring, however, also requires the input and acceptance of all of the stakeholders.

As the initial step in the actual planning process, the records manager must first inventory what functions exist within the organization. The only way to ensure that all functions are captured is through high-level interviews with key personnel. Those individuals can be identified through the organizational chart and then through additional recommendations provided by those interviewed. Functions are not departments, however, and may not be clearly reflected in an organizational chart. Departmental names may be misleading; good examples are Accounting and Tax. In addition to performing standard bookkeeping and accounting activities, an accounting department may manage financial instruments and treasury activities (treasury activities typically manage foreign exchange transactions). A tax department may collect information for an outside company to use in the preparation of tax forms, it may actually prepare the tax forms, and it may also manage audits. A function may be outsourced as, for example, an insurance company's use of an actuarial consultant to create rate books and develop new products. Note that the outsourcing of a function does not mean the function itself is nonexistent within the organization, because someone within the organization must manage the company that performs the outsourced activity.

The interviews that constitute this functional inventory have several purposes. They identify serious concerns and business requirements for any future records management projects. They help to identify the level of risk management that each interviewee regards as appropriate for their functional area. The interviews are also an opportunity to educate interviewees about the scope of records management within the organization, serving to identify and prioritize records-related problems within the organization. The interviews reveal the interviewees' understandings of how serious their records-related problems are, as well as revealing the extent to which the organization is dependent upon outside entities for its key information. They clarify what relationship, if any, the interviewees believe records management has with the organization's IT function. Finally, the functional interviews also identify additional employees to interview in a subsequent, second set of interviews in order to obtain a thorough understanding of the business processes within the organization.

The second set of interviews will reveal the business processes and how records intersect, assist, get created, or are output from each process. Records are an input, an output, or a decision tool for each process. This activity, the second interview, is ordinarily called a records inventory, but it serves as the primary opportunity to gather information for every other records program that the organization may want to implement. The inventory can be the beginning of a number of different programs, such as an enterprise taxonomy, an electronic records program, vital records and business continuity planning, forms management, electronic forms management, correspondence management, reports management, content management, enterprise reports management, and email management. The inventory also provides yet another opportunity to identify the level of risk tolerance among employees of a particular department, as well as the level of knowledge that they may have about the organization's existing policies for records management.

Irrespective of the type of program that will be implemented or the medium of the records, the most successful program will divide responsibility for management of information life cycles equally in the hands of all stakeholders. The records manager is the project manager for each records series' life cycle; no single person can manage the life cycle of every records series within an organization. No single person can know everything about a records series' life cycle to make all of the decisions and take all of the actions that are necessary. The responsibilities of each party must be made clear.[26]

Creating teams for each records series means that any inventory must include a description of its life cycle so that each individual on the team understands where his or her responsibility begins and ends, as well as what that responsibility is. This can be accomplished during the interview phase of the inventory, where employees describe from whence each item of information comes, what is done with it, and where it goes. These descriptions can then be included in a discussion of where the information fits into the departmental business processes, and diagrams and flowcharts of both the departmental business processes and the records series' life cycles can be outlined.

Before each interview, it can be useful to send a survey to gather basic data identifying candidates for records series within that employee's department. The survey should also ask what prescribed limiting factors are required for each records series candidate. The survey should request basic identifying information about the person completing the form. The subsequent interview can then serve as a gap analysis for the survey, addressing questions that were not completed, and also serve as an opportunity for the interviewee to reveal any limiting factors that he or she may feel uncomfortable about writing down—such as concerns about confidentiality or a particularly complex issue that has been politicized.

As the business processes and records series life cycles are outlined in the surveys and interviews, deficiencies in handling and opportunities for improved management can be identified. For example, the question of volume helps an organization create priorities to determine what information should be automated. Details about limiting factors can then be used to ensure that automated information arrives in the appropriate form to the appropriate persons at the appropriate time and place—and to no one else.

A separate survey and interview should be performed with representatives of the appropriate IT department to provide a description of the current technology environment and any changes that may be on the organization's strategic plan for the IT function proposed for the department. Such plans can be reviewed for compliance with requirements, limiting factors, and opportunities to improve management. Another important part of this particular interview is to discover whether IT has any information management policies and procedures. Many information systems security professionals within IT departments have created excellent email policies and procedures that require only minor tweaking to serve the purpose of records management as well. But one of the most important aspects of this interview with the IT department is to discover where the existing technology may be foiling the best efforts of management to maintain a smooth transition from one phase of the life cycle to another, or where the transition from one type of storage device to another leaves gaps in knowledge of content or location. A particularly arduous problem in high-volume information management, for example, is the point at which files or data are transferred from on-line devices such as random access to inexpensive disks (RAID) to off-line tape or optical disk. An off-line reel of tape or optical disk has the same accessibility as a drawer or box of paper: the contents must be inventoried, the location carefully tracked, and its destruction or preservation documented. The IT interview is an excellent opportunity to discover any copy-control problems that may arise as a result of ignorance or the IT department's lack of knowledge concerning the difference between archiving and backing up of information. Even when employees know that a back-up is a type of copy, they may not realize that it is not a medium that can be easily searched to find a single document—that it is actually a disaster recovery device.

The information collected during the interviews can then be analyzed for opportunities and concerns. That analysis should be performed with various stakeholders, including physical security, IT security, corporate counsel, department heads (including those in charge of global departments, audit, risk management, and regulatory affairs), and the CIO. By performing this information gathering and analysis activity every few years, both the business processes and the life cycles can be reviewed in the "as-is" form. By performing the life cycle information gathering and analysis with the business-process information gathering and analysis, the organization learns that records series' life cycles are business processes. The organization also receives the benefit of knowledge of its own processes and can obtain the type of process innovation for which many organizations strive.[27]

This repeated analysis and improvement resembles the "capabilities maturity model" found in systems analysis and design, which leads to continuous improvement.[28] Unlike other true phases of the life cycle, this phase anticipates all other activities in order to ensure the other phases are executed optimally for the organization. The analysis must also include the other phases in the life cycle and how well those are being or can be executed. Once the analysis is complete, an appropriate report can be produced documenting the findings and suggesting strategies for implementation.

Another document that should result from the information management planning process or that should be revised is the organization's records retention schedule. The schedule should cover every type of information within the organization, including databases, and should be usable by every individual within the organization. Achieving this requires the creation of a classification with a clear taxonomy. The classification is the basis for adding procedures for the time periods that each records series should exist, where they should be stored, what method of destruction is required or what archive, and what policies constrain each records series through security, privacy, or standards. The retention schedule is a planning document as much as it is a policy document, because it, together with the policies and procedures that go with it, is the culmination of all information about captured information within the organization.

Essentially, the activities of the information management planning phase create the processes that information will enter when it arrives, however it arrives. Those systems include introduction to a business process, current filing, distribution, user access, privacy, security, encryption, storage, vital records or business continuity, and records retention. Management within most companies, agencies, and non-profits understand that information must get to its appropriate business process. Many understand (or are coming to understand, as the result of legislation or disaster) the concept of information getting to its appropriate system of privacy and storage systems. The increasing utilization of these privacy and storage systems is an indication that management is beginning to understand records as both intangible assets and as potential sources of risk.

CREATION, RECEIPT, AND CAPTURE

Creation of information is complex and requires many more controls than receiving and capturing information. We will discuss receipt and capture first in order to pave the way for the complexities of creation. Receipt of information happens without effort by anyone. Mail is delivered; email arrives in the mail box; someone leaves a voice message for an employee; a copy of a report is placed in an employee's in-box. A claim on an insurance policy arrives in the mail. Each piece of information initiates a process. A product order is received in the mail and forwarded to the order fulfillment department. Junk email is deleted. The employee receiving the voice mail must leave the office immediately, requiring the assignment of the second-in-command as in charge. The employee receiving the report files it in the appropriate folder. The insurance claim is passed to a claims agent.

The first step in any of these processes is the same: information is sorted and forwarded to the appropriate location, whether an appropriate department or the deleted files directory; or it is deleted entirely from the phone system or is filed in a folder and routed to an appropriate employee. Sometimes a department handles these activities like the mailroom; sometimes an employee performs the filing. "Capture" has come to refer to the sorting, imaging, and forwarding of paper documents within organizations or to the introduction of preexisting electronic documents to an automated process. High-volume processes requiring paper documents with a signature—such as claims processing, loan processing, and check clearing—require a phase wherein the documents are received, sorted, and prepared for imaging. This preparation activity can include removing staples, removing duplicates, and placing documents in the appropriate order. The documents are then scanned and converted into electronic images, and various fields of information from the document, such as a check and account number, name, address, or claim amount, and information from the process, such as a claim number, are entered into a database.

The fields that are entered into the database are part of what archivists call the "metadata." Businesses refer to this information as tracking, indexing, identification, and audit trail, among other names. Sometimes the information is captured through automatic means using software technology such as optical character recognition (OCR) for printed information and intelligent character recognition (ICR) for handwritten information. Documents called "forms" that have very regular, well-defined features can be identified by the scanner and the appropriate fields can then be captured through OCR or ICR in a process called "zone" capture. The captured fields and document can then be routed electronically to the appropriate persons for action.

When preexisting electronic documents are received electronically within an automated process, this is also called capture. A common and very high-volume example of an application in which this automated capture takes place is email. Email may be delivered to the desktop or to a server. In either case, most email does not enter an organization through an automated process forwarding it to the appropriate person other than by the address on the email. Products specifically designed to take email addressed to a generic address (such as customer_service@organization.com) and route it to the appropriate person has been available since the mid-1990s and has demonstrated a high degree of success. Attempts to classify all other types of email, including the filtering of junk email, and application of an automatic, appropriate action have met with varying degrees of success.[29] Generally speaking, individual employees have had the burden of classifying their own emails and filing or deleting them appropriately.

Having discussed the relatively simple parts of this phase, let us now look at creation. Creation of records describes the process by which information is created by the organization itself, in contrast to receipt and capture that describe the arrival of information from the outside. The process of creation can last for decades or seconds. Creation of records includes creation of individual documents, copies, drafts, versions, and the accumulation of various documents making up an entire project. As the discussion in chapter 3 indicated, a record is not synonymous with a document. A record can be the equivalent of rooms full of documents worked on and gathered together over decades. How those records are created is part of the life cycle.

Let us begin with the creation of a single, complex document that may, in and of itself, be a record. In several different types of industries, such as engineering and architecture, law firms, accounting, and publishing, documents are the result of highly structured methods of collaboration called "document control." Each individual on a team is assigned a different role: researcher, drafter, reviewer, reviser, proofreader, approver. In some instances, a single individual may play multiple roles—for example, the researcher, drafter, and reviser may be the same person. The research may be performed on a pre-existing building or concept. The person drafting may be creative, as when an author writes a book; may be following a template, as when an administrative assistant creates architectural specifications; or may be following the research performed, as when an attorney drafts a contract or court paper. The reviewer may be checking for quality control items or looking for plagiarism. The proofreader may be looking for consistency of standards applications or errors in a predetermined code that must be corrected. In every one of these instances, however, the approver takes ultimate responsibility for the originality, correctness, quality, or force of the final document.

In the process of creating the document, controls are placed on who may view the work-in-progress. Distribution control and copy control are used to ensure that the audience for the document being reviewed is limited and the time during which the document is being reviewed is also limited. To understand the importance of distribution control and copy control within the creation process, consider the example of an organization or a government agency, such as the Office of Civilian Radioactive Waste Management (OCRWM). When OCRWM creates, repairs, or manages something that presents dangers to the public, such as the Yucca Mountain project to hold all nuclear power plant waste material, the entire life of the project is expected to be documented in order to ensure accountability to the public. "Yucca Mountain" is not just a place in Nevada; it is also a set of highly engineered documents. Every single item that will go into the making of Yucca Mountain must be thoroughly documented: its drawing, its method of manufacture, the manufacturing of the object, its transportation to the mountain, its installation, its maintenance, its replacement, and its destruction or storage. In short, the life cycle of the document itself from its creation to its final disposition must be thoroughly documented.

Continuing with this example, let us look at a sample of a container for radioactive nuclear waste. Research is performed as to the effects of a particular type of radioactivity on materials and current design trends. A team is assigned to draft a drawing of the container. The drawing is assigned a version control number so that everyone knows the precise document to which to refer. A single copy is made for each reviewer. The reviewers make their comments on the document and are required to return their review copy to the drafting team. The reviewer may not make her own convenience copy, although she may make a copy of her comments. The drafting team is required to ensure that every review copy is returned. The drafting team makes a copy of the current version and gives it a new version number. The new version receives revisions from the reviewers. The process of drafting, version control, copy control, and distribution control continues until a satisfactory final version is created. The final version is given to the approval team, which may request more changes. Following any additional changes, the final version is then provided to all appropriate persons and organizations. In the case of the Yucca Mountain project, OCRWM also makes a TIFF version of the final document and publishes it to the web.

This document creation process may be as elaborate or as simple as the organization requires. In a large law firm, the previous versions, called "drafts," may be kept or disposed of, depending upon the desires and experiences of the attorney or the needs of the firm. The documentation for distribution and copy control may be carefully maintained or destroyed. In an architecture firm the drawings may be maintained for reuse, training, or even destroyed because what the client really needs are the "as-builts," the drawings depicting what the end product actually was. Creation of a record that consists of more than one document can be as simple as putting documents into a folder as they are created. For example, in a doctor's office, patient medical tests are placed in the appropriate patient file. Where multiple folders make up the file, each folder represents a separate type of document. For example, correspondence with those outside the organization may be kept in one folder, and communication with those inside the organization may be kept in a different file. As noted in chapter 3, document type here means format as well as function.

In a large engineering firm, a single record can be made up of millions of documents. Imaginethe number of documents that went into the design and building of Hoover Dam, an immense project that required planning and design, budgeting, accounting, ground preparation, steel and concrete construction, massive plumbing, and electrical systems taking many years to complete. The loss of a single document can destroy the organization's understanding of the project or its accountability to citizens. The records life cycle phase of creation, receipt, and capture can describe entire processes that last years and include millions of documents, or the phase can describe the opening of a single email and its filing in an appropriate location. The activities making up this phase can be performed by many different actors. How carefully the activities are performed is dependent upon the records management needs of the organization. When the needs are great, those activities should become part of job descriptions and performance evaluations.

The formalization of a creation, receipt, or capture process may begin at the conception of a document or after the document is finalized. The process may be completely manual. The ability to automate the conception and creation of a document inside a process is referred to as business process management (BPM). Most BPM software applications are created with a particular industry market and specific industry applications in mind, such as ISO 9000 regulated manufacturing or pharmaceutical new drug applications, which require minimal human intervention for exception processing and are thus good candidates for automation using BPM. In contrast, other business processes are simple and require only a few steps and approvals, such as the processing of a travel expense form. This is commonly called administrative or ad hoc workflow. Still other processes, such as check clearing, can require a very complex workflow, with multiple approvals, subflows, and voting. These workflows are commonly called "production" workflow. Not every workflow software product can perform all of these functions. Currently email is known as "poor man's workflow," used in many organizations to route documents for review and approval. Because it was not designed for this purpose, however, it lacks the controls, audit trails, and management features of a business process management application.

The pages of an organization's website are a good example of a "document" that can benefit from workflow. A single web page may have many different parts, potentially supported by different departments within the same organization. Using workflow, these departments create, approve, and update or publish content to their respective portions of the web page. The software products that perform these tasks are called content management applications. (One should note that many vendors have extended the term "content management" to their document management applications to give them more caché—albeit in many cases without giving them any further functionality.) The best content management applications are document management applications with a component that assists in the creation of HTML and with workflow that then publishes the content to the web.

Some documents, such as engineering drawings, can require multiple versions and approvals before the document is finalized. Electronic engineering drawings are usually created in computer-aided design (CAD) software products. The drawings themselves have multiple layers, standardized notation, and references to other documents, such as specifications. The creation process takes as many versions and approvals as are required to provide a final document containing all the requirements and specifications needed. Each version and each approval must be clearly documented, as well as what changes were made to each version of the document. The approvals may consist of anything from a signature on a hard-copy document, a data field indicating that the approver hit a particular button on the keyboard (a generic electronic signature), or the application of a hash and audit trail information to the electronic version—a digital signature.[30] In any case, the type of approval required is agreed upon by the parties in the contract, according to each party's risk assessment.

When documents are associated with a group that performs organizational functions such as project management or research and development, a great deal more functionality is required in the document creation process. For example, notes about the current status of a project or news affecting the project may be important as supporting information, documenting the justification behind a particular decision or change. Some software products provide so-called collaboration functionality, permitting the creation of a project space that will permit the sharing of links, news reports, and status updates, as well as providing version control of documents under creation and complete access to all information associated with the project to designated project team members.

This discussion has focused on electronic documents and their creation in order to emphasize that the creation of records is the creation of documents as records. Each document, irrespective of its format, must at some point be assigned to a particular records series. This association may occur as part of the entire life cycle of the document, whereby no affirmative action must be taken by the employees manipulating the information. The association may alternatively take place in the form of an affirmative action taken by an employee assigned to create appropriate metadata or place the document into a particular folder. In the electronic environment, creation of metadata for a document may automatically place the document in the appropriate "buckets." In the majority of organizations, however, electronic documents are created in the absence of a document management application that would require the creation of such metadata. Product managers of document management software applications report that employees are loathe to create what are called "profiles" without precise policies and procedures created by upper-level executives directing them to perform such acts. Profiles assign the correct metadata. In contrast, within the hard-copy world, an individual within a workgroup or department typically is assigned to handle the documents produced—which brings us to the particular challenges of creation, receipt, and capture within the electronic world.

Back in that hard-copy world, the secretarial handbook was as much about the format and tone of all types of communication as it was about proper phone etiquette. Now, everyone is their own secretary for both internal communication and a great deal of outside communication. The business process for catching information has changed—it has nearly disappeared. One difference between the electronic and hard-copy environments is that a hard-copy document gets in the way and must eventually be disposed of. Nevertheless, I have seen many offices containing so many documents and folders that a path to the desk is the only space kept clear. The piles are covered with dust, and coworkers complain about the persons who keep such offices because they are constantly losing documents. In contrast, electronic documents do not create a pile that must be cleared in order to walk across the room. The consequences of this basic environmental difference are that, unless directed to do otherwise, every employee becomes an electronic pile-maker, with his or her own ideas of what constitutes a distinct and individual pile.

Among the most unwieldy of these electronic "piles" are those for email. The only documents that have any likelihood of being found are those that are kept in email as attachments, and then only if the employee can recall who sent the document and the time period in which the document was sent. Most office workers move important email to an appropriate folder within the email system. As noted in chapter 3, this is one of the main sources of confusion concerning email and records series. Email cannot be maintained within the same electronic folder as other "desktop" documents without losing potentially important information, nor can it always be printed without losing some information. These defects do not make email a records series or even a document type requiring that they be stored together and deleted according to the same retention. Email is many different records series trapped inside of inadequate software.

Both email and instant messaging are particularly pernicious because of the current cultural practices we have for them. The delivery mechanism for the email on these devices can make it nearly impossible to manage at the enterprise level, and the products for email have been difficult to integrate with document management applications. Our current cultural practices regarding email include an assumption that motivates all other actions: we treat email the same way we treat the telephone—we are casual, we use more idioms and colorful language, we make questionable statements that we assume no one else will ever hear or see.

As for the telephone, we do not record our phone calls in the normal course of business, nor do we treat voice messages as records—primarily because the technology has not yet arrived to permit us to do so individually on a regular basis. However, voice over IP (VoIP; i.e., voice delivered using the

Internet Protocol) will create many problems for records managers to solve. Phone calls can be formal or informal, but they are considered conversations, not documents or records. The informal tone of phone conversation is carried over to email and instant messaging. The business press reports individuals having "conversations" by either of these two methods, i.e., email and instant messaging, while doing other things, such as participating in a conference call. Because these methods are less intrusive than a phone call that requires immediate attention, or a personal visit that will require more time to complete, they present an additional opportunity for brief communication that resembles conversation more than it does the visual format of the email: a memorandum.

Because of the manner in which these new vehicles of communication have come to be used, employees have difficulty identifying either email or instant messaging as being a record. This is true even of employees in organizations that have deployed document management applications, and is in part a result of some peculiar language that these organizations have adopted concerning the relationship of documents and records. As we learned in Chapter 3, nearly any information that is captured within an organization is a record. Document management and content management software applications have a procedure called "declaring a document a record"—a procedure that, as we have seen, is absurd: if it is captured information, it is a record; it has a life cycle; it must be classified, filed, and retention applied. The precise origin of this odd terminology is unclear, but it contributes to the poor risk management of many organizations, as well as to employees' illusions that their work output either belongs to themselves or is not a record unless they say so.

ORGANIZATION

This phase consists not of the creation of a system of organization, but rather of the registration and placement of an item of information into those systems of organization. (The creation of systems of organization occurs in the initial phase of the records life cycle, the Information Management Planning phase.) Those various systems of organization include introduction of the information to a business process, current filing, distribution, user access, privacy, security, encryption, storage, and records retention. Depending upon circumstances, the actor performing the registration can be many different employees within an organization. In instances where employees are not well trained or the organization does not recognize this phase as either reducing risk or adding value to an asset, the Organization phase is performed only as well as the personality and immediate demands of the employee allow. Unfortunately, this phase is ordinarily quite brief in comparison to most other phases of the life cycle, and it also happens to be the phase whose activities are crucial to the ability to retrieve an item at a later time.

In many instances, all that is required of an employee is to place the item in a specified "bucket" that already contains the appropriate indexing information to associate it with all other appropriate systems. An electronic document placed in an electronic file folder is immediately placed within its appropriate current filing, user access, privacy, security, initial storage and records retention systems. When the organization of an item requires further work on the part of the employee, such as completing an index field or a profile, the chances of the item reaching its required destination are reduced, unless this activity is part of the employee's job responsibilities and performance evaluation.[31] Completing an index field requires identifying the item as a part of a particular records series. By identifying the records series, the user identifies the item as a document within a particular workflow. In many instances that document receives a tracking number; for example, in insurance, a claim is associated with a particular policy number, assigned a claim number, and is then routed to the appropriate claims adjuster.

Completing a profile requires completing more index fields, such as author or sender, date of the item, date of receipt, subject line, and records series. Conversations with vendors of document management and records management software applications indicate that employees are loathe to complete such a profile unless it is a clear part of their job duties. One of the products of redesigned business processes is the reduction of fields required for the capture or the automated capture of elementary indexing fields. Creators of the most current records management applications have recognized the labor-intensive process of filing/classifying electronic records and have designed ways to remove this burden from the employee. However, these methods require ingenuity, considerable work on the part of the implementation team, and a lot of laborious customization, which in turn would be difficult subsequently to maintain and upgrade. The instant a document or process changes, the rule that was previously created to help the employee file/classify records is in danger of no longer working. In addition, some employees, particularly managers, are engaged in processes that are not good candidates for these rules because their processes are not regular enough.

Many organizations are beginning to have questions about how to apply retention to email and instant messaging. This issue is an extension of the old hard-copy problem of how to classify correspondence and memoranda. Classification systems—also called taxonomies, as will be discussed below—are based upon function. Prior to the advent of email, most of the documents that an individual would be likely to file were neither correspondence nor email; they were forms. Forms have a clear function that can be determined by the visual appearance of the form, as well as by means of a number or title. Correspondence, however, has only one visual appearance, as does a memorandum. For those not old enough to remember, correspondence was used for communication outside the organization, and memoranda were used inside an organization. Either of these could have multiple functions—for example, negotiation of a financial transaction conducted via correspondence, a transmittal attending attached documents, notification of an important situation or knowledge. Within an organization, a memorandum could announce the company picnic, state a policy, present research for a project, announce a transfer or a hire, or state an opinion. The only way to determine the function of the correspondence or memorandum was to read it.

Email was originally used for internal organizational communication, hence its format as a memorandum. Again for those too young to remember, "cc" is the abbreviation for "carbon copy"—the way that copies were made before photocopy machines. Another line, "bcc," is the abbreviation for "back carbon copy." The back carbon copy was sent to someone who needed to know the content of the memorandum, but whose identity was hidden from the recipient in the "to" line. This made two "originals"—the one sent to the recipients in the "to" line, and the one kept by the writer but also sent to the recipients on the "bcc" line. On both correspondence and memoranda, the initials of the author and the typist were included at the bottom of the memo in addition to a notation that an attachment was included. The title of the attachment generally was not noted at the bottom, as it was typically referred to in the body of the communication.

The archival community has focused on metadata and particularly the presence or lack of metadata associated with email as an important issue. For example, David Bearman states that "the printing of electronic mail messages would have resulted in the loss of structural and contextual information required to understand their significance including the names of recipients and senders, the date and time of receipt, the link to prior messages, full distributions lists, and so on."[32] The reader can see from the description above that the hard-copy environment cannot be idealized and then compared to the electronic environment, as Bearman has done here. Not all basic information is contained in an "original" memorandum or email, such as a list of all recipients, if you are not the recipient of the "bcc" copy—and this applies to both the hard-copy environment and to today's more "metadata-friendly" email applications. Hard-copy memoranda did not have the names of all recipients, the date and time of receipt, links to prior messages, and full distribution lists. If hard copies were incomplete, why are we asking so much more of electronic copies? Too often, an idealized hard-copy world is held up against an electronic environment and the electronic environment is held wanting. Records managers and archivists willingly report deficiencies within the hard-copy environment.[33] Those deficiencies should be simple guides for us to perform better in the electronic environment.

As stated previously, the form of communication in correspondence and memoranda gave no clue to its function. This is the case now with email and instant messaging. To determine how the email or instant message is to be classified, its contents must be read and a determination must then be made by an employee. In a past position as the records manager for a large law firm, I found that the most pernicious problem was identifying to which file each piece of correspondence and memorandum belonged. In many instances, the secretary working for the attorney could not determine into which file a document was to be placed because several similar matters were being performed for the same client. Not only was this a time-consuming problem to resolve, but quite often it required the attention of the individual with the highest salary to resolve it.

Form, in information, does not follow function. This is nowhere more evident than in the use of the term "document type" in document management systems. A document type is a format, in many instances a word-processing template. Templates exist for correspondence and memoranda that function as described above in numerous ways. The point here is that, in the paper world, employees would not have tossed every hard-copy document that looked like correspondence into a single bucket. Each would have been evaluated for the department it addressed and its function and would then have been appropriately filed.

The reader can see that this phase, Organization, and the previous one, Creation, Receipt, and Capture, can be confused because in the practices of many organizations they are often combined. When the mailroom opens a letter and places it in the appropriate employee's inbox, a manual and tacit form of indexing has occurred. When a letter is scanned by the mailroom, then indexed and routed to the appropriate employee, the indexing is explicit. The manual and tacit approach may actually be just as speedy in getting the letter to the appropriate employee in the correct business process, but this act will not have introduced the document to any other electronic system required for tracking or business intelligence. In any case, for the artifact itself to have value above and beyond its tacit participation in a business process and to avoid what David Shenk so aptly named "data smog,"[34] it must be indexed.[35] The question is when and by whom.

Archivists, librarians, and museum curators use the term "metadata" to include the term "indexing." Metadata is, for these groups, any information about information artifacts. Records management practices have long ensured that appropriate descriptive data are associated with records series. The classification of a set of documents as a particular records series is an explicit association of a particular life cycle and office of record to that set. Data that managers associate with information artifacts are specific to each set of records. For example, when policy forms are imaged in an insurance company, the only "metadata" associated with it, other than details of the imaging process, is the policy number. All other relevant information will have been put into the insurance company's other databases. By adding only the policy number during the imaging process, only the information required to associate the policy with the database information is entered, streamlining the process and making it less expensive.

Other business processes may not require a great deal more metadata, but the organization itself could benefit from attaching even more metadata. For example, many document management applications permit a user to complete a large number of index fields so that a document can be found using different key words. From the standpoint of the user who subsequently seeks to retrieve the document, those key words function as much as a filing system as the folder icons on the screen. In highly regulated organizations, metadata is added related to document control, quality control, or approvals. In organizations or departments where creative work is being done, an entire project area may be created with information areas that are neither truly data nor documents, but more similar to headlines. The members of the project team may agree to add indexing fields to documents in order to organize and find them more easily. Applications that permit these activities are often called "knowledge management" applications or components to document management and content management applications. These applications go beyond the simple assignment of metadata for routing and finding, to using not just those fields already assigned but also additional fields to permit innovation and increase an organization's ability to utilize the knowledge contained within its documents. As the reader can see, the fields associated with a record are directly related to the records series and the purpose to which the organization puts the records. It is just as possible to have too much metadata as it is too have too little. Too much metadata adds to "data smog" in the same way that too little metadata contributes to lost or poorly documented records.[36]

As noted above, electronic records can be a resource for the organization with the appropriate metadata, but this also requires the appropriate document management application. Document management applications that manage electronic records must have a repository. The repository must be able to contain and manage whatever type of object the organization requires. For example, some repositories are designed to handle only TIFF files. Some organizations, such as engineering and architecture firms, have extraordinarily complex objects that must be managed, and the repository must be able to handle those. The application must also be able to associate the object with the appropriate number of metadata fields. An organization that chooses to include author, title, date, subject, and a few key words will exhaust the number of available index fields of many of these software applications. The document management application must also have appropriate search capabilities. Most applications have simple Boolean search capabilities that permit a few relationships in a search. Search capabilities could also include truncation, "wildcard," and proximity searching. Another capability that some products have is auto-abstracting. While students of library science may scoff at this functionality, the auto-abstracting feature generally provides enough information for a business user to distinguish one record from another and to decide whether to open the document.

Irrespective of the metadata we have and the rigors of the search engine, people like the visual simplicity of file folders as an icon for organizing documents on our desktops.[37] This is certainly a carryover from the hard-copy environment. Folders are sets of logical relationships. Creating a filing system that makes sense to everyone who must encounter (and use) the records can be a challenge. However, conversations with numerous users of Microsoft Exchange, which permits a workgroup to set up folders, indicate that even agreed-upon folders can miss the mark. This happens most often when users attempt to establish what are called "subject matter" files. Filing systems for documents we work on during a business process, such as leases, policies, and tax papers, are typically much easier to create because these generally reflect the size of an organization and the way that it does business.

For example, a large law firm with many different practice areas would ordinarily segregate each client and the work done for each client, called a matter. In the hard-copy environment, the type of work being done might be reflected in the color of the jacket holding the folders and documents. The information is corralled by color to distinguish the type of work being done and by number to distinguish the client and matter. Inside those distinctions, the documents are divided by their function: client papers, court papers, appellate papers, instructions to jurors, correspondence with the client, research memoranda, internal communications, and so forth. A smaller firm performing one type of law for its clients would have no need to use colors for determining practice area, but instead might use colors to correspond to different functional types of documents, and use number to determine client and matter. These small differences make a world of difference in helping employees to find what they need and file what they have.

The classification that is used in the retention schedule is a very different type of organization of information. It is important to note that the master classification plan is not a file plan. A file plan is designed for the use of a specific work group or department to handle a single records series or a closely related set of records series within the business process and for a short time after the records series are no longer required for the principle business process, but for secondary or related business processes. Those secondary or related business processes are ordinarily not customer-driven, but are driven by various management reporting requirements. Where reference is motivated by the customer relationship, most often the reference activity will be because of an exception or an error.

A master classification plan (MCP), business classification scheme (BCS) is designed for the entire organization. Every employee from the CEO to the janitor must be able to use the MCP. The MCP must be created with utmost simplicity and care for the "mental models" of the employees within the enterprise. Those mental models reflect the functions found within the organization, not the departments, as departments are methods for organizing people, not information. After functions, the MCP must reflect business processes. Business processes are methods for organizing work; hence they are also methods for organizing information. Finally, within business processes records, series can be identified according to how they are created and used and according to their final disposition.

As shown in table 5.1, each level is named, its purpose within the classification, whether it is real or a concept, whether it names an action or an object, and any additional considerations.

One of the most important policies that the MCP establishes is a schedule for assigning responsibility for a records series. The work group that is assigned responsibility for a particular record is called the "office of record" for that record. The office of record may not have originated the records series, but it is the locus of control. For example, the ultimate source of an invoice issued from Accounts Receivable may be Sales. Sales, however, is never the office of record for invoices; Accounts Receivable is, because it performs different activities from those of Sales. Accounts Receivable receives and deposits funds, creates accounts receivable reports, and sends unpaid invoices out for collection. Sales may issue the invoice, but its role ends at that point in most organizations. There will be different offices of records for different record series.

An office of record is responsible for maintaining its designated records series within the organization, determining when a date set of the records series should be transferred to another storage medium or area, when a litigation or audit hold is required to halt disposition (including transferring sets to

Table 5.1.   The Master Classification Plan

Level	Description	Conceptual or Real	Action or Object	Additional Considerations
Function	Major activity within organization	Concept	Action	Must be clearly articulated and identified within organization as separate
Business Process	Name of method within company by which work gets done	Concept	Action	Must be identifiable to employee, not just executives
Records Series	Group of documents with similar creation, use, and same retention	Concept	Object	Security Privacy Retention Separate use
Document Types	Documents called out separately within records series for easy finding by workgroup	Real	Object	Defined by workgroup as important enough to call out separately

archives), and for approving final destruction. The office of record is also responsible for limiting access to its records series. Some access limitation is a matter of convenience. When an Accounts Payable specialist wants to see "invoices," the chances are quite slim that an Accounts Receivable invoice is intended. The Accounts Payable specialist is primarily interested in bills that need to be paid—i.e., invoices from the companies that are billing the organization. Limiting access this way is helpful to the Accounts Payable specialist because he does not need to plow through entire sets of documents that are of no value to him.

The office of record is also responsible for assigning access to its designated records series on the basis of privacy, security, and use. These access rights must be determined for categories of information, not for individual documents. Employees cannot be individually assigned responsibility for determining privacy, security, and use of individual documents the same way they cannot be assigned responsibility for destruction of individual documents. Each of these access assignments is established through policies created in association with the MCP, as enacted in the records retention and disposition schedule. Records series are the point of application for these policies, not individual documents. Note that the office of record of a particular record is not the "owner" of that record. While ownership may appear to be a convenient term for identifying the relationship between the business unit and a set of information, it implies the wrong relationship. The organization owns the information. People manage information. Assigning responsibility, not ownership, is a function of management.

USE AND DISSEMINATION

The next phase of the records life cycle, as listed in the description provided by the National Archives of Canada, is Use and Dissemination. Use and Dissemination is not truly a phase because records can be used and disseminated at any point from the beginning of their creation. When the format of a document is being decided upon, a draft is being circulated, or copies are made for an internal meeting, information is being used and disseminated. The idea that this is a phase comes from a peculiar and specious notion that some individual or group "declares a document a record," at which point the record is distributed—a notion that has been promulgated most recently by vendors of document management software products. By "declaring a record," document management vendors and archivists mean to change phases, a document's status, from the Creation to the "Use and Dissemination" phase. What they actually intend to describe is the point when the document leaves the hands of its creators and is then sent to its final destination.

In the previous discussion on the Creation phase, we saw the many ways in which a chunk of information can be used and disseminated before it is finalized. What we did not address there is one of the current greatest problems: copy control. As the author writes, the issue of copy control has reached crisis proportions. The primary culprit is email. When an employee sends an email, the chances of multiple copies of that email existing within seconds of sending are astronomical. No other type of information creation and transmission has this quality of spawning duplicates of itself automatically and uncontrollably.

Systems for creating and sending email create copies automatically. When an email is sent, most email applications create a copy in the sender's "sent" box. If the email is not responded to before either sender or recipient have the chance to delete all their copies, a back-up will probably be made. Even if one of the parties deletes all their copies, there is no guarantee that all copies have been deleted. The back-up is ordinarily not a copy in the sense that it can be easily identified and produced from the back-up medium; rather, it must be "restored." Irrespective, for the purposes of complying with a subpoena, the back-up is a copy.

Any search using a standard search engine will present results that include every one of these duplicates—that is, if the email application is formatted as Internet Mail Application Protocol (IMAP). IMAP is a protocol that places the email on a server where the employee will view it. Post Office Protocol (POP), which is used less and less now, is a protocol that places the email on the employee's desktop, laptop, handheld, or mobile phone. A search within a POP-formatted email application requires searching every single device. Lotus Notes email is a combination of both protocols, although it is more IMAP than POP. Emails are delivered to the device as POP, but a version stays on the server. When the device and server are "replicated," the two come back into alignment. This means that an employee's device may temporarily have a slightly different set of emails from that stored on the server, but this is only a temporary situation. Either IMAP or the Lotus Notes format are preferable to POP for management of emails because they create an authoritative centralized repository.

Unfortunately, unless employees are trained to aggressively manage their emails, any search on an IMAP or Lotus Notes email application (and now the Google Device for searching all drives), will produce a huge number of duplicates. Every one of those duplicates must be reviewed when a subpoena arrives. The burden on an organization under such circumstances can be, and for some organizations already has been, disastrous for productivity. Efforts such as "The Sedona Principles," authored by a group of legal professionals and technology experts who want to affect positively the problem of electronic document production,[38] are attempts to reduce the destructive power of electronic document production. Those principles are not law, nor are they yet widely accepted judicial practice.

Because a solution to this problem requires a great deal of records management expertise and technology knowledge as well as knowledge of the current capabilities of document management and records management software products, and an organization with the ability to create and enforce policies and procedures as well as a training program, the chances of implementing a successful email management program are quite slender. The reader can also see that the problem does not begin the instant the employee hits the "send" button "declaring the email a record" and disseminating the record for use. The problem exists in every phase of the life cycle, from creation of an information management program to creation, organization, storage, and destruction.

MAINTENANCE, PROTECTION, AND PRESERVATION

This phase is often referred to as "storage," "semiactive," or "inactive" in other versions of the life cycle. Maintaining, protecting, and preserving do not comprise a phase in the same way that use and dissemination do not make up a phase. Every phase requires maintaining, protecting, and preserving. Every phase of the records life cycle also requires storage. In any phase, a record may be more or less active. For example, when a record is being created, it may sit idle or even be off-loaded to a different medium. A record may even reverse course from having been inactive for years to becoming very active—as is the case when litigation resurrects information from its slumber. The essential point of maintenance, protection, and preservation is that the choice of format, medium, and storage environment is crucial to ensuring that a life cycle can happen at all. Those choices, however, are a matter of risk management.

Any chunk of information enters an organization or is created in an organization via a format and a medium. The format is the system by which the information is kept ready for viewing. It may be directly readable by the human eye, it may require assistance from magnifying lenses, or it may require translation by computer software and hardware. Ink or other methods for making marks on paper is a format. Etching a metal plate is a format. The human eye can read the zeroes and ones of the digital format when it is printed on a computer screen or paper. Those zeroes and ones can be translated by a human, but only through great effort. Hardware and software are required to translate one format—zeroes and ones—into the words, sounds, pictures, lines, colors, and so forth, of which a human can make sense. In the case of digital formats, we keep them ready as zeroes and ones so that we can manipulate them into a human eye-readable format—when that is our purpose.

A storage medium is the physical layer on which information is laid down, such as paper, the computer screen, or a magnetic tape. Paper is storage, just as is micrographics. The computer screen is storage, albeit a temporary and easily manipulable one. A hard drive is storage; the cache and buffers of a computer are also storage devices. The storage medium itself requires maintenance, protection, and preservation so that the information on it may be maintained, protected, and preserved. Depending upon the medium, translation devices may be required to translate information quickly from one format to another for easy readability. Any storage medium requires "maintenance, protection, and preservation" to make information last from the instant of creation or receipt. Consider, for example, the facsimile (fax) machines of the mid- to late 1980s. Many of these fax machines required the use of a coated paper called thermal paper. The problem with this paper was that it faded, irrespective of how carefully it was handled—sometimes within hours. Many organizations learned this by finding their key documents faded within a day following their receipt. The solution that many organizations devised was to copy the fax immediately and use the copy as the original, disposing of the thermographic copy.

One medium that we do not save is voice mail; indeed, many organizations have had to implement aggressive destruction campaigns. When voice mail systems were implemented, storage of the voice mail files was expensive. Voice mails themselves are quite large in comparison to other types of files. Even when storage costs declined in recent years, storage of voice mails was still prohibitive because of the size of the files. By the time the cost of storage came down, most organizations had trained their employees to manage their voice mails by deleting them as well as having automatic deletion programs, typically after thirty days.

Just as voice mail storage began to be affordable, another medium and format came along: email, which, as we have seen, then assumed many of the functions of the phone and voice mail. We now tend to use email for non-immediate communication (although some use it for immediate communication, apparently with the mistaken notion that everyone is sitting in front of an always-on email account). As noted above, email is not easy to delete, nor is it easy to organize, making it an extremely poor method of storage. Applications exist that can manage email by organizing and applying appropriate storage methods, but successful implementation of those applications requires both records management expertise and technology expertise. Most organizations still believe or would prefer to believe that technology is the only component of the solution.

Other media, such as optical disks and magnetic tape, are used by many organizations to store and retrieve information. These media do not have the longevity of micrographics, but when well maintained, they usually serve the purposes of the organization. The key is maintenance, because even microfilm, when not well maintained, has poor longevity.

Paper presents particular maintenance issues—issues with which the library and archival communities are quite familiar. The longevity of paper is dependent upon the composition of the paper itself and the composition of the ink, as well as how the paper is handled. Many books from the nineteenth century are literally crumbing to dust because the paper used has a high acid content. The library and archival community are justified in their concerns about longevity because they are concerned about preserving documents for hundreds, even thousands of years. Records managers do not have the luxury of such worries, because the vast majority of documents that we manage are kept for a total of six years or less. We have our own horror stories about not being able to maintain information for this brief period of time, but our task is much less onerous than that of our colleagues.

What is the longevity of any medium? That is determined by the quality of the underlying medium, the care with which the medium was imprinted, and the care with which the medium is maintained. The question of media longevity arises when the imprinted information must last longer than prudent maintenance methods can maintain any medium. When nineteenth-century books were beginning to crumble to dust, some repositories decided to sacrifice the current books by copying them. The books were torn apart and the pages copied on a copier machine. When magnetic tapes show signs of beginning to wear, the contents are copied to another tape.

In each case of transference from one medium to another, many questions arise. A copied book is not the same book. The medium of paper has been preserved, but the document only represents the original; it is not an original. The new tape to which information is transferred may be a different format. However, where book copying produces a copy that can easily be assessed for readability and completeness, tape copying does not unless the actual tape is thoroughly tested for completeness and readability. This is the major difference between eye-readable media and media requiring intermediate technology: we can easily check the first, but not the second.

Archivists are understandably concerned with what they call "recordkeeping" because the records with which they deal typically have retentions of forever. Within an organization, retention will be only as long as program requirements—for example, life of organization, life of asset, thirty years. Very few items have retention of life of organization; these include articles of incorporation, by-laws, and minute books. In contrast, government entities have records with a much longer retention. Government records, such as the U.S. Constitution, require more than prudent maintenance; they require active methods of conservation. Business records rarely require more than simple conservation, generally no more than refreshing the information by copying it to another medium (migration) or reformatting it to a more currently readable form (conversion).

We accept that hard-copy documents are subject to wear and tear, that they must be carefully handled and preserved. We show no patience, however, for electronic records. The results of our impatience are pronouncements of "functional requirements" or of "recordkeeping systems"[39] that are meant to help us manage all electronic records for all time. Records managers do not have the same requirements for records longevity. In addition, such requirements demonstrate none of the exquisite detail and attention we have traditionally paid to hard-copy documents.

This is in part because archivists usually get records only after they are useless for the organization. One of the earlier works of archival practice, Muller,

Feith, and Fruin's *Manual for the Arrangement and Description of Archives*, was first published in Dutch in 1898 and served as the basis for Jenkinson's and Schellenberg's tomes—the classics in Great Britain and the U.S. In a revealing footnote, Muller et al. discuss that sets of documents are living organisms: "At least an organism which has lived, for the archivist generally receives the archival collection into his custody when it is dead, or at any rate only the parts of it which must be considered as closed."[40] In striking contrast to this view are the comments of Patrick Cadell, former Keeper of the Records of Scotland: "The archivist's principal concern is with the future rather than with the past. This point always comes as a surprise to the creator of archives. Yet while archives illuminate the past, and explain the present, the whole purpose of keeping them is to guide the future. This is true whether we are talking about the archives which we all hold for our own needs, or about the archives of the corner shop, local government, or the nation itself. For example, it is a matter of no historical interest to know exactly when we took out an insurance policy on our house; what is important is to have the document that allows us to assert our right to payment when in the future some disaster occurs. Likewise the nation needs to be reminded of its duties, needs to be able to assert its rights, and perhaps most important of all, needs to have the means of examining past decisions so as to avoid mistakes already committed, or working again through problems which have already been disposed of."[41] Cadell holds that historical research is ancillary to the purposes of archives. He believes that the real purpose of an archive is to serve the organization itself. The instances of which he speaks are national archives that have served the administrations to which they are attached. Among the topics he discusses is the new purpose of archives, to serve the citizens through public records acts.

The result of this situation is that archivists have had to find out how organizations work and to learn about the remainder of the life cycle—specifically, those phases that lie outside the maintenance, protection, and preservation phase. The results have not been entirely encouraging.[42] A document is authoritative because of the business processes and information management applied to it. If those have not been carefully managed, no recordkeeping system ever imagined could make a document authoritative. (Remember also from Chapter 4 that business documents are authoritative if someone within the organization who has care of the documents says so.) An authoritative document is an end result of a business process and information management, not a characteristic that can be attached or created like metadata. Authoritative records are not on the radar screen of companies unless government regulations, litigation, or a specific business deal require it, as recent experience with the Sarbanes-Oxley Act has demonstrated.

Archivists do have cause for complaint. For more than 40 years, archivists have been receiving dysfunctional sets of information in electronic form from government agencies. The most infamous were the emails from the Reagan and Bush administration concerning the Iran/Contra affair.[43] Those emails were just that—the text of the emails, lacking thorough lists of recipients and attachments because the email system simply did not maintain this information. As noted above, these problems are not unique to emails. One of the methods proposed by the archival world for managing the archivists' predicament is the Records Continuum.[44] This reflects a viewpoint that the archivists receive records when the records are dead and that what archivists often receive is not well organized. The management of records must account for every aspect of those records from a spatial as well as a temporal dimension. The life cycle addresses primarily the temporal existence of a record, from conception to ashes. Properly understood, it does not address every phenomenon occurring to records. As noted above, maintenance, protection, and preservation do not constitute a phase but occur at every phase.

The other life cycle phases discussed within this chapter generally fall into the rubric of active, semiactive, and inactive. If one were to criticize the life cycle using this rubric, one would have a great deal to criticize, as proponents of the Records Continuum do.[45] Active, semiactive, and inactive represent not management concepts, just observations. However, this rubric is an excellent foil for discussion of storage.[46] It is an excellent foil because it does not ascribe different levels of value to each of the three phases. The major problem with the Records Continuum is that it does not address business processes. It addresses the context of the program of records management, but does not take on business processes.

Organizations have demonstrated their lack of interest in storage problems, as witnessed by high-profile court cases such as Arthur Andersen and its destruction of quantities of records related to the potential SEC investigation of Enron. The major problem storage creates for properly managing the life cycle is that the method of storage required to maintain and preserve information is not necessarily the best method of storage for retrieving information. Some compromise must be struck. That compromise may be staged electronic storage from on-line hard drives, then to on-line RAID or spinning write-once, read-many (WORM) media, then to near-line tape or optical disk, and finally storing tape and optical disk off-line. A related technology is hierarchical storage management (HSM) that measures activity on sectors of hard drives and then moves the inactive sectors to optical disk. Options could include migration from one medium to another, conversion from one format to another, or both. Migration is essentially the same document in the same format in a different place—for example, a Microsoft Word document on a disk drive as opposed to on an optical disk. Conversion is a change in format, not necessarily in a different place—for example, changing a document format from PDF to TIFF on the same disk drive.

Both migration and conversion present risks. The primary risk is loss of information in the form of lost documents or lost metadata. A secondary risk is loss of the ability to use an index for finding a document, primarily because it has been moved and the index pointers cannot follow it. A tertiary risk is loss of metadata because the new medium or format cannot maintain the metadata fields, a risk which was the concern when the Archivist of the United States passed a regulation saying that printing emails was acceptable. The argument by the opposition was that valuable information was being lost because the header was lost, as was the ability to search the contents.[47] This Archivists regulation still stands because it is not unreasonable. We do not have the same information for hard-copy correspondence; why should we maintain it for email, "just because we can?"

No storage medium is ideal. Knowing that there are trade-offs, any organization must assess its own risk in determining what medium to use at what point in the life cycle, as well as whether and when to migrate or convert information and how to store the resultant media.

RETIREMENT

The records life cycle model of the National Archives of Canada does not call for a Retirement phase, yet I would argue that it is deserving of designation as a distinct phase because it is the point in the life cycle at which the greatest damage tends to be done to records, particularly to their organization. Damage is done primarily to context, but also to unity of the individual record. Retirement is the migration of records from one, higher-priced location where they are not being used very much, to another, lower-priced location where they are either not being called up for use at all or not called up very often. Moving records is at minimum a migration, and at maximum it is both a migration and a conversion. Records may be converted to a TIFF or PDF image for long-term electronic storage. Retirement is also the partial severing of records—whether paper or electronic—from their office context. By taking files out of drawers or off of servers, part of their context is being removed. The following are some examples of how that context is not preserved.

A look through nearly any organization's list of records in box storage will bring up boxes labeled with titles such as "John's desk" or "Lucy files." Sometimes the organization knows what these titles mean, but more often than not, John and the people who put the records in the boxes are no longer working for the company. Most often the case is that John left, someone cleared out his desk, put everything in boxes, and sent the boxes to storage. When a particularly onerous discovery subpoena involving John's workgroup arrives, the boxes must be inventoried.

Another problem is whether the records in storage, either hard copy or electronic, are actually complete. Many tech-savvy employees boast that they keep "everything" in electronic form. Unfortunately for their colleagues working on the same project, those electronic records are likely to be in the tech-savvy employee's personal work folders. The not-so-tech-savvy colleagues print their documents and send them to "the file." Another, over-worked employee, however tech-savvy, files the printed documents, all five copies of the identical document, in "the file." Under these circumstances, there is no way to know whether "the file" is complete or whether it is filled with multiple copies of only a few documents.

Yet another common problem is when different records series are placed in the same box, tape, or optical disk for storage. Records series are defined by a number of different elements, but one of the elements is how long the records are to be kept in storage. When some documents in the container can be destroyed after three years and others can be destroyed after seven years, the documents with the lesser retention have a negative value. Their value is negative because they are taking up rental space and, should there be a subpoena regarding these records, they will have to be recalled, indexed for litigation, photocopied, and presented to opposing counsel—at the very minimum.

Archivists commonly complain of not getting appropriate contextual metadata—a problem that occurs most often during the Retirement phase, for all of the above reasons. The problem appears worse with electronic records because the records are wrenched from the software, hardware, and the people required to read the records. The situation is comparable not only to taking away an employee's reading glasses, but taking away her knowledge of a foreign language. Even if we can see the records, we may not be able to make anything out of them because we cannot read the "language" in which they are written, just as we cannot read the Mohenjo-Daro script or Cretan Linear B. Calling hardware, software, and knowledge of the particular computer language involved "metadata" is a stretch, but once we have defined "metadata" as the tools we need to make sense of a document, we have no way of shutting off the flow of context. This problem gets worse with migration and conversion of records during the natural course of preservation.

Any one of the above problems can be alleviated with appropriate policies, procedures, and technology management. Unfortunately, these policies and procedures tend to arise within organizations only after an organization suffers a spectacular disaster. Indeed, records management consultants and companies that peddle "records management" software products report that organizations and governmental entities that show interest in such services and products are generally those that have experienced some type of adverse situation regarding their records, as such, one could say that records management is a religion that is adopted by only the prodigal son.

DISPOSITION

Disposition is a phase of every records series. The term "disposition" stems from the concept of a record's existence vis-à-vis the organization, not from the concept of "disposal," as in "to throw away." The phase is strictly related to the organization's needs with regard to the continued existence of information. Information that is of no value to an organization is destroyed. The key component of disposition is making a determination of the value the information is to the organization.

Information may be valuable because it is a patent for a new drug that will cure a disease or alleviate the symptoms of a disease that is widespread. Information may be valuable only because it must sit on a shelf for a certain number of years because of a regulatory agency's requirements. Information may be reused and reworked on a regular basis within an organization because it addresses current needs. New information may lead to a new corporate strategy or abandonment of an old one. A piece of information may, in and of itself, have no value, but when placed within a context may lead to a great discovery or to prevention of a disaster.

Information may also have a negative value. Information that existed before it is convenient may be damning. Examples of this type of information include company memoranda demonstrating knowledge that the product the company grows, mines, manufactures, or sells—such as asbestos or tobacco—is harmful to humans.[48] A set of information may develop a negative value by being implicated in potential—not actual—litigation, such as the emails concerning Enron that were destroyed in 2000 by Arthur Andersen's Houston office. Bill Gates's email, in which he stated that Microsoft's competition must be crushed by any means, was produced and made public during Microsoft's antitrust trial, is another example of information that develops a negative value.

Records can also have no value. Consider the example of a large bank that was growing by merger and had amassed more than a million boxes in storage. Of those million-plus boxes, the content of 100,000 boxes was unknown.

In 1995, The bank asked for advice from a records management consultant, who gave three options. The first two options were very expensive: the bank could immediately inventory the boxes, or the bank could wait for litigation and inventory the boxes as part of the discovery process. The third option was less expensive. As the bank had no knowledge of what was in the boxes, it was as if the boxes had never existed. Because of the way the banking industry functions, it is highly unlikely that the boxes held any information of value; hence the bank could destroy the boxes without inventorying the contents. The bank chose this third option—to destroy the boxes without inventorying the contents (much to the chagrin of the commercial box storage company it used). This option may no longer appear attractive, because opposing counsel could argue that the bank did not make sufficient effort to maintain and inventory the materials in the boxes. The choice, however, is a measure of risk management. The costs of storing and inventorying 100,000 boxes may considerably exceed the cost of settlement and fines.

Records management is ordinarily associated with the negative value of records. Organizations lay off records management employees during recessions, except when high-profile cases and regulations bring it to the attention of upper-level executives. Recent examples include the Sarbanes-Oxley Act of 2000, which was motivated in part by the previously cited destruction of email by Arthur Andersen and the production of Bill Gates's email during the Microsoft antitrust case. Records managers are called in to make order out of the chaos created by a complete lack of a records management system or by a company's failure to enforce the systems it has in place.

As we saw in chapter 1, the two Hoover Commission reports recommended developing a records management program when the volume of records becomes too great to manage.[49] This is a good example of records with no value getting in the way of access to records that still have value, either positive or negative. Recently, this issue has also been one of the reasons that organizations have brought in records managers: email systems are full of irrelevant emails. One of the symptoms is that searches for relevant emails bring up lists of so many irrelevant emails that too much time is spent sifting for what is of value.

To repeat, information can have a positive value, a negative value, or no value. Information that is not organized has a negative value or no value depending upon context. If the bank with a million boxes mentioned above had received a subpoena while pondering what to do with the 100,000 boxes with unknown content, the boxes would immediately have received a negative value because the contents may have had to be inventoried. The appearance of destroying so many boxes with a document discovery order in hand could be extremely damaging.

When records have value outside of a clearly defined institution, such as a company or a government agency, the records are in many instances sent to an archive. Records may have no value for a company, but they do have a social or cultural value. Histories of business and management work with company archives. Alfred D. Chandler could not have written his great history of recordkeeping practices, *The Visible Hand*, had private industry not maintained records that were of no business value to the organization.[50] Companies do not keep records past their usefulness to the organization for many different reasons, among them a lack of understanding of the goodwill created, a desire to keep potentially unsavory information out of the public view, or a lack of interest in social and cultural issues. Many companies are made aware of the potential historical value of their records only when a records retention schedule is created or revised by a records manager. To include in the retention schedule notations that documentation is historical, create procedures for handling those records, and then create an archive for such historically valuable documentation are typically not very expensive activities, and organizations should be encouraged to consider taking such steps.

Government institutions are also a mixed lot with respect to archives. Having possession of records has been a source of power since the idea of records was created. Historically, government institutions have not necessarily been associated with the keeping of records, however. Religious institutions such as temples and then monasteries were frequent loci for records. Until the Reformation, reading was not required even for worship, so having a record was of little value. Indeed, the idea of a public records act is very recent. The Archdiocese of New Orleans, for example, holds many public records created before Louisiana became a state. Those records include marriage licenses and birth certificates. The archivist for the Archdiocese must go to court on a regular basis because the parish and the state keep trying to obtain the records held by the Church. Then consider that Gwinnett County in Georgia threw away its historical records in the early 1960s. The local private historical society was able to retrieve most of those records by rifling through the dumpster. For historical information about property titles, births, and deaths before the 1970s, a citizen in Gwinnett County goes to the private historical society to retrieve the information. These examples show opposite attitudes by governmental institutions concerning the value of historical records.

What makes a record historical? When a citizen researches a family tree, the purposes may include desire for personal knowledge, proof of inheritance, and demonstration of lineage for receipt of a scholarship or service. In other words, the records are not solely of cultural value. The records have different values for citizens depending upon the context. What the records have in common for the citizens is that they may not be accessed for generations, but when access is desired, the records have a very high value. Unlike the records of private organizations, dormancy of public records is neither an indication of value nor of life cycle stage. Whereas organizational records that are accessed less frequently than once per month are candidates for storage and are considered "inactive" by some life cycles, access of less than once per century is not considered inactive for public records.

Government institutions have the same relationship to records as private organizations. Consider minute books, which contain decisions and reasons for decisions for an organization. A private organization is required to maintain its minute books for the life of the entity. Government institutions typically last longer than private organizations. Unlike private organizations that are merged into other organizations and lose their identity entirely, government institutions do not lose their identity, even when they disappear. When West and East Germany merged, for example, the records of numerous past governments were revived to resolve the conflicts created by the political partition of the country after World War II. What this tells us is that the records do not represent the government so much as they represent people. As long as people require records to settle disputes, the records have value. Correlating this to the life cycle, the active phase of government records lasts until the people decide they have no value. The piles of rock Abraham built are records of the extent of his "property," and the Israelis and Palestinians are today disputing those boundaries.

Records in companies, on the other hand, represent the company and the owners or shareholders. What differentiates government records from organizational records is that the stakeholders have two sets of values for records: as records performing an act and records memorializing an act. Each record does both. Government as an administrative entity—whether the agency, bureau, office, legislature, or court—has an administrative use for the records. That administrative use is similar to a private organization in that the records are being used both to perform line-of-business work and to manage the department. Line-of-business records perform an act and memorialize an act or assist in either of these activities. Records of the management of the department record how well citizens' money is used. The citizenry of the land associated with the government have two uses for the records: as a record of how well the department was managed and as a collective memory of acts in the past that affect the present. The first use measures how well the citizens' money is used. Records such as deeds or birth certificates or drainage board meetings and zoning ordinances affect an indefinite future, so the citizenry have a stake in the records as memory.

Government management records do not lose their value in the same way that any organization's administrative records lose value: once an organization has been audited or an employee has left and regulations complied with, the records have no value. In contrast, government records that memorialize what the department does never cease to have a value, either to the government entity or to citizens. Those government records are a collective memory, similar to the minutes of boards of directors that memorialize the actions taken by the governing council of an organization. These minutes constitute the collective memory of an organization and are kept for the life of the organization. The organization, where government is concerned, is not the governmental department, but the citizenry of a geographical area. When the citizenry ends, so does the value of the records to the citizenry.

The value that scholars place upon government records as well as on the records of other organizations is capricious. What is fashionable to study and whether the scholar has funding to study records will determine what records are studied. For example, as I write, there is little funding to study records management within business. Making an argument that records should be kept because they may be of value to scholars is an argument to be made to a benefactor, not to a corporation or a government entity. A corporation or a citizenry may decide that such a purpose is appropriate, but it is an ancillary and subsidiary purpose for those records.

The real problem with disposition is not keeping the records, but ordering them for retrieval—as discussed above—and destroying them. Seamus Ross of the University of Glasgow described in a conference talk[51] how he was asked by NASA to work on recovering information from the tapes in the Challenger disaster. The tapes had been at the bottom of the ocean for six months before they were recovered and, of course, had been through a fiery explosion. Ross was able to recover 90 percent of the information from those tapes. At the end of a lecture on data persistence, an audience member asked Ross how to destroy information. He responded that it must be crushed and burned. Many corporations report adverse experiences with the law of salvage. It is illegal for an individual to go on corporate property and sort through papers, computer disks, and tapes found in the trash on the property. That information having been recovered, however, it now belongs to the scavenger. Records can be recovered in less obtrusive ways. Detective agencies report recovering valuable corporate information from trash bags left on the street for pick-up by the rubbish company. The sidewalk is public property. Anyone may pick up trash from public property. Entire books are written on computer espionage.[52]

Disposition as a phase of the life cycle presents particular challenges because it branches in two different directions: archiving for continued corporate or government purposes or destruction. Providing that activities of all previous phases of the life cycle have been performed properly, an organization should not find archiving to be a challenge. Destruction, however, requires an evaluation of the records from the perspective of competitive intelligence—business intelligence as well as from the perspective of intellectual property. Companies rarely examine the social, cultural, or historical value.

The focus of management of the life cycle of information is in improving productivity.[53] Because the information life cycle does not coincide exactly with any business process, yet is a key factor in every business process, it is a requirement for meeting productivity objectives. As a metalevel management practice, it is more difficult to explain because it requires a bird's-eye view of the organization.

Records managers are not concerned with issues of authenticity, reliability, and trustworthiness—nor should they be. Those are outcomes of properly managing records life cycles in relation to business processes. Once a record lands in off-site storage or the archives, it cannot be made to be authentic, reliable, or trustworthy. Application of fundamental records management principles, a sound understanding of the technology involved in managing records in different formats, and the cooperation and support of the organization are required to create the outcome authentic, reliable, and trustworthy.

As we saw in chapter 4, these are also issues of risk management. If an organization, whether government or privately held, chooses as part of its risk management strategy not to manage some aspect of the record life cycle, no amount of haranguing by low-level administrators called records managers or archivists will be able to change that strategy.

ARCHIVING

Archiving is the activity performed to preserve and present information for purposes outside the organization that are social, cultural, historical, or even governmental. Records managers rarely participate in these activities because the vast majority of organizations we are involved in have little interest in this. However, I know of no records manager, myself included, that does not urge their organizations or the ones for which they consult to either maintain or do effort by business historians to sensitize us to what may be of interest.

NOTES

1. Thomas H. Davenport and James E. Short, "The New Industrial Engineering: Information Technology and Business Process Redesign," *Sloan Management Review* 31, no. 4

(Summer 1990): 11–27; and Michael Hammer, "Reengineering Work: Don't Automate, Obliterate," *Harvard Business Review* 68, no. 4 (July–August 1990): 104–112. David A. Garvin, "The Processes of Organization and Management," *Sloan Management Review* 39, no. 4 (Summer 1998): 33–50.

2. Helen L. Chatfield, "The Problem of Records from the Standpoint of Management," *American Archivist* 3, no. 2 (1940): 93–101, 100.

3. Mark Langemo, *Winning Strategies for Successful Records Management Programs: Proven Strategies for Developing New Programs and Improving Existing Ones!* (Denver: Information Requirements Clearinghouse, 2002).

4. Mary F. Robek, Gerald F. Brown, and Wilmer O. Maedke, *Information and Records Management,* 3rd ed. (Mission Hills, CA: Glencoe, 1987); David O. Stephens and Roderick C. Wallace, *Electronic Records Retention: New Strategies for Data Life Cycle Management* (Lenexa, KS: ARMA, International, 2003). The latter book has the term in the title, yet, curiously, it plays no role in the text.

5. William Saffady, *Records and Information Management: Fundamentals of Professional Practice* (Lenexa, KS: ARMA, International, 2004), 5.

6. Judith Read-Smith, Mary Lea Ginn, and Norman F. Kallaus, *Records Management,* 7th ed. (Cincinnati: South-Western, 2002), 14–15. Ira A. Penn, Gail B. Pennix, and Jim Coulson, *Records Management Handbook,* 2nd ed. (Aldershot, Hampshire, UK: Gower Publishing, 1994), 12–18.

7. Elizabeth Shepherd and Geoffrey Yeo, *Managing Records: A Handbook of Principles and Practice* (London: Facet Publishing, 2003), 5–10.

8. Peter F. Drucker, *Management: Tasks, Responsibilities, Practices* (New York: HarperCollins Publishers, 1974), 403–418.

9. Evidenced by the lack of articles on databases and reports management in the industry journal, *Information Management Journal,* formerly called the *Records Management Quarterly.*

10. Robek, Brown, and Maedke, 1987, 494–511.

11. Penn, Pennix, and Coulson, 1994, vi, 187–207.

12. Personal experience, in consulting engagements with public and private organizations.

13. Robek, Brown, and Maedke, iii–iv.

14. Penn, Pennix, and Coulson, 13.

15. U.S. National Archives and Records Administration, "About Records Management, The Life Cycle of Records," http://www.archives.gov/midatlantic/fed_agency_services/records_management/about_records_management.html (31 December 2003).

16. National Archives of Canada, "Records and Information Life Cycle Management," http://www.archives.ca/06/0625_e.html (31 December 2003).

17. United Kingdom Parliamentary Archives, "Records Management Policy Guidelines May 2000," http://www.parliament.uk/archives/policy/policy1.htm (31 December 2003).

18. International Council of Archives, "Guide for Managing Electronic Records from an Archival Perspective," http://www.ica.org/biblio/guide_2b1.html (31 December 2003).

19. William Saffady, "The Document Life Cycle: A White Paper," and "Film-based Imaging in the Document Life Cycle: FAQs for Best Practice," both published by AIIM International (Silver Spring, MD: AIIM, 1997).

20. Stephens and Wallace, 25.

21. Shepherd and Yeo, 5–7.

22. Catherine Hare and Julie McLeod, *Guide pratique: Mettre en place le records management dans son organisation* (Paris: Archimag, 2003).

23. Shepherd and Yeo, 8.

24. See the CMPros listserv, who are blissfully unaware that they perform records management; also, personal conversations with consultants and analysts in this field.

25. Personal conversation with ARMA board members. To quote one, "We've been trying to catch that train for twenty-five years. Now that we've caught it, we have so much work, we don't know what to do!"

26. In many consulting interviews within various types of organizations, I have noted a lack of desire on anyone's part to be responsible for information in electronic form. In many instances, the staff of the IT department would say that as they are not responsible for the content, they cannot be responsible for the life cycle management of the files or databases. The departmental employees would retort that they cannot be responsible for the files or databases because these files and databases are on the computer, and the IT department is responsible for the maintenance of the computer.

27. For example, Six Sigma is not just about the diagnosing of problems using methods and statistics from the social sciences; it is also about innovation and continuous improvement.

28. Capabilities Maturity Model, created by Carnegie Mellon, Software Engineering Institute, http://www.sei.cmu/cmm/cmms/cmms.html (11 April 2005).

29. Personal conversations. As with all failures, the companies experiencing the software failure and the companies that developed the applications do not like to appear in public.

30. James K. Watson, Jr. and Carol E. B. Choksy, "Digital Signatures Seal Web Deals," *Information Week* 804 (September 18, 2000), RB26–RB28.

31. Even when there are consequences to not performing those activities, some employees either do not perform them or find ways around them. The metadata utopia of library and information science is impossible in the world of documents (and organizations).

32. David Bearman, "The Implications of Armstrong v. the Executive Office of the President for the Archival Management of Electronic Records," *American Archivist* 56, (Fall 1993): 674–689.

33. Marcia Stepanek, "From Digits to Dust," *Business Week* 3574 (20 April 1998): 128–130.

34. David Shenk, *Data Smog: Surviving the Information Glut* (San Francisco: HarperEdge, 1997).

35. For an excellent book on how to work indexing into business processes, see Susan L. Cisco and Tom Dale, *Indexing Business Records: The Value Proposition* (Silver Spring, MD: AIIM, 1998). Library and Information Science use the term "metadata" rather than index. Business uses the term "index."

36. Kristan J. Wheaton, *The Warning Solution: Intelligent Analysis in the Age of Information Overload* (Fairfax, VA: AFCEA International Press, 2001).

37. Discussion with managers at Ricoh during review of their eCabinet document management product, July 2001, at Ricoh Silicon Valley. They had not originally intended to create an interface with folders, but decided to do so as a result of consumer requests.

38. *The Sedona Principles: Best Practices Recommendations & Principles for Addressing Electronic Document Production,* 2004, was created by the Sedona Conference, a group of attorneys, judges, professors, and technology experts, http://www.thesedonaconference.org (29 March 2004).

39. See the Pittsburgh Project, http://web.archive.org/web/20000818163633/ www.sis.pitt.edu/~nhprc/ (13 April 2005); University of Indiana projects, http:// www.indiana.edu/~libarch/ER/ (13 April 2005); InterPARES project, http://www .interpares.org/ (13 April 2005), all of which demonstrate a lack of understanding of the records life cycle, of business and technology requirements, and of the reality of managing records within the organization.

40. S. Muller Fz., J. A. Feith, and R. Fruin Th.Az., *Manual for the Arrangement and Description of Archives* (New York: H. W. Wilson, 1968), 19f. This work was "drawn up by direction of the Netherlands Association of Archivists."

41. Patrick Cadell, "Access and Information: European Attitudes and Anxieties," *Archives: Journal of the British Records Association* 28, no. 108 (April 2003): 3–13, 7.

42. The various studies on the subject, such as the Pittsburgh Project, the Indiana University Project, and the InterPARES Project, have emphasized authoritative recordkeeping.

43. See *Armstrong v. Bush,* 721 F. Supp. 343, 345 n.1 (D.D.C. 1989); *Armstrong v. Bush,* 139 F.R.D. 547, 553 (D.D.C. 1991); *Armstrong v. Executive Office of the President,* 807 F. Supp. 816 (D.D.C. 1992); *Armstrong v. Executive Office of the President,* 810 F. Supp. 335 (D.D.C. 1993); *Armstrong v. Executive Office of the President,* 1 F.3d 1274 (D.C. Cir. 1993); *Armstrong v. Executive Office of the President,* 877 F2d 690, 715 (D.D.C. 1995); *Armstrong v. Executive Office of the President,* 810 F. Supp. 335 (D.D.C. 1993) at 341.

44. See the Records Continuum Research Group at Monash University's website at http://www.sims.monash.edu.au/research/rcrg/publications/index.html (1 April 2004) for a large collection of articles on the Records Continuum, including Frank Upward's "Structuring the Records Continuum, Part Two: Structuration Theory and Recordkeeping," *Archives and Manuscripts* 25, no. 1 (May 1997): 10–33; "Structuring the Records Continuum, Part One: Postcustodial Principles and Properties," *Archives and Manuscripts* 24, no. 2 (November 1996): 268–285; "In Search of the Continuum: Ian Maclean's 'Australian Experience' Essays on Recordkeeping," 110–130, *The Records Continuum: Ian Maclean and Australian Archives First Fifty Years* edited by Sue McKemmish and Michael Piggott (Clayton, Australia: Ancora Press, 1994). Upward's now famous rendering of the Records Continuum is in "Structuring the Records Continuum, Part One."

45. See, for example, The State Records New South Wales, "The Records Continuum," *For the Record* 12, (November 1996). http://www.records.nsw.gov.au/publications/ fortherecord/ftr12/ftr12.htm (31 March 2004).

46. See, for example, William Saffady, "The Document Life Cycle: A White Paper," (Silver Spring, MD: AIIM, 2003), http://www.documentconversion.com/news2.htm (31 March 2004).

47. *General Records Schedule 20; Disposition of Electronic Records*, 60 Fed. Reg. 44,643 (1995); *Public Citizen v. Carlin,* 2 F. Supp. 2d 1 (D.D.C. 1997); *Public Citizen v. Carlin,* 2 F. Supp. 2d 18, 20 (D.D.C. 1998); for the final 1999 D.C. Circuit Court of Appeals decision ruling in Carlin's favor see http://caselaw.lp.findlaw.com/scripts/getcase .pl?court=dc&navby=case&no=975356A (1 April 2004).

48. A good source for understanding the essential case law on this is Donald S. Skupsky and John C. Montaña, *Law, Records and Information Management: The Court Cases* (Denver: Information Requirements Clearinghouse, 1994). See also the Sedona Conference, http://www.thesedonaconference.org (19 April 2004), as well as Randolph A. Kahn and Barclay T. Blair, *Information Nation: Seven Keys to Information Management Compliance* (Silver Spring, MD: AIIM, 2004), for court cases regarding records found in an electronic environment.

49. Emmett J. Leahy, "Paperwork Management: Part I, In the U.S. Government," *Commission on the Organization of the Executive Branch of Government* (Washington, D.C.: U.S. Government Printing Office, 1947); and "Paperwork Management: Part II, The Nation's Paperwork for the Government, an Experiment," *Commission on the Organization of the Executive Branch of Government* (Washington, D.C.: U.S. Government Printing Office), 1955.

50. Alfred D. Chandler, *The Visible Hand: The Managerial Revolution in American Business* (Cambridge, MA: Harvard University Press, 1977). Alfred Chandler could have performed none of his research without the organization and preservation of records within the great companies he studied.

51. Seamus Ross, "Acting to Avoid Loss, But When Disaster Strikes Relying on Digital Archaeology," presented at the Managing Electronic Records Conference, Chicago, IL, November, 1998.

52. See, for example, Joel McNamara, *Secrets of Computer Espionage: Tactics and Countermeasures* (Indianapolis: Wiley Publishing, 2003).

53. Nathaniel Bulkley and Marshall Van Alstyne *Why Information Should Influence Productivity.* (Cambridge, MA: Center for eBusiness@MIT, 2004). http://ebusiness.Mit.edu/research/papers/202_vanAlstyne_Productivity.pdf (6 May 2004).

Chapter Six

Creating Value: Organizing Records

By defining information as something that will change us, we might assume that information has an inherent value. A single datum has no value in and of itself. All information requires context to give it meaning, value, and form. What is lacking in information can be illustrated by a pointed pun. In French, the term *"informe"* means "formless." The English "inform" could also mean "formless" because the prefix "in-" can mean "without"; hence "inform" can mean "without form." In and of itself, a chunk of captured information has no ability to change us. Indeed, a great deal of the modern art portfolio is about using formlessness as a vehicle for creating meaning within a defined space, yet not creating form.[1] The challenge of records managers within organizations is identical: to provide maximal form to information so that it can change us.

As we saw in chapter 2, the context with which information arrives within the organization or the context we give it is what gives meaning to that information for us. Organization is the act of preserving or providing that context. Whereas archivists protect context, it is the role of records managers both to provide and to protect context. Context provides form to information, just as context provides meaning to words. Attempts to evaluate the truth or falsity of statements such as "The king of France is bald" failed because there is no context—there is no king of France. Attempts to evaluate the price of sugar in the U.S. as compared to the price of sugar in Great Britain are dependent upon context: the U.S. uses English tons and the British use metric tonnes.

Captured information does not have meaning through some semantic, hence symbolic, characteristic for which we have knowledge. The meaning within captured information is usually iconic: a person's name, a reference

159

number, transaction. In other words, captured information has meaning only because it points to a context that we have preserved in some measure. The object signifies by pointing, even if its signification is unclear to more than a few people.

The bloody glove in the O. J. Simpson case is an excellent example of the importance of context. The signification of the bloody glove was unclear because of the glove's handling by the police. The context of the glove's finding and subsequent handling made unclear its manner of coming into being as a signifying object—how it came to have blood related to a high-profile murder case on it. What it pointed to was unclear, and members of the jury regarded it as such.

THE VALUE OF INFORMATION WITHIN THE ORGANIZATION

When information is created within or arrives at the organization, what is to be done with that information is known only within the organization. While the fact of the information's existence may be of value to other organizations (competitive intelligence, for example), in most instances, information has meaning only to and within that organization. Information has meaning within an organization. But does it have a value? Most information held within an organization has no market value: it cannot be sold at an auction or via any other market device. Some information is so valuable we buy it and sell it as we do intellectual property and industry analysis. Some information is so valuable we protect it from others as we do our credit card numbers and medical information—consider, for example, trade secrets such as the formula for Coca Cola. Most information within a business, however, has a limited value for a short period of time. For example, once an organization has paid an invoice, the invoice has value for a short time: prices change, the need for the product may change, or a different vendor may be used. Any longer-term use of information is likely to rely almost entirely on the information stored in databases, as an organization may use data mining as an internal effort to analyze current captured information and compare it to historical captured information in order to identify trends or problems. Currently, such analyses are automated only with information stored within databases. Documents are not even on the radar screen.

If information has value for a corporation, it is as an intangible asset.[2] Much has been written recently on the value of intangible assets, asserting that at least part of the run-up in stock value in the late 1990s was due to the inclusion of the value of intangible assets in the stock price. I doubt that anyone included the quality of an organization's records management program in that evaluation of intangible assets. Yet having consulted in many different organizations and many different industries, I can tell you that there are corporations that I would not invest in, nor work for, precisely because their records management programs are in such disarray. In most instances, the situation does not appear to be that the companies made a decision not to have a records management program, based on a thorough and precise risk assessment. I have never seen an organization, in either the private or the public sector, that had serious records problems that did not also have a high-level executive who believed it was appropriate not to manage information.[3]

As intangible assets, records have a "value" that is relative. Other intangible assets—patents, copyrights, formulas, brands—are valued for their presence; records are valued, i.e., obtain clear value, primarily when they are lost (and need to be found). Costs for executive time looking for documents, costs to re-create the document, costs to pay fines for not being able to produce a document are totaled up and circulated in our discipline every five to ten years. These numbers result in a flurry of activity to organize information—a flurry that lasts a few months and is not revived until the next disaster. The only exception is when an organization or a manager raises the profile of records management high enough to put it on every employee's radar screen and to ensure that funding is allocated to put the necessary program in place.

Clearly, organizations place value on the availability of the systems that house business-critical information. Disaster recovery has certainly seen its profile rise in recent years, not the least in the wake of the events of 9/11. A key part of the portfolio of information systems security professionals is to establish costs for disaster recovery purposes. As listed by Poore and Ozier in their Guideline for Information Valuation, the basic measures are utility, exclusive possession, cost of creation or re-creation, liability, convertibility, and operational impact. Consider "utility," for example, which refers to information important to the organization for operating, in the absence of which the organization will be disabled. A good example of this is Accounts Receivable. A company needs the information to continue operations, because without it, the company would not know what it was owed. "Exclusive possession" refers to information that has value because it is either known or has been gathered by only one organization. Trade secret information has this quality. "Cost of creation or re-creation" is self-explanatory, except in those instances where information cannot be re-created easily. Project reports, given their complexity and the multiple sources and software applications on which they are based, are a good example of information that cannot easily be re-created. As a metric for establishing disaster recovery costs, the last measure, "liability," is perhaps the most complicated. Evaluation by this facet depends upon the content, the timeliness, and the lack of value contrary to expectations, as well as confidentiality, availability, and integrity. Liability is difficult to assess because it is an element of risk management that is always dependent upon probability. "Convertibility" refers to the intrinsic value of the information, as in the case of patents or copyrights. A marketplace value for these could be established, but not without some effort. Finally, "operation impact" refers to the importance of the presence or absence of the information, such as correct inventory count.[4]

The assessment of value of information assets as represented in the listing above may seem clear and precise, but actually establishing those costs for litigation is not easily done when destruction of records is one of the points of the case. One of the more recent efforts to evaluate information was presented by two attorneys representing Exxon/Mobil Oil and the other First Union National Bank, respectively, in assessing damages to those companies resulting from destruction of their records by fire in a facility of Diversified Record Services, an off-site storage company.[5]

Exxon/Mobil's destroyed records were determined to be of value only to Exxon/Mobil. There was no marketplace to establish value for the information. Exxon/Mobil lost seventy thousand boxes and was awarded a total of US$20,750,000, including US$7,406,558 in lost tax deductions; US$3,000,000 for loss of a marine engineering library referenced for various projects; and US$1,347,654 in lost reimbursements for an underground storage tank remediation program. The remaining US$8,995,788 was awarded on the basis of a calculation of the clerical time required to process a box of records for storage, send it to storage, retrieve the box (using real-time assessments), and destroy the box, all totaling US$150 per box. In contrast, First Union's records were determined to be of value to both the bank and to its customers, debtors, and employees. First Union lost 150,000 boxes and was awarded US$20,500,000, including US$9,500,000 in costs to reconstruct personal and charitable trusts for which the bank was the principal trust officer.

While these two perspectives on the value of records, Exxon/Mobil's and First Union's, are different, they do not show up in either organization's balance sheets. Both assessments were created solely as a result of the attempt to recover costs from the catastrophic loss of the Diversified Record Services fire and both were arrived at rather quickly and haphazardly. Organizations never manage tangible assets the way they manage information generally. They keep strict inventories; they know the locations of all tangible assets and even maintain a specific, assigned location for each. They know the replacement value versus the historical cost of assets, for amortization purposes.

They take actions to prevent efforts to dilute the value of those assets. Indeed, organizations do as much as they can to enhance the value of their tangible assets by assigning managers with skills specific to the asset's maintenance requirements. In Chapter 5, we compared the records life cycle to product life cycle management. As records management is practiced in most organizations today, the similarity ends there, as even the development of the product in product life cycle management (Research and Development) is perceived to have value. Products in development are intangible assets and are valued sufficiently highly that a specific manager, a product manager, is assigned. In many instances, the stock values of pharmaceutical company are tied directly to the number and promise of products in the research and development "pipeline." Entire suites of applications are devoted to product development and product life cycle management.

Yet with information that does not belong in the category of intellectual property, organizations do not know what they have; they do not know the location of what they have; they have no specific, assigned location for any of the information; they cannot even guess at the historical cost, yet are quick to guess the replacement value. In the Diversified Records Services court case noted above, the attorneys said they had no precedent for determining value. I have seen estimates for how long it takes for the average executive to find a document, twenty to thirty minutes, and then an evaluation made on the executive's time. I have been in offices where documents that had been lost for months were found when a records management professional analyzed the situation of the office at the point when the document was lost and then found it within minutes. In other circumstances, I have seen attorneys panic at the loss of a multimillion-dollar contract because they said they would be embarrassed to ask the other party for a copy, not because the document per se had value.

In general, organizations manage their debt better than they manage their records—despite the fact that records can become as much, or even more, of a liability. Records become a key source of risk for any organization. Mismanaging records, in fact, costs more money than managing them. Consider discovery, the first activity performed when litigation arises, which requires that all records associated with the topic of the litigation be produced within a short period of time, generally thirty days. Mismanaged records cannot be produced quickly, even if headcount is increased to sort through the records in question—and particularly if those records include email.[6]

Another problem that organizations face is recent changes in law and in government regulations. Numerous of these laws and regulations have had the effect of extending the life of much information without improving its value, specifying additional documents that must be retained as records for extended periods of time. Called "compliance" by information technology

(IT), now part of a larger compliance function within the organization, this one small segment of the records life cycle is left completely in the hands of records managers. This wrongly associates records management only with the management of information when that information is of no value to the organization other than for purposes of its interface with the government.

One part of records management has been raised to heights of executive decision-making: what is currently called content management. Content management is simply the management of the first half of the records life cycle—the period of their active use within the organization.

Few records managers are involved in this activity. The reasons are historical. After World War II, as the profession of records management began to find its identity, the advent of computers enabled organizations to tabulate information more quickly in databases. Until relatively recently, computers have been very expensive and have required expenditures from the capital budget—hence information technology was regarded as a capital investment, with costs that could be amortized over the life of the hardware and software. In contrast, records management being a practice, not a technology, received its funding from the operations budget.[7] Thus the decision-making for the "information conduit,"[8] the hardware and software, became divorced from the day-to-day practice of managing information. From the standpoint of the organization, the resource was understood to be the technology, not the information. The expertise believed to be required was in hardware and software, not in concepts for managing information.

One of the by-products of this attitude toward information technology was a belief that records found in an electronic environment were somehow different from hard-copy records. They were not records; they were "documents," or "content." This belief became solidified subsequently, as vendors of content management solutions began to add records management functionality to their software products. In the parlance of these vendors, documents and content had to be "declared" records in order to be managed by a records manager. Hard-copy records had a lesser value because of their association with the operating budget and records management, as opposed to the capital budget and IT.

Irrespective of how valuable information may have been, in most instances "records" are considered nearly worthless because they are believed to be records only when the business process is finished with them and the approach taken by enterprise content management (ECM) vendors reinforces this. This is evidenced by the uninformed notion that many employees have that "records" are only paper documents.[9] Another is the IT supervisor who stood up in front of her peers at a recent IT conference and proclaimed that email are not records.[10]

One of the more interesting symptoms of this trend is the belief that some-how the technology will manage, i.e., organize, the records. As a consultant, I have been in many companies where the introduction of technology to man-age documents/records—the so-called EDMS (electronic document manage-ment) or ECM products—has led to the breakdown of any information or-ganization in every electronic repository: document management, images, email, etc., because the same controls used to control documents in the paper system were not imposed. The departments and IT did not know such controls were as important in the electronic world as in the paper world. After all, the product is called electronic content management.

To exacerbate the problem, because paper records are no longer perceived as having value, no one pays attention to them anymore. Whatever organiza-tion may previously have existed among the paper documents has been lost. Records management employees managing paper are eliminated because the ECM system is supposedly managing the documents now. Whatever paper makes its way to the "file"—there is no longer an official medium or reposi-tory for documents—are simply tossed into a folder with all other documents relating to the same issue because there is no longer enough time to ensure that duplicates are eliminated and the documents are in chronological order. Only the few workgroups with a strong bent toward records management still maintain order within their files.

The net result is that only persons with a natural ability to create search algorithms—and, yes, there are search algorithms for paper[11]—can find what they want. The executives and administrators in a company or government entity have no idea that the key to protecting and preserving the value of their information was, in fact, in the records manager. The managers in informa-tion technology simply provide bigger, faster, and more extensive plumbing. They do not provide organization.

The net result is that the perceived value of records has come to be associated with both their place within a business process as well as the media involved. In addition, the value of employees who handle a particular medium has been den-igrated and their portfolio circumscribed while the value of those handling an-other medium has been raised—with disaster recovery of systems the only sig-nificant addition to IT's portfolio. The inherent value of the records is irrelevant.

PRACTICAL GUIDANCE: DESIGNATING VITAL RECORDS

One of the ways in which records managers manage the value of records is to distinguish vital records—i.e., those records which are necessary to do business the next day—from those that are not necessary. Considering that a disaster can be everything from the overflowing of a janitor's closet to a complete destruction of a facility, the solution for business process continuity must include a review by every department of as many potential scenarios as possible. Far from being a burden, this activity can be interesting and even fun if a group tackles it.

Each set of records may be handled differently, as the role that each plays within business processes tends to differ. For example, the existence of by-laws is more important than their accessibility, so these can be maintained in a secure location. Copies of by-laws are not official. The record copy may have an affirmation by the secretary of state for the state of incorporation. In the event the original is destroyed, a company may need to present copies and proof of the destruction of the originals to get the copies affirmed. Compare this to records of Accounts Receivable, which must not only exist, but their details must be easily accessible; consider that in the wake of a disaster, little is more important than ready funds, as insurance policies may not pay out for months or years. Other vital records include lists of employees and their contact numbers, as they will be important to get an alternative site up and running.

An organization must determine for itself what its list of vital records looks like. Other documents that may be of value to the organization for consideration in the vital records program include:

- Contracts
- Intellectual property
- Mission-critical process information
- Intelligence
- Audit support
- Reusable knowledge
- Litigation support
- Cultural artifacts (government and historical)

The preceding discussion leads us to the following formula I call The Primary Value of Information, figure 6.1:

Value of information = existence + retrievability + ease of identification as relevant + ability to present in appropriate form + known place in process + appropriate level of protection

---

Figure 6.1.   The Primary Value of Information.

"Existence" requires techniques of preservation. Preservation will require creating copies in a remote location that is not subject to similar disasters.

(Preserving copies of records in Tampa because the Miami headquarters is subject to hurricanes is not appropriate.) The records must also be preserved in appropriate temperature and humidity and protected from vermin. It would seem that all of these requirements be obvious; however, many organizations do not apply even these minimal standards to the preservation of their records.[12]

"Retrievability" and "ease of identification as relevant" require that records be accessible and easy to identify. Storing many boxes, microforms, tapes, or disks in a secure site with no vermin is good, but not keeping an index of what is at that site is comparable to not keeping them at all. For disaster recovery purposes, the documents must be easily accessible. Back-up tapes are useful when only a few need restoring, but for business to continue on a next-day basis, a mirrored site—complete with computers, applications, work stations, printers, data, and documents—is required. Each group of electronic information must also be examined for those issues that will help identify the right document. Titles of documents, thumbnails, groupings into the right folder, an appropriate search engine, and appropriate index fields (metadata) can all contribute to this.

"Ability to present in appropriate form" requires that the documents be presentable in a form that can be used within an appropriate period of time; if no microform reader is readily available, for example, presenting the documents on microfilm will not help. Many business processes in financial services are regulated and require information be stored on write-once, read-many (WORM) media. The mirrored site must also have the appropriate media presentation.

Having information at the appropriate place within a process makes the process more efficient and the end product more valuable. The "known place in the process" requires that information be available to those who can make best use of it. For example, information concerning the cost of the parts that go into the new product design should be available to the research and development group. Having the cost of constituent parts at the point of manufacture makes the manufactured product less valuable to the company. What if the cost of the parts is more than the company can charge for the finished product? If the research and development group had known the finished product could not be sold for a reasonable profit, they would not have continued with the design.

All information must be protected in some form. The "appropriate level of protection" may be as simple as choosing acid-neutral folders or as arcane as using an electron microscope to read the microetchings on a nickel bar. That protection may require going after those who have infringed on a trademark or used copyrighted material without permission. Protection may require locked doors and strong encryption. Each organization must determine the optimal and most cost-effective method of protection for each group of its information.

In recent years, several highly publicized events have transformed the understanding of organizations with respect to both the value of records and what constitutes a record. Among these are Bill Gates's email during the Microsoft antitrust trial,[13] the enactment of the Sarbanes-Oxley Act of 2002 in response to the destruction of Enron-related email at Arthur Andersen, and the heightened awareness of personal privacy through the scandalous losses of personal information by trusted sources.[14] Whether the increased awareness of the importance of records management will prevail remains to be seen, but many corporate records managers now find themselves speaking and working with higher-level executives than previously.[15] Analyst firms such as Gartner, IDC, and Forrester track records management products and functionality. Technology vendors such as IBM and Oracle are working to create certifications in records management for database managers. Systems analysis and design, however, have yet to discover that much information is either found within documents (records) or must be maintained as documents (records).

HOW RECORDS MANAGMENT DIFFERS FROM ARCHIVES

How do we evaluate information within an organization, and what value do records managers provide? Nongovernment archivists and librarians evaluate information for cultural purposes only—for the value that history and posterity will make of it. Government archivists value information for cultural and social purposes—for the value that history and posterity, as well as the citizenry, will make of it. Organizations, in contrast, do not value information for cultural purposes. Their evaluation is much more complex. The information, such as a patent or copyright, may have a market value. The information may have value only to the organization or to a government regulatory agency or standards body. For this reason, records managers do not "appraise" records. We evaluate records according to a complex algorithm that is different for every organization and that may change over time. For example, technology gives us greater access to information now than it did even ten years ago. Regulations change and force us to keep or handle information differently. Practices such as strategic intelligence that were used by only a few individuals two hundred years ago are now considered good business practice by large corporations.

The archivists have gotten it right, and wrong, that managing context in the electronic world is more complex. The archivists are wrong in treating the provenance of an electronic document essentially identical to the way they would treat a pot shard—i.e., by scrupulously documenting the layer and location of the shard throughout its life. Generally, records managers find that separating an electronic document from its context is one of our most vexing problems. Software applications magically create and restore information unbeknownst to the authors of that information. The applications used to create documents often hold on tenaciously to various properties or edits, much to the bewilderment of the documents' users. Such software features have nearly brought down governments, as was the case with the 2003 British intelligence assessment for the second Iraq War, which contained authorial properties; in other instances, the inadvertent preservation of edits effectively smeared the authors themselves (the Starr Report published to the web as an HTML document restored previous edits, making it different from the printed report that was submitted to Congress). Another area in which the archivists have been mistaken is in the area of preservation. The complete destruction of all instances of an electronic document has proven to be a challenge beyond the capabilities of many organizations. The use of terms such as "delete" by operating systems and applications is in fact misleading, as the only thing deleted is the pointer to the information. The file still exists, will continue to exist, and can be recovered—sometimes for more than a month following its supposed "deletion." Employees in charge of disaster recovery do not understand that in the process of making their daily system back-ups, they are actually creating copies of information. While it is true that the copies that result from these backups cannot be easily read or retrieved, they can and are used as copies.

Email systems do not force employees to manage their sent and received messages in the same way that the hard-copy world does. As we have seen, paper documents get in the way and must be disposed of either by filing or throwing away, but email messages gather—both in "Sent" boxes and even in "In" boxes. When employees do file their email, they ordinarily do so through personal folders that they have established themselves. But each person to whom an attachment is sent may, depending upon the email system, keep a copy of an email in a separate folder. How would you find copies of each attachment?

These are just a few examples of the ways in which information technology foils our attempts to manage information. Litigation attorneys use techniques based on these shortcomings of information management to gather information through a method called computer forensics. These bits and pieces of information are valuable precisely because they hold enough "provenance" to be used as evidence—evidence in a court of law. The difficulty that records managers have with most electronic evidence is that it is not *informe* (the

French for formless), it is well-formed. The document and its context continue to exist despite our best efforts to destroy them.

MANAGING THE ORGANIZATION OF INFORMATION

Records management manages the value of information by managing the organization of information. Organizing information is a complex activity because it is both conceptual as well as practical. We arrange the order of documents in a folder and the order of folders in a project or case. We select index fields. We create, restrict, and manage keywords. We create organization-wide classification systems. We create search strategies. We define optimal locations. We determine which employee will select a location for an information item. We improve business processes. We restrict business processes. We determine user access. We control the creation and capture of information. We gather information together during litigation. We determine when information is to be destroyed. We determine how information is to be destroyed. We ensure that information goes to archives. In short, everything we do to manage the records life cycle is intended to manage the value of captured information. All of these activities are limited by the requirements dictated to us by our organizations. We cannot do what our organization believes is of low priority, nor can we perform our activities without the necessary funding. Records management itself has been a low priority for most organizations. Arguments of the business benefits associated with effective records management—such as greater productivity, reduced costs of litigation, reduced exposure to litigation—tend to fall on deaf ears. Experience has shown that enlightenment usually comes with disaster or litigation. We do not even deign to raise issues such as authenticity, reliability, and trustworthiness as reasons for funding a records management program because these are of no perceived value to the world of records inside the organization.

When we organize records, we manage them in space, in time, in speech, and conceptually. We manage records in space by providing a logical, spatial presentation. We manage records in time through our management of the records life cycle. We manage records in speech through the creation of control vocabularies, keywords, indices, thesauri, and so forth. We manage records conceptually through policies, classification, procedures, and employee training. Of these four ways of organizing records, managing speech and concepts have become the most important. In a hard-copy world, we manage using time and space. At a particular moment, a document will be found in a particular place with other, similar documents. Within that place, the documents will be in a particular spatial order—a spatial order that is relevant to the department using those documents. For example, within a city or county planning department, a permit may be located by its permit number, plat, lot, or subdivision number or name; by its street address; or by the requestor of the permit—depending upon how the department needs to have it ordered. As the permit undergoes its rounds of approvals in each subsequent department involved in its processing, it may be placed in numeric, alphabetic, geographic, or even temporal order—i.e., the order in which it was received in that department or the order in which it was issued.

Within those orders, employees must determine how logically to arrange the documents in a file plan. A file plan is a kind of "social compact" among an employee workgroup to ensure that every document goes into the right place for further work in the business process or for purposes of subsequent reference work. For example, within geographic order it may be more logical to separate Puerto Rico from the United States, or it may be more logical to keep the two entities together. In alphabetical order, it may be more logical to put "van Ives" after "Vanivar."[16]

An electronic filing system has few differences from hard-copy records filing systems, but those differences are almost insuperable. Records (and documents) in an electronic environment are more difficult to manage than paper records because the records manager's ability to organize the information is more dependent upon the technology than on standards of good practice. Another dramatic difference between the hard-copy and electronic worlds is that hard copies force themselves into our consciousnesses by being in the way. Electronic records, however, are not in the way; they simply form a list that can be ordered chronologically, alphabetically, by sender, etc., from which the employee can choose, many of them using the familiar file-folder metaphor that users continue to find highly intuitive.[17]

What may be intuitive to the end user, however, may not be possible within the technology. Replicating for electronic files the same filing functionality that users characteristically find most effective for their hard-copy files can prove to be a daunting task for software developers. Case or project files are a good example. Paper documents from many different applications need to be put together in the same "bucket" so that they can be examined together as a complete story. Within the case file, those paper documents are separated by function, not by the software application in which they were generated. When transmittals, for example, have been created in word processing and fax, as well as email, ideally the document management software would permit these documents to be held together and examined chronologically in the same virtual "folder" or repository; only recently has the technology been developed to provide this specific functionality.[18] Previous to this, electronic document management (EDMS) or enterprise content management (ECM) software products could keep the documents generated by desktop productivity applications (such as Microsoft Excel, Word, Visio) together in the same repository, with the notable exception of email. Irrespective of the email application —whether Lotus Notes, Microsoft Exchange, or Novell GroupWise—few EDMS or ECM products could even integrate with them, much less manage the emails and attachments inside them and permit a unified view of email and other desktop productivity documents. Very few attempts to create "public folders" in Exchange, for example, have proven successful in providing buckets for employees to "file" their emails.[19] Typically, an employee will have a personal filing system in her own directory and will file documents there. The best example of the project file problem in the hard-copy world is architecture and some engineering drawings that are printed on enormous sheets of paper so that all details are clear. Those sheets do not fit into a letter- or legal-sized file folder; they must be folded up. In many instances, however, sets of sheets must be kept together that simply cannot be folded; instead, those sheets are hung on a rack or laid in a niche or a drawer for reference. The file folders and the rack or drawers make up two separate repositories for the project file that simply cannot be integrated.

DOCUMENT CONTROL/REPOSITORY MANAGEMENT

This must lead to what I call "repository management"—the "silo" of documentary information referred to by ECM product vendors and analysts. The first activity we would perform to actually inventory all captured information within an organization is to inventory all repositories. Each C-drive is a potential repository. The drives assigned to a specific department are repositories. Each USB drive, floppy disk, personal digital assistant (PDA or handheld), and "smart" phone is a repository. Every CD storage unit, tape storage closet, optical jukebox, and RAID is a repository. Most organizations have no record of every official repository, much less the various "rogue" repositories now proliferating within organizations. Many USB drives, smart phones, and PDAs are purchased by individuals for personal as well as professional purposes and then "smuggled" into the office. Electronic documents typically do not maintain a record of the repositories they have been copied to or "visited." Most organizations do not require the collection of that information. Finally, most organizations have no policies or procedures concerning such devices or their use. This means that the loss of an unofficial repository, such as a PDA, by an employee can mean the loss of anything from the loss of personal emails to documents that are of value only to the organization, to client lists or trade secrets.

Repository management is only the newest of a set of valuing and organizing activities called "document control." Found in its most robust form in nuclear records management and in the records management programs of highly classified U.S. research centers such as Los Alamos National Laboratory, this is the basic practice missing in the knowledge of most records managers—primarily because the portfolio of most professional records managers has been management of the end of the life cycle.[20] Nearly every problem we identify in "electronic records" already has a corresponding practice in the area called "document control."[21] This practice is also found in engineering as well as in law firms, accounting firms, and consulting firms.

Document control is the business process of how a group creates a document. Those processes require policies and procedures for each step in the creation phase. When we put policies and procedures into place before we create a document, we are performing an act not contemplated by traditional notions of the life cycle—notions of the life cycle that have generally begun following a document's creation. Under policies and procedures for document control, we are performing the "family planning" phase of the life cycle—i.e., we are determining what documents or records are going to be created within the organization and by what method. This can be a very important aspect of business processes, even for organizations that create documents as their final product. Engineering, architecture, accounting firms, construction, and law—essentially any type of work requiring a project or case file—are examples of the types of processes that perform this act. Governments are also in the business of creating documents as final products—documents such as deeds, marriage certificates, bills, and treaties. The central importance of the final document to the business process is the key indicator as to whether document control will be instituted within any particular business process—or, indeed, within a particular organization.

The basic premises of document control are: ensuring that every document has a clear path through creation, that appropriate reviews and approvals are in place at specific steps, that each document used is the correct one, that only the appropriate people have access to those documents, that documents are kept together to provide a complete record of a project or case, that annotation does not create additional documents other than the intended final, that documents are maintained in the correct medium, and that documents meet a timely and complete end. Document control is one of the strengths of "content management" software products—including the workflow functionality, the so-called library functions, as well as the creation of a "team space" where workgroups can find information relevant to their project.

The creation of documents is the creation phase of a record. Within processes that require document control, the creation of a particular type of document will require its own business process. That business process will include documentation of every change occurring to the document. This documentation of changes may require signature approvals, separate documents that inventory the changes made, and numbering systems for each document (called "versions"). Some processes may call the versions "drafts," and may differentiate them further as to whether they have been presented to an outside entity such as a client; for example, many industries call their documents "versions" only if they are published to an outside entity. Each one of these versions and each one of these drafts has a different life cycle, according to the needs of each industry and business process.

Deal-related documents—those related to a transaction requiring more than a receipt or a single contract—in a law firm are instructive. Law firms call their successive documents "drafts." Drafts are circulated within a firm to appropriate persons, and changes are collected. The changes are then filtered through one individual who is responsible for authorizing the changes. The next draft is then circulated. When the team of attorneys believes a draft is appropriate for showing to the client, the client is presented with it. Subsequent drafts may need to be made and circulated, until finally a draft is approved for showing to the other side in the deal. That draft is said to have "crossed the table." Each of these groups of drafts—those that are internal to the law firm, those that have been shown to the client, and those that have been shown to the other party—has a different life cycle.

Clearly, one of the problems with having different versions and drafts floating about is the need to ensure that the correct persons are working with the appropriate version. The first technology for managing this process was Standard Generalized Markup Language (SGML), which, as we discussed in Chapter 4, was invented in the world of engineering to manage sections of manuals or paragraphs in electronically produced documents, as in the case of the massive maintenance manuals associated with jet aircraft. Because individual jets have a slightly different configuration, each requires a slightly different version of the maintenance manual. The only way to ensure that the correct paragraphs got into each manual was to keep a type of computerized list of sections of the document that could be assembled quickly when the jet was ready for delivery.[22] This method of dividing a document up into pieces and then updating separate pieces is the same concept behind technology currently called "content management." SGML is also the precursor to HTML and XML. These are all designed to separate the content from its presentation.

The current vocabulary for software products that manage document control can be very confusing. The category of products that provide the functionality to manage most of the life cycles of electronic documents is called

Enterprise Content Management (ECM). Those products include content management functionality (document control functionality), which handles the creation, approval, indexing, storage, and publishing of web content; document management functionality, which handles the creation, approval, indexing, storage, and collaboration of documents; forms management functionality, which handles the creation, data validation, imaging, approval, indexing, and storage of electronic forms; imaging functionality, which handles the imaging and indexing of hard-copy documents; print/output management functionality, which handles the workflow and management of printing and copiers; digital asset management, which handles the indexing and storage of complex objects such as graphical objects, photographs, or film clips; digital rights management functionality, which manages trademark and copyrights for electronic objects; workflow functionality, which automates the processes surrounding content, documents, and other electronic objects; storage systems, which manages where, when, and what type of storage device an electronic object goes to; and records management functionality, which manages retention of any captured information and deletion of electronic objects on on-line magnetic disks. Over the years, vendors have sought to bring multiple areas of functionality into their ECM solutions, as "suite" products that are capable of meeting a wide range of the requirements for document control. Yet the concatenation of all these various areas of functionality under the rubric of "enterprise content management" is confusing, at best.

Another aspect of document control that has become nearly impossible to manage is copy control. This is a broad set of management practices meant to ensure that extraneous copies of documents do not circulate for purposes of confidentiality, security, business process requirements, and/or compliance. One of the most deleterious problems in any organization is the convenience copy. Employees may have a copy of an email attachment on their hard drive or smart phone; they may have a copy of a final document in their files for reference. When a new version is published, containing new information, those previous copies do not necessarily disappear and may continue in use — along with the incorrect information. Copies of sensitive documents may circulate surreptitiously, damaging reputations or ruining the potential for a deal to be signed. Documents may survive past their intended retention periods and be called up in document discovery. While the contents of the documents may not be damaging to the organization, the production of those documents may be time-consuming and costly for that organization.

Of course, the ease with which copies can be made is not new, nor is it solely a characteristic of electronic documents. The advent of the press copy, invented in 1780 by James Watt and coming into general use in the late nineteenth century, created one copy for an organization to keep as a record of letters it had sent. The carbon copy, invented in 1823 by Ralph Wedgewood, was used successfully to make adequate originals of any document and several copies, using the typewriter, which in turn was made commercially successful in 1784 with the Remington No. 2.[23] A visit to the Early Office Museum[24] reveals that a great deal of technology in the latter half of the nineteenth and twentieth centuries was devoted solely to making copies. By the end of World War II, however, the first Hoover Commission was decrying the vast numbers of documents created and copies maintained.[25]

The digital revolution notwithstanding, we are scarcely any closer to the paperless office today. According to a white paper issued in 2004 by Iron Mountain, "paper consumption by U.S. businesses has risen 20% per year over the last decade, peaking in 1999 with a consumption level of some 6 trillion pages."[26] The facsimile, the photostatic copying machine, and then the network-attached printer increased the ability of any employee to generate paper copies on demand.[27] The use of email did not change how much we print; it changed only when and who does the printing: instead of printing, copying, and sending, we now send, and the recipients print. The result has been a change in the ratio of copier to printer installation; "between 1988 and 1993, the worldwide installed base of copiers increased by only 5 percent, whereas the worldwide installed base of printers increased by 600 percent."[28] Unlike a century ago, however, the problem with this latter practice is compounded by the fact that not only do we still have paper copies, we now also have numerous electronic copies.

Several electronic methods have been employed to mitigate these problems. Printers and copiers have been programmed to create a background "draft" watermark on all documents, with the exception of those documents specifically requested to be free of it. Paper documents are printed with expiration dates indicating when they should be destroyed. Retention schedules have an extra column indicating when convenience copies should be destroyed. Electronic copies may have a programmed destruction date, at which time they become encoded and cannot be read. None of these practices is particularly effective. What is effective, however, is training and enforcement within an organization. A convenience copy readily qualifies as a record made during the course of business and fits the best evidence rule. An effective electronic method of copy control is to place a document on a shared drive or other location where everyone who needs it can access it, and then send a link to the document rather than a copy. This does not stop anyone from copying the document electronically or from printing it, but it does limit the proliferation of attachments—and thereby extraneous copies—that linger unmanaged in email boxes.

A copy may or may not have all of the same properties that are associated with the original. Some word-processing programs permit the creation of a copy that eliminates the trail of revision histories and edits. This is an extra step in the document finalization process that most employees are either unaware of or unwilling to take on a regular basis. The copy that is kept by the organization is the "record copy." This copy may be an original, as in a signed letter received by the organization, or it may be a copy, as in an image of that same signed letter. All other copies are considered convenience copies. Disposal of all convenience copies is urged as soon as possible. The "record copy" may not have superior signs of being "authentic" as the archivists would have it. The record copy is official because it is maintained by a department that can most thoroughly manage the remainder of its life cycle. The key idea behind the record copy is not authenticity; rather, it is responsibility.

Extra information about a document is dubbed "metadata" by the information science community, primarily the archivists and librarians, one of whose chief objectives is the creation of a worldwide virtual catalog.[29] For this community, the standardization and thoroughness of metadata is vital. Its definition of metadata is equally grand; according to the Working Meeting on Recordkeeping, metadata is to be defined as: "Structured or semi-structured information which enables the creation, management and use of records through time and within and across domains in which they are created. Recordkeeping metadata can be used to identify, authenticate and contextualize records; and the people, processes and systems that create, manage and use them."[30] Under this definition, "metadata" would include programming for the operating system and would stop only at the hardware.[31]

As we have noted above, records managers have the dual problem of both trying to get rid of extraneous information about documents, as well as ensuring that we have appropriate information. For us, metadata management is as much about destroying information as managing what we have. Unlike archivists or librarians, we deal with information that is primarily of value only to the organization, not with a worldwide system. When we do deal with information of value to other organizations, our primary job is to ensure its protection against accidental or covert revelation. Because we manage captured information to ensure that it can be shared by no one outside a limited number of clearly defined persons, we have a different set of challenges. We provide a context for and manage what people do; we do not document subjects as librarians do with the Dewey Decimal and Library of Congress systems. We examine how employees do their work using all information, primarily documents, not what the content of those documents is. As Glenda Acland, Barbara Reed, and Sue McKemmish put forth in their discussion of the Australian Recordkeeping Metadata Schema (RKMS), "[e]lectronic recordkeeping and archival systems provide such mechanisms. They are fundamentally concerned with identifying, describing and classifying the functions, activities and transactions that records document. This can be contrasted with the fundamental concern with subject classification in library and information systems. Records document actions, not subjects . . . "[32]

We are concerned with ensuring that the metadata for any captured information is appropriate for a concrete set of users. Business intelligence and knowledge management practices have expanded the potential users by permitting managers and executives to ask questions about internal information for decision-making they did not previously have access to, but those users of information remain primarily users who are inside the organization. Documents, however, have rarely risen to the level of "mining" that for years has been applied to data, irrespective of the amount of metadata that might be captured. Records management is more concerned with enabling business processes through links from documents to business applications, passing audits through adequate usage and information protection, and easy litigation production through adequate classification, indexing, and locating. None of these are called "metadata" by either end users or records managers.

What records managers might call "metadata" refers primarily to business process information. For example, an insurance policy does not have an author in the same sense that a government document might. Key information on the insurance policy document is captured in a database, and the document is imaged for reference. The imaged document must have the policy number and capture date as metadata to link it to its database record and for management in the document repository. Similarly, an accounts payable invoice will also have information captured from it into a database, and the document will be imaged for reference during the business process. The metadata associated with the imaged document will include a unique identification number that will be used to associate it with the database record. How often the invoice is referenced will be more important to its life cycle than who authored the document. Through hierarchical storage management, inactive records are written from hard drive to optical disk, irrespective of any other metadata. Records managers are also interested in linking the insurance policy to other documents, such as claims and cancelled checks (i.e., structural information) and in who has seen the information and their actions taken (i.e., audit trail information).

The metadata that records managers end up managing for purposes of preservation more closely resemble those in a data warehouse than those in a library or archives catalog.[33] Other, more records management-oriented programs, such as the Australian RKMS, are very thoughtful, but too much in some ways and too little in others. For example, one of the metadata elements is "Title." What is the title of an invoice or an insurance policy? Another record metadata element is "Abstract." What is the abstract for a journal voucher or a quarterly financial report? On the other hand, where within this schema is the metadata element for hyperlink name or for client name?[34]

Each grouping of documents has its own context to which it refers and from which it gains meaning and value. No list of metadata could exhaust every possible requirement within an organization. To determine metadata elements for each records series requires a determination of what each stakeholder group needs to ensure thoroughness. For example, the quality group will need information specific to the process to demonstrate appropriate standards. IT will need information about behaviors. Records management will need information about records series classification, user access, and a use audit trail. The nearest metadata standard to this type of thorough analysis required is the Metadata Encoding and Transmission Standard (METS) developed by major research libraries and put in its present form by the Digital Library Federation (DLF).[35] This standard was developed for what the library and information science community calls "digital objects" and the IT vendor community calls "digital assets"—i.e., complex digital information that is not print.

One of the reasons that many metadata standards are inappropriate is that libraries constantly search for ways to share information and create better forms of information representation. In contrast, other organizations, such as those in private industry, are constantly searching not for ways to share information, but for ways to protect their information in order to achieve a competitive advantage. Enlisting metadata standards used by the entire world opens the door to theft of valuable intangible assets, confidential employee information, and corporate planning. Government may be interested in sharing information, but must also protect confidential employee information. Lists such as the Australian RKMS are useful checks for records managers, but cannot substitute for conversations with application vendors and internal IT, and discussions with users concerning their respective business process.

What we end up managing for purposes of preservation resembles the metadata in a data warehouse. Because metadata is data and is found in a database, few of us have the skills to manage these adequately. Familiarity with database problems as well as preservation problems in data warehousing is part of our path,[36] but collecting appropriate information for each document grouping for each phase of the life cycle and communicating that information well to the organization's information technology group is the only solution. There are no quick fixes or premade lists that can replace hard work or an understanding of the precise context for each document group.

CLASSIFICATION

Records managers create classification plans, or taxonomies, for organizations.[37] Each organization has different functions, different ways of performing business processes, and different histories, so the process of creating a

classification plan must be performed anew with each organization. Two organizations could, conceivably, have the same classification; however, this
conclusion could only be arrived at inductively. The process we use to determine the classification plans for other organizations would still have to be
performed anew each time.

Classification plans are different from file plans. File plans are groupings
of documents for day-to-day use of employees performing work on business
processes. Classification plans, in contrast, are created from a much higher
viewpoint for the purpose of creating "buckets" for all types of information
that exist within an organization. Claims within a life insurance company are
a good example. Each business process managing claims must be different.
For example, marine property claims require a different process from home
or auto claims. Marine property itself may sink to the bottom of the ocean and
may or may not be worth salvaging, whereas a home or auto can be inspected
to determine the extent of damage. For the purposes of a file plan, these different property groups will also require different types of documentation and
review. For purposes of a classification plan, however, these are all the same:
they are all property claims. Property claims are created the same, have similar use and distribution, and have the same retention; hence they belong to
the same grouping.

A classification plan is a life cycle tool, a metalevel management tool at the
thirty-thousand-foot level. In contrast, a file plan is a business-process tool, a
line management tool at the ground level. Classification plans organize
records series according to how work is done within each workgroup. The
classification must be recognizable and usable by every member of the organization, from the janitor to the CEO—not by just a particular set of clearly
defined stakeholders. Records series are groupings of documents that are created similarly, used similarly, and have the same retention. To put it more suc-
cinctly, records series are groups of documents that are differentiated by their
life cycles.

Records series may be kept together physically or virtually for convenience, but it is possible for two different departments of an organization to
have identical records series. For example, a manufacturer may make several
different types of electrical appliances and have separate processes for the
manufacture of each. The engineers who design those appliances may work
in separate workgroups corresponding to those separate processes. Each
workgroup will create change orders when necessary for the manufacturing
process to continue. Each engineering workgroup may have a different name
for those change orders, and the change orders will be kept in separate locations. The documents perform the same function in each workgroup and have
the same life cycles. The two sets belong to the same records series. Records

series have characteristics of being ideal, but of also being directly related to something real—that is to say, real sets of documents exist. While document sets have similar life cycles, they may be located in different places. Two records in a records series may appear to be quite unlike, yet belong to the same series. Consider personnel files within an organization. These files represent every individual, yet have different numbers of documents, even substantially different documents, yet have the identical life cycle.

Nor are the document groups that are found within the records series a sure guide to the records series. For example, a set of documents relating to the sale of a property is identical to those relating to the acquisition of a property, but the life cycle of a sales file is completely different from that of an acquisition. The sales file may be kept for a few years and then destroyed; the file from the acquisition will be kept for as long as the property is kept, possibly for hundreds of years. Records series may also be differentiated by their respective security requirements. For example, the Health Insurance Portability and Accountability Act of 1996 (HIPAA) requires specific handling and reporting for health-related documents. The set of health documents, however, may contain an even more sensitive set of documents, such as mental health documents, that an organization may require be treated even more securely and with additional restrictions. The names of the document groups are also not a guide. The project files kept by the accounting department may be entirely different from those maintained by the project workgroup. While those two sets of files may refer to the same project and even have some documents in common, they serve entirely different functions. One file is financial and the other is a business function. They also have different life cycles. They are created and used together, but their retirement is dependent upon very different criteria. The financial project file is required for the creation of financial reports and financial statements and for an audit. The business project file, however, may be subject to any of a variety of retention policies: it may be disposed of immediately, or kept until conditions change or the work product is reused, or the file may be kept together and referred to years later, should additional work be desired or in the event a product defect is found.

In effect, records series are the species of our information ecology. This may seem like a gratuitous statement about biology. How we distinguish records series is determined by how we create our classification plan. Our methods of creating classification plans more closely resemble the methods used in biology than they do those used in library science. As an example, consider the Dewey Decimal system. The Dewey Decimal system is what is called a "faceted classification."[38] The essential features of a faceted classification are that the criteria be exhaustive and mutually exclusive. As the reader will have noted above, records series are certainly not mutually exclusive, as documents found in one are found in another and identical documents may belong to different records series. The life cycle itself does not distinguish records series as document sets with the same life cycle, but different functions belong to different records series.

What records managers do in terms of organizing and classifying information has a stronger resemblance to biological methods of classification. We use a single primary differentiator, function, to make distinctions down to the penultimate level, at which the life cycle is then imposed to distinguish sets of documents into records series. We have species—records series—that belong to population sets, not concepts or ideal types. Knowing how we understand our classification subject matter helps us to create more consistent classification plans; as Paul Q. Hirst observes in his *Social Evolution and Sociological Categories*, "the very objects to be classified are constituted by definite social theories and those theories also provide the conceptual means of classification. The objects classified are not given independently of theory—categories of classification . . . are products of specific forms of theory."[39]

A collection of records series found within a particular department may be a faceted classification. Within project-based departments such as an engineering firm or law firm, the files may be organized on the basis of how the work is done.

What is classification? It is the creation of order out of chaos. It is the creation of knowledge—not just its organization through the creation or enhancement of a context. Classifications describe, define, and explain. In some ways, they are the very basis of human thought and communication. Every culture and language can be defined by its sets of classifications—its methods of dividing the world. We are profoundly changed when the classifications making up the foundation of our thought processes are challenged or changed. The Copernican revolution of the mind, the Darwinian revolution, the study of the Bible as a book—all were just such revolutions. The examples above are profound, yet we depend upon classifications to navigate our everyday lives: the Yellow Pages, cookbooks, organizational charts, Yahoo!, taxes, your sock drawer. Within the profession of records management we have many common classifications, such as media types, media longevity, file plans, and event-based versus time-based retention.

METHODS AND PRINCIPLES OF CLASSIFICATION

Our most important classification system is the Master Classification Plan (MCP). An MCP is the basic ordering of all the information assets within an organization by function, method of creation, and retention. The reasons we do this include improving customer service, increasing productivity, reducing time to market, ensuring quality, ensuring compliance, and managing risk. An MCP functions as an enterprise information architecture (EIA). This is not the organization of information on a corporate website;[40] this is the organization of all captured documentary information within an entire organization. An EIA is the information correlate to an enterprise architecture (EA): "Enterprise Architecture is about understanding all of the different elements that go to make up the enterprise and how those elements interrelate."[41] Where EA is concerned with technology and information flow, EIA is concerned with categorizing all documentary information. Each is concerned with standards for exchange of information, security, user access, and privacy.

Classifications create a metalevel context for information. Records information management (RIM) classifications define the context for creation of information and the larger organizational purpose for which the information was created. File plans relate information to its immediate work context, to defining relationships, establishing priorities and causes, and creating solutions. Because file plans work at a more microcontextual level for a particular group of people, there is no way to create one file plan for every workgroup. Indeed, even the same work being done by different workgroups may require different file plans. Because classification plans address the same issue in every organization, however, their overall structure is the same.

Let us dissect a hierarchical classification such as the one used by records managers. The parts of a classification are the domain, the rules for its creation, a hierarchy, the rules for the creation of the hierarchy, the rules for its order and rules for additions to the hierarchy, the elements, the rules for creation of elements, and the rules for the order of elements and the rules for the addition of elements. The domain is the specific area to be ordered—whether that area be Thanksgiving leftovers to be eaten first, political systems, or the weather patterns predicted by the rings on a woolly worm caterpillar. In our case, that domain is all of an organization's documentary information assets. Defining this domain is very important to creating a successful classification. For example, should dynamic databases be included in the inventory of an organization's documentary assets? Should Java server pages and Active server pages be considered part of the document for the purposes of archiving?

The term "taxonomy" is currently a popular term for describing classifications of information other than the library catalog. This is not the case in academia, however. The term "typology" is used in the social sciences to describe an ordering of objects into groups, as compared to a description or a causal explanation.[42] When a typology is created from statistics, theoretically without pre-determined notions, it is then called a taxonomy.[43] Social sciences deals with difficulties unlike our own because that area of study is classifying human beings or human behavior. Typologies of human beings are apt to lead to stereotypes and the reification of those types.

Librarians use classification systems and must distinguish those systems from other methods of ordering and identifying information for retrieval and use. Navigating the library literature is not quite as easy as understanding Aristotelian, Linnean, and Darwinian classification—in part because library science must classify all of human knowledge rather than a neatly defined subset. Boris Mirkin, a Russian statistician, says of library science: "This is the only field where authors allow themselves to title their monographs with the name of 'Classification,' as they feel they are the only people dealing with 'classification in general' because they classify the knowledge universe."[44] Librarians themselves do not agree about what it is that we—records managers —do. Elin Jacob would call what we do "categorization": "Indexing is both a process of representation through the systematic assignment of surrogates (descriptors or category labels) that model, or point to, the intellectual content of a group of documents and a process of categorization (grouping like things together to create order)."[45] As we organize according to the life cycle, not the content of objects, it is difficult to determine whether this is a correct assessment. Phyllis A. Richmond disagrees and would place records management firmly on the grounds of classification: "[C]lassification requires patterns of relationships and rather strong structure, and partly because classification is used in most American libraries only for shelf arrangement. Indexing is freer and can be almost structureless."[46] What we do is certainly highly structured, but bears no relation to shelf (or box) arrangement. David M. Liston and Murray L. Howder would also place us in the category of classification: "Classification, when considered carefully, can be seen not to be an indexing process in the same sense as the other indexing processes. Classification actually consists of subdividing a field of knowledge into hierarchical sets of classes, sub-classes, etc."[47]

The field of biology has the most expertise in methods of classification. Beginning with Aristotle's methods of classifying animals and plants, biology has developed soaring theories of classification. The method developed to create classifications of plants was borrowed and changed to create classifications of animals and languages.[48] These various systems argued among themselves as to the taxa that should be used to define a group or a classification—whether a single feature, analogous function, some type of essential coherence or similarity, or place within the grand chain of life. The great Harvard zoologist, George Gaylord Simpson, describes the step taken in the twentieth century to remove the individual entity from the mix: "Populations, not individuals, are the units of systematics and are the things classified. . . . Taxa, at all levels, are not in principle

defined by membership but by relationship . . . by implicit or explicit specification of relationships among those individuals."[49] Similarly, when we are creating classifications in records management, we are truly not interested in the individual document, but in groups of documents for which end users have given
a name, such as "accounts payable files," "engineering change orders," and so
forth. We are, in effect, the "botanists of information" inside an organization. We
do not determine the function of these document sets; we only observe and
record them. In this way, we are like anthropologists observing how information
is actually used.[50]

The Russian statistician Mirkin's definition of classification, based on John
Stuart Mill's, is very helpful: "Classification is the actual or ideal arrangement together of those which are like, and the separation of those which are
unlike; the purpose of this arrangement being primarily; 1) to shape and keep
knowledge; 2) to analyze the structure of phenomena; and 3) to relate different aspects of a phenomenon in question to each other."[51]

Ontologies differ from records management classifications in that they are
used to constrain and specify a classification, i.e., they are the rules for the
classification. A Master Classification Plan describes. An ontology is a
"shared understanding of some domain of interest which may be used as a
unifying framework" to promote communication, interoperability and enable
systems engineering.[52] As such, it is a method for creating a standard among
a group for identifying what systems may exist, what relationships among
systems are called, how they may be used, and what the constraints are. For
a business, a Master Classification Plan is a formative document within this
structure, because it captures the current state of functions, workflows, document groupings, and terminology. A Master Classification Plan is a type of
ontology because it does constrain and specify what can be created, but not
for purposes of interoperability. The Master Classification Plan is as much a
method for ensuring that employees place objects in the correct category as it
is a way to order information—i.e., it is as much a way to get objects ordered
as it is to order them.

A hierarchy is the structure for distinguishing elements. A hierarchy does
not signify levels of preferment which exclude, but larger classes subsuming
smaller classes. As an example, the social hierarchy indicates presumed exclusive levels of preferment, as indicated in the observation, "The Lowells talk
to the Cabots and the Cabots talk only to God."[53] A hierarchy in a classification is inclusive. It is multidimensional, functioning along at least two axes
and potentially more. The rules for a hierarchy are the principles by which the
layers of the hierarchy are determined and by which those layers are related.
A good example is the manner by which phone directories are organized. We
are familiar with our "white" pages, which are ordered alphabetically by last

name and then first name; and our "yellow" pages, which are ordered first by type of organization, and alphabetically within each type.

Elements are the conceptual objects being ordered into classes. Elements are concepts because we classify populations or groups, not individuals. No group of individuals is so closely similar that they can be unambiguously placed in one category, so we borrow from the modern biological systematicians and work with populations.[54] Elements are groups of individuals sharing traits. No individual within the group need have all the traits defining the element; hence the idea of a population of similar but non-identical individuals, as in a human population.

The rules for element relationships are the principles for making distinctions. The records management profession is being presented with numerous examples of problematic elements. Among the problems for records managers today are email, web objects, and document management document types. How, for instance, are we to determine the records series that email represents: by brain-storming, by corporate policy, by draconian procedures? With respect to web objects, how are these objects to be determined, and how are we to determine the records series those objects represent? As for document types within a document management system, when do they translate into records series, and when do they identify a format (correspondence, memoranda)?

The rules for the hierarchy and the rules for element relationships are part of the taxonomy. Differentiating the populations that define elements is an example of the rules that should be decided upon before undertaking a classification. For example, in some law firms the closing books, those sets of documents that are bound together and shelved, are considered trophies by some attorneys and valuable reference sources by others. Are the closing books part of the population, or are they trophies? The rules for the hierarchy are that it is enterprise-wide, top-down, and functional. Hierarchy is enterprise-wide: begin at the top with the high-level, idealized, corporate functions that are found in an annual report or comparable document for the entire enterprise.[55] To understand these functions, we work with key personnel for finer-grained distinctions. We do not describe departments, as these are artifacts of history, not functions. Departments can be duplicates by product line or experimental organizational elements. The hierarchy is also top-down. Define those overall functions first; do not define those functions with an organizational chart. Hierarchy is functional: it will contain idealized functions, discrete units with clear purpose.

These functions will not be the same for all organizations. It depends upon how important and how fully expressed a function is. For example, in Accounting and Finance, is Accounting separate from Finance? Is Accounting separate from Treasury? Is Accounting separate from Tax? Is Tax separate from Audit? Separating these requires analyzing the extent to which separate functions are elaborated within the hierarchy viz. functions = tasks to be accomplished, workflows = how tasks are accomplished, records series = information by and through which tasks are accomplished.

The elements classified are idealized populations of records, each of which is called a records series or a record type. Records series or record types are concepts, not real groupings of records. They are concepts that may indicate a single grouping of records or they may refer to groups of records in many or in every department: such as change orders in a construction company which has oversight of many different groups of engineers, or in a manufacturing plant, where design change orders and manufacturing process change orders have the same retention, but different end products. This classification is the basis for all the work we perform, including vital records, active records, document control, retention scheduling and disposition, and so forth. It is also the basis for any knowledge management program. Only now are individuals involved with knowledge management coming to realize that information without its context—i.e., its place in the MCP—has little value to the organization.

Many records managers use the term "unified classification plan," but it tends to refer to a bottom-up method of creating a classification. This is performed by creating classifications for each department separately, and then concatenating them into a single list. Although this is an appealing method for creating a classification plan because it does not require any department to have to deal with the vocabulary or business process issue of any other department, it presents a number of problems. The first problem is that rules are not created for the elements before they are classified into the initial departmental classification, and in many instances each departmental classification has its own set of rules. When these separate classification plans are brought together, the resulting classification plan is not unified, because of the disparate naming conventions and importance placed on the same document in different departments. In other words, while a "unified classification plan" may be called a classification, it does not have a corresponding taxonomy to go with it—i.e., it does not have a set of precise rules for its creation.

A hierarchy describes or explains its elements. It creates or enhances a context. The hierarchy we use in records management has three basic levels. The top level describes Functions—the tasks to be accomplished. The second level describes Business Processes—how the tasks are accomplished. The third level describes Records Series—the information by and through which tasks are accomplished. Records Series are elements. The first two levels describe the context for the third level.

THE ISSUE OF RECORDS SERIES OR RECORD TYPES

This raises the issue of records series or record types. Robek, Brown, and Maedke define a records series as: "A group of identical or related records that are normally used and filed as a unit and that permit evaluation as a unit for retention scheduling purposes."[56] A records series or type is a conceptual population of records that serve the same function and participate in the same business process as an input, an output, or a decision tool, and are evaluated as a unit for retention scheduling purposes. At a finer level, however, this begs the question of the records series versus the document type. The document type is a recognizable, standardized page format such as a memorandum, accounts receivable invoice, engineering change order, or correspondence. Its importance lies in document control, the objective of the creation phase of records management. The electronic counterpart is called document management. A records series is an idea defining the purpose of records groups. For example, a memorandum can serve many different functions: general office, policy announcement, brainstorming. A records series, in contrast, serves only one function.

Another aspect of the issue of the records series versus document type is where different document types have a different process of delivery, but the same purpose. Consider the transmittal form, a document that is used to demonstrate what was sent and when it was sent. In today's business world, the transmittal form can be exemplified by a memorandum, a facsimile cover sheet, or an email message. As transmittals, these three different document types serve the same function, have similar workflows, and are considered as a unit for retention scheduling purposes. This problem is particularly pernicious in such delivery methods as email and instant messaging, which are used for everything from emergency notifications to contract negotiations and transmittal forms.

The next challenge to the subject of records series are file formats. A file format is the architecture or structure of each unit within a records series. A file format appears to be a factual observation, but in more complex types of records such as case files and project files, it is as conceptual as a records series. The same holds for any records series having more than a single document type that must be kept separate. To be a single records series, the units must be used similarly (i.e., have the same function); be created similarly (i.e., have the same business process); and be retained and disposed similarly.

Elements help to define the hierarchy. Records series are defined primarily by purpose to an organization; fulfilling the tasks of an organization's functions as an input, an output, or a decision tool for a business process. Related concepts include the list, index, cross-reference, and thesaurus. Some librarians claim that classifications, cross-references, and thesauri are indices; some claim that indices, cross-references, and thesauri are classifications. Although the issue has been overstated, this is something we must look out for ourselves. We must look to our own skills and the needs of the organizations that employ us.

Many of us are more in awe of skilled librarians than skilled records managers. However, most librarians do not classify "the knowledge universe;" they apply a predetermined classification to individual items. Nor do we "receive" a classification in provenance, as archivists do. We must create, for each organization, a new classification. We truly create knowledge for the purposes of the organizations employing us.

For records management, a list is a collection of objects which may or may not be related like a shopping list: eggs, apple juice, bread, milk, orange juice, sweet rolls, cheese. An index is an ordered list of objects which may or may not be related: apple juice, bread, cheese, eggs, milk, orange juice, sweet rolls. An index can act similarly to a classification when the objects are related. In many instances, an index to a book acts as both an ordered list and as a classification when it has higher and lower orders of terms and concepts.

A classification contains objects which may or may not be related, that are ordered by groups: juices, apple juice, orange juice; dairy, cheese, milk, eggs; bread, wheat bread, sweet rolls.

A cross-reference is an object leading to another object. It may be an alternate name, or it may be part of an object. A cross-reference list may be an index or a thesaurus. A thesaurus is a type of classification with specific elements, including alternative names, potentially with broader, narrower, and related terms: juice, fruit drinks, cordials; bread, rolls, croissants; eggs, egg substitutes, powdered eggs.

An index is any additional information attached to an object so that it can be found again or so it can be grouped with other objects.

We must be clear about what we mean when we refer to these. Insular professional language will only confuse our most important audiences: upper-level executives and the end users of records management policies and procedures. Here we must examine an important issue about current jargon—specifically, the terms "content, structure, context" and "metadata." The content of a document or record is understood as much by its context and structure as by the linguistic content found there. An excellent example of this in everyday language is what is called "deictic" terms such as the word "I"; or shifters, such as verb tenses. Such terms are understood only in context. Structure also provides meaning; as we saw in chapter 5, a hard-copy memorandum is primarily a formal, intraorganizational communication; as an extraorganizational communication, it is informal. Email has blurred this distinction internally and externally, but a signed letter from an individual in an organization is always formal. The formality of a communication imparts meaning to content. Attempting to neatly separate these three aspects—content, structure, and context—confuses issues that we in records management already know must be kept separate. The document or record must signify and it must have a medium—a *support,* as the French say— and a context.

Metadata is by definition context, but as we have seen, the context is required to understand the meaning of the record. In a sense, XML is intended to be a thesaurus for all our separate "metadatas." The unfortunate history of metadata is that it began its life as the referent for defining the information in a column for a database table—e.g., its size, format, links, and so forth. It began to be used to refer to other information that described unstructured data, what we used to call the "audit trail." It has now become so broadly defined that one could actually include software applications under its rubric.[57]

Records information management is also a critical component of any organization's knowledge management strategy, as it creates reusable knowledge, which is now considered a critical element in any organization seeking to achieve an advantage over its competition. This activity is highly intellectual, requiring the practical understanding of how records are used, how businesses function, how processes work, and how divinely inspired classifications are.

Search is a method of organizing information on the fly, on an "as-needed" basis. Technologies for search methods are changing rapidly because researchers are now beginning to examine how different groups seek information. Most people have by now experienced the fruitlessness of full-text search. In many instances we cannot find even our own documents, because we cannot remember what we called them or what terminology we used inside them. More advanced methods permit us to request information using combinations of terms and header fields, but these are all still full-text search. Different algorithms for finding desired information, such as the one used by Google, look at how much others have referenced information through links and how many times such information has been requested. Yet searching Google is becoming a more and more complex activity.[58]

Natural language processing uses context and thesauri to differentiate how terms are used in context. For example, such searches could differentiate, "I'm having lunch with Sue and you," from "I'm going to sue you." These distinctions are important, particularly in production of emails for purposes of complying with a discovery subpoena. Even natural language processing, however, cannot aid some types of searches. Because emails are used to conduct conversations and to pass news articles and jokes as well as to conduct business, many terms can appear that may initially appear to be leads for incriminating evidence. For example, nearly any organization searching its email archives for the search term "Enron" is likely to get many hits. While few corporations were actually involved with Enron, it will take many costly hours of attorney time to sift through all those emails.

Information technology has actually made it difficult to organize records so that they are easily useful for employees. As processing speed increases and our applications do more, our expectation that we will be required to proactively do something to aid the process correspondingly decreases. The situation presents several consequences. Employees must either receive more training or become more technologically savvy, and organizations must impose more strictures on creation and use of electronic records (or documents, if you must) than employees are likely to be willing to volunteer. Organizations must also become more technologically adept at responding to discovery.[59]

NOTES

1. Yves-Alain Bois and Rosalind E. Krauss, *Formless: A User's Guide* (New York: Zone Books, 1997). This is a translation of *Inform: mode d'emploi,* published by Editions de Centre Pompidou in 1996. It is the catalog of an exhibition held at the Centre George Pompidou in 1996 and curated by Bois and Krauss.

2. Baruch Lev, *Intangibles: Management, Measurement, and Reporting* (Washington, D.C.: Brookings Institution Press, 2001). Jonathan Low and Pam Cohen Kalafut, *Invisible Advantage: How Intangibles Are Driving Business Performance* (Cambridge, MA: Perseus Publishing, 2002). Richard Hall, "The Strategic Analysis of Intangible Resources," *Strategic Management Journal* 13, No. 2 (February 1992): 135–144. Baruch Lev, "Sharpening the Intangibles Edge," *Harvard Business Review* 82, No. 6 (June 2004): 109–116. John J. Ballow, Roland Burgman, and Michael J. Molnar, "Managing for Shareholder Value: Intangibles, Future Value and Investment Decisions," *Journal of Business Strategy* 25, No. 3 (2004): 26–35.

3. When the records problem is electronic, my experience has been that employees believe that the technology manages, i.e., organizes, information (cf. chapter 4).

4. Ralph Spencer Poore, "Valuing Information Assets for Security Risk Management," *Information Systems Security* 9, no. 4 (September/October 2000): 17–23. Poore and Will Ozier created the very valuable *Guideline for Information Valuation,* published by the Information Systems Security Association (ISSA).

5. One of the latest is a webinar offered by ARMA, International, Inc. by Richard Stabinski and Mark Zingarini, "Calculating the Intangible Cost of Lost Records: A Legal Perspective," 30 June 2004.

6. See *Zubulake v. UBS Warburg LLC*, No. 02 Civ. 1243 (S.D.N.Y July 20, 2004). In this request for sanctions, the judge examines the entire story of how UBS and its attorney mismanaged Zubulake's request for emails.

7. Tom Wilson, "Towards an Information Management Curriculum," http://informationr.net/tdw/publ/papers/infmagt89.html (27 April 2004).

8. W. R. Synott, *The Information Weapon: Winning Customers and Markets with Technology* (New York: Wiley, 1987).

9. As recently as March 2004, an attorney at a major law firm responsible for clearing up an expensive email problem asked why I, a records management consultant, was speaking authoritatively about the lack of policies and procedures about documents in an electronic format when all I was responsible for was paper records.

10. Personal experience.

11. For example, knowing what day work was performed on the document permits the searcher to look at all folders worked on that day. One of the most common problems with paper is that it gets tucked under another document and gets filed with that other document. Another example is knowledge of how people use files within a company. People use files to do work, but they also use them to prop open doors and as footrests beneath their desks. Files used as doorstops become doorstops in the mind of the person thus abusing them, so when a call goes out for that file, the abuser believes she does not have them. This method requires learning who has handled the file recently and searching their offices.

12. Personal experience. I have been in many organizations whose records storage facilities are physically and geographically situated poorly. The temperature and humidity controls may be adequate, but they have large numbers of vermin.

13. *United States v. Microsoft Corp.,* 84 F. Supp. 2d 9 (D.D.C. 1999).

14. Most recently Choicepoint and Lexis-Nexis.

15. Personal conversations and observations.

16. As a particularly arcane example, in one organization in which I performed work, it was clearly more logical to order the records according the last three digits of a five-digit primary classifier, then by the first two digits. The order would have been: 11325, 20325, 10326, 09327. The reason for doing this was to ensure that growth occurred as evenly as possible throughout the records. The organization had two miles of shelving, and the growth was both in particular numbers where large amounts of activity were taking place, or at the end of the numbers where new business was being added. This worked very well for the organization in question. It did not work in similar organizations.

17. In a consulting engagement for Ricoh Silicon Valley, I learned that product designers of Ricoh's eCabinet were told by clients that they preferred a file folder structure to word association (indexing) as a method of filing and finding documents. This same preference for representing documents or content by folders is also reflected in every other ECM product.

18. Only this year (2005) have software vendors begun to advertise products that will perform this function. Having been involved in such a project, I can assure the reader that it is with bated breath that even the programmers wait to see if the products will function the same way a hard-copy file folder works.

19. Personal experience, based on consulting engagements in many different types of organizations.

20. This practice continues to be reflected in the educational offerings of ARMA, International.

21. "Document control" is the term used by the nuclear industry for the creation phase. In legal, architecture, and engineering firms this is also called "document management." Because the vendors and analysts have already claimed this term, I will call this "document control."

22. Dawna Travis Dewire, *Text Management* (New York: McGraw-Hill, 1994).

23. JoAnne Yates, *Control through Communication: The Rise of System in American Management* (Baltimore: Johns Hopkins University Press, 1989), chapter 2.

24. http://www.officemuseum.com (21 April 2005).

25. Emmett Leahy, "Paperwork Management: Part I, In the U.S. Government," *Commission on the Organization of the Executive Branch of Government* (Washington, D.C.: U.S. Government Printing Office, 1947), 3.

26. "The Myth of the Paperless Office," Iron Mountain, http://www.ironmountain.com/resources/resource.asp?svc1_code=1&resource_key=263 (3 Aug. 2004).

27. Abigail J. Sellen and Richard H. R. Harper, *The Myth of the Paperless Office* (Cambridge, MA: MIT Press, 2002), 13, "In a survey of 150 companies in the United States, information technology (IT) managers reported that introducing networked access to the Internet and to the company intranet caused a noticeable increase in the amount of printing in their organizations from desktop and work group printers."

28. Sellen and Harper, 14.

29. For example, one of the ways this has been speeded up is by university reference departments downloading a book's or document's listing in the OCLC—also called WorldCat—instead of creating a new listing. This ensures that the OCLC has up-to-date information on all copies of books in university libraries and ensures the listings for each library are the same. This makes OCLC the de facto candidate to become the worldwide book listing.

30. Margaret Hedstrom, "How to Proceed? Presenting the Results of a Working Meeting on Recordkeeping Metadata," (summary of the Working Meeting on Recordkeeping, Wolfheze and Castle Bergh, the Netherlands, June 5–7, 2000), 2. http://www.archiefschool.nl/docs/hedshowt.pdf (3 August 2004).

31. For clarification of how complex this issue is, see W. H. Inmon, "Toward a Unified Theory of Metadata" *The Data Administration Newsletter,* July 2004, http://www.t-dan.com/specialfeature.htm (19 July 2004), 4.

32. Glenda Acland, Barbara Reed, and Sue McKemmish, "Documenting Business: The Australian Recordkeeping Metadata Schema" (paper presented at ADCS '99, Australasian Document Computing Symposium, December 1999), 2.

33. See, for example, Simon Cox, "A Guide to the Dublin Core Datamodel with Some Notations for Recording Dublin Core Metadata," Dublin Core Metadata Initiative, 5 May 1999, http://www.agcrc.csiro.au/projects/3018CO/metadata/dc-guide/ (22 July 2004).

34. See in particular Sue McKemmish, Glenda Acland, Nigel Ward, and Barbara Reed, "Describing Records in Context in the Continuum: the Australian Recordkeeping Metadata Schema," *Archivaria* 48 (Fall 1999): 3–43.

35. For a thorough description and primer, see the Library of Congress website http://www.loc.gov/standards/mets/ (23 August 2004). A comparison of various standards can be found at http://www.niso.org/metadata (23 August 2004).

36. See, for example, Arun Sen, "Metadata Management: Past, Present and Future," *Decision Support Systems* 37, no. 1 (April 2004): 151–173.

37. Classification plans are sometimes referred to as taxonomies. I will not use the term "taxonomy" in this discussion, as this is not a common term in everyday language or in business. It is currently a very fashionable term. My experience is that employees are so confused by the term that its value is quite low. "Taxonomy" is also a troubled term in academia, particularly in its primary home, the social sciences, as the following discussion

will describe. Knowledge Management uses this term to describe optimized indices for business intelligence. Most of those "taxonomies" are subject matter-focused and are what any special librarian would create for a particular set of documents. Those types of tax-onomies bear little or no resemblance to the "Master Classification Plan" or "Business Classification Scheme" created by the records manager, because they are focused solely on research. Records management classifications are based on function and life cycle.

38. S. R. Ranganathan, *Colon Classification* (Madras: Madras Library Association, 1933).

39. Paul Q. Hirst, *Social Evolution and Sociological Categories* (New York: Holmes & Meier Publishers, 1976), 11.

40. Richard Saul Wurman, *Information Anxiety* 2 (Indianapolis: Que, 2001). See also, for example, http://www.google.com/search?hl=en&ie=UTF-8&q=%22enterprise+information+architecture%22 (12 August 2004).

41. Definition from the Institute for Enterprise Architecture Developments, http://www.enterprise-architecture.info/ (12 August 2004).

42. See Edward A. Tiryakian, "Typologies," in David L. Sills, editor, *International Encyclopedia of the Social Sciences* (New York: Macmillan and Free Press, 1972) and Kenneth D. Bailey, "Typologies," in Edgar F. Borgatta and Marie L. Borgatta, editors, *Encyclopedia of Sociology* (New York: Macmillan, 1991).

43. Kenneth D. Bailey, *Typologies and Taxonomies: An Introduction to Classification Techniques* (Thousand Oaks, CA: Sage Publications, 1994).

44. Boris Mirkin, *Mathematical Classification and Clustering* (Dordrecht: Kluwer Academic Publishers, 1996), 4.

45. Elin K. Jacob and Debora Shaw, "Sociocognitive Perspectives on Representation," 131–185, in Carlos A. Cuadra, *Annual Review of Information Science and Technology* 33 (New York: Interscience Publishers, 1998), 160.

46. Phyllis A. Richmond, "Document Description and Representation," 73–102, in Carlos A. Cuadra, *Annual Review of Information Science and Technology,* 7 (New York: Interscience Publishers, 1972), 88.

47. David M. Liston, Jr. and Murray L. Howder, "Subject Analysis," 81–118, in Carlos A. Cuadra, *Annual Review of Information Science and Technology,* 12 (New York: Interscience Publishers, 1977), 87.

48. Patrick Tort, *La raison classificatoire* (Paris: Editions Aubier, 1989).

49. George Gaylord Simpson, *Principles of Animal Taxonomy* (New York: Columbia University Press, 1961), 65.

50. Archivists, because they are not concerned with litigation discovery, are more like horticulturalists. They are interested in a subset of information: that which may have an enduring value, that will nourish the culture.

51. Mirkin, 2.

52. Mike Uschold and Michael Gruninger, "Ontologies: Principles, Methods and Applications," *Knowledge Engineering Review* 11, no. 2 (June 1996): 93–155.

53. From John Collins Bossidy's toast at the Holy Cross Alumni Dinner, 1910, entitled, "On the Aristocracy of Harvard."

54. Gaylord, *Principles of Animal Taxonomy.*

55. Chandler, *Structure and Strategy.*

56. Robek, Brown, and Maedke, 569.

57. If metadata is anything required to read a document, then those needing reading glasses must include their eyeglasses as metadata. Microforms require some type of magnifying glass with a light source. Are the light source and magnifying lens metadata? With electronic documents, a slew of hardware and software are required to read documents, so they must be included as well. Because we would probably say "no" to the eyeglasses, the magnifying lens, and light source as metadata, are the hardware and software much different?

58. As an example of just how complex searching Google has become, my husband recently helped my son search for a way to get into a cave in a Pokemon game. They got many hits, and the first few pages had offers to give the information in exchange for a child's email address. My husband and son concluded that such information could not be found on the Internet without interacting with a pedophile. After several days I coaxed my son back to the World Wide Web and used the classification search in Yahoo! We found the information and he was inside the cave in less than five minutes.

59. A good example of end-user savvy is when numbering documents. Computer applications most often evaluate numbers from left to right unless one has a special field that is a number. This means that 1,000,000 comes after 1 and before 11 unless the user put in leading zeros. As an example for litigation production, in one recent consulting engagement I was told that 1,000 hours of attorney time were spent reviewing emails that had been required to respond to a third-party document production subpoena. See also Ariane Johnson, "Spoliation and Electronic Discovery," *Indiana Lawyer*, June 30–July 13, 2004; and http://www.thesedonaconference.org.

Chapter Seven

Conclusion: New Requirements for Records Managers

Knowledge of technology is now a requirement for records managers, as the information and communications technology (ICT) industry continues to find ever newer ways of creating documents and tucking them into every hardware unit manufactured and into every information system, from phones to personal digital assistants (PDAs). Text messaging, Blackberry pin-to-pin emails (emails that do not use the organization's email system, such as Outlook or Lotus Notes, but go through a server from one Blackberry to another), the way instant messaging is configured, to name a few, are among the most current accidents waiting to happen, from the records manager's standpoint. As long as the ICT industry takes no notice of records management, it will be developing better and newer ways to create risk for all types of organizations.

Only within the past five years have IT departments become widely aware that some of the information that they help to manage is subject to government regulations, as evidenced by the way storage products are now being advertised as products to achieve "compliance."[1] Consequently, for IT, the term "compliance" has come to mean regulatory compliance. At the same time, plaintiffs' counsels have discovered that many documentary "smoking guns" lie hidden within corporate IT hardware, operating systems, caches, applications, hard drives, etc. Judges have been educated by requests for discovery that include what is called "electronic evidence." Corporate general counsels and compliance officers have also been getting an education concerning electronic evidence. Unfortunately, however, when an order for "compliance" is handed to IT departments from the organization's General Counsel or Compliance functions, the result is confusion about what is being requested. IT departments believe they are complying when they help to produce what they are calling the "official records"—i.e., line-of-business records or records that

196

are regulated—when in fact, as every discovery subpoena requires, every captured piece of information that is relevant to the case must be produced.

Another problem that has affected many companies' ability to manage information effectively is the terminology that vendors of software tools that manage unstructured and semistructured content use to describe their products. Records management is concerned with the complete life-cycle management of all captured information within an organization. Unlike a judge in court proceedings, records management is not concerned with what is in employees' heads, but rather with information that could be broadly understood to be a document or an electronic object. For example, web content is a document when it is viewed on a web page, even though that web page may be made up of a Java server page, web services, HTML code with content, and a dynamic "edge-side include". The Java server pages and HTML snippets are electronic objects that can be managed as documents. So, too, is voice mail.

Unfortunately, many of the software vendors and software analysts consider the term "records" to be passé. To make their products appear to have nothing to do with "records," vendors use other terms, such as "document management," "imaging," "content management," or "information life cycle management" (ILM). They go even further and borrow from government the idea that documents or content are "declared records" by the end user—i.e., that it is an individual who decides when a document is a record, hence subject to business, statutory, regulatory, legal, and standards issues. This particular conception of records management leads IT departments to believe that they are not dealing with records other than when documents are ready for longer-term storage. It also leads IT departments to conclude that "compliance" requires only the careful maintenance of a tiny set of information in its final form. When a discovery subpoena arrives, no group is more surprised than IT, because they had no idea that all the material in all of the unstructured and semistructured software products that they handle are, in fact, "records."

For the most part, other employees are no better educated than those in IT. As we have seen, ICTs have created even newer ways for employees to make piles of records. Unlike the paper world, electronic documents do not get in our way by piling up on our physical desks or inboxes and do not demand some form of management simply because of the physical space they occupy, frequently getting in the way. A further problem is that technology empowers each employee to create and maintain copies in many different formats and places. The result is that achieving compliance in the electronic environment is a much greater challenge than it was in the paper world. Part of the problem is that most people believe their computers are "managing" information, when in fact computers cannot manage information; they are designed only to transform, extract, and transfer information.

In this electronic environment, end-user interfaces, training, policies, and procedures all must be created with the idea of encouraging the end user to comply with circumstances no more extreme than when we used typewriters. However, in the absence of physical documents that get in the way, as noted above, the methods employed must require registration/classification/filing of a document using some method. At times, that method will require an action by the employee, and the organization must use threats of employee discipline to ensure a 97% success rate. When any technique is too complex, end users find ways around them or ignore them completely. The various categories outlined within records management policies, for example —such as the classification of documentary information into "nonrecord," "transitory or administrative" records, and "legal or regulatory" records—are too cumbersome for end users to be able to use successfully, even if the categories made sense. End users need a small number of clear choices— particularly where litigation compliance is concerned—and all information must be classified by retention, irrespective of how records management policies and procedures define them. Categories such as "nonrecord" add a level of unnecessary complexity to handling that end users find frustrating.

IT must use its knowledge of human-computer interaction (HCI) to present the appropriate records management categories in the end-user interface. If the interface takes more than about three clicks to register/classify/file any document, end users will be less likely to comply. On the other hand, records managers must create policies, procedures, and categories that permit IT to create an intuitive interface. Another skill required of records managers is keeping track of litigation discovery issues—i.e., being current about what is being requested of organizations in general in discovery, the responses of those receiving discovery subpoenas, and the adjudication of the judge.[2] We must be concerned with learning where all possible copies of documents are held and whether new documents such as logs and caches have been created and may be required in document production. A related skill is tracking current court cases where the presence or absence of records is a major issue.[3] In addition, we should be concerned with whatever opposing counsel could conceivably ask for in a discovery subpoena and how costly producing those documents could be. It is also the duty of the records manager to bring this knowledge to the attention of managers and corporate counsel. Another skill required is concern over security and privacy. This may require technology knowledge or simply working with the information systems security officer. Information security has two concerns: theft and disaster recovery/business continuity. Each of these concerns affects the organization's ability to do business. Addressing both of them requires imagination, policies and procedures, and enforcement. In addition, privacy issues require knowledge of the law as well as an understanding of weaknesses within any system used to manage information.

It is also important that records managers have an understanding of business processes. Records are an input, and output, or a decision tool for a business process. Each life cycle intersects with a business process in a different way. To map the life cycle requires mapping how the life cycle intersects with the business process. The records manager must know what business processes exist for his or her organization, how to map each one, how to measure each one, how to improve each one, and the impact of ICT on all of those processes. Just as important, however, is knowledge of how to manage change. As more technology to manage records and documents is introduced into the organization, each employee's world is affected in a personal and individual way. Having knowledge about good business practices for how people generally react to change, how negative reactions can be mitigated, and how to ensure that such negative reactions do not negatively affect technology projects, can ensure a higher degree of success.[4] This requires communication skills and an understanding of how corporate culture affects strategies for change.

A records manager must have communication skills that would permit her to address strategic issues with executives as well as tactical issues with the lowest-level employee. Historically, this skill has been one of our weakest. While in general we have been very good at dealing with "how-to" requests from employees and in supervisory skills for our departments and direct reports, we have been very poor at measuring and summarizing problems and accomplishments for executives. In part this is because we have not been given portfolios that look strategic within the organization, but neither have we developed skills that would make us look strategically important to the organization. Most important of all is knowledge of what a record is, what a document is, how the life cycle functions from creation to disposition, how to organize records, and what value each record represents. Staying on top of this last set of skills in many instances brings improvement in all or most of the other areas.

We have looked at how complex the objects we manage can be, how the history of records management is part of the history of modern management, how what we manage is different from archivists' definitions of records, how our work intersects with business processes at a visceral level, and how we bring value to the organization. Throughout this discussion, I have pointed to places where upper-level management has stymied the business benefits of records management through misunderstanding, and how information technology and IT professionals have, through their own ignorance of records management principles, created opportunities for records managers to shine.

I have also discussed how trends in electronic records management technologies—variously called document management, knowledge management, and content management—have excluded even basic practices of records management that would have made those software products more successful and useful to the organizations which deploy them. This exclusion has taken place through the strenuous efforts of software vendors and industry analysts to convince their customers that their products do not have anything to do with records management. The recent trend among ECM software providers to buy up records management vendors and bolt the technology onto existing ECM solutions only compartmentalizes records management further. The vendors sell records management as the endnote of their solution, not as a way to help manage a Freedom of Information Act (FOIA) request or to respond to a litigation subpoena. However, only part of the problem that software companies and industry analysts have created is intentional; the rest is the result of ignorance of what records management is—an ignorance that is shared by upper-level executives.

Electronic records are a challenge because records managers do not have the life cycle knowledge, the management skills, or the portfolios to manage them. The challenges are only exacerbated because electronic records have been excluded from our purview for so long, that the disorder we now confront and need to clean up has become even more complex and changing. Records managers have asked themselves for at least the past twenty years whether we have the skills and knowledge to manage electronic records. Our conclusions have always been negative, as we have become more marginalized. I posit that the skills we lack are not the special skills required for information technology, but rather the special skills for records management that most of us never learned—i.e., skills involving the first two phases of the life cycle: 1) planning and 2) creation, receipt, or capture. ECM software products will take us only so far. Document control is what the ECM products enable. Those of us who have had experience in engineering, architecture, nuclear records management, or the law know this area well. Copy control, a part of document control, is one of the first areas we need to address. Another is linking the creation phase with organization, registering information into the life cycle management system as soon as is reasonably possible. Having appropriate policies and procedures and then helping our organizations to follow them is also vital.

An area where we have not done well is our understanding of what skills and knowledge we need as managers—and if we have fallen short, it is entirely our fault. CEOs are managers; so are office supply room managers—

but their skills as managers have little in common. Many of us have modeled ourselves more on the office supply room manager than on the CEO. We do not dress for success, learn how to make appropriate small talk, or learn how to make executive presentations. We object to aligning our departmental objectives along the lines of the organization's business objectives—which is to say, we do not see our roles as strategic. How strategic, I would ask, were the records management departments of Arthur Andersen or Credit Suisse First Boston? In short, we are not assuming a higher profile within the organization, despite the fact that our profession has itself achieved a higher profile. We must learn to address business requirements. Business requirements are an organization's strategic, "big-picture" goals: for example, increase the time to market, or lower the risk of litigation. Much is made of functional requirements for records management applications. But functional requirements are useless without understanding what the organization's purposes are and where leadership wants to take it. Functional requirements are tactical rather than strategic. The extent to which we assist the organization in achieving its business goals is also a measure of success. If we have not, first and foremost, addressed the business requirements, we have not succeeded.

We must also learn to focus our language on the language of business. Words such as "continuum," "metadata," and "taxonomy" are jargon that confuse employees and turn off executives. What we manage are intangible assets, and we must learn to discuss and manage records using that terminology. Business terminology is also the only way that an executive will understand the potential impact to the top line. The life cycle is a set of similar business processes that intersect with other business processes. We must begin to discuss what we do in those terms. We must also stop playing the role of Chicken Little. We have predicted doom and gloom for our organizations when they have not taken our advice, and nothing has happened. Bad things have happened to other organizations such as Arthur Andersen and Microsoft, but our warnings cannot change what a few rogue individuals did. Some organizations do care what is happening, but others do not care what risks they are taking with records; taking risks is part of being in business. Unless we quantify those risks, no one will pay attention to us.

Where we report within the organization also limits what we can do. What records managers do crosses many boundaries within the organization. The only other person with the organization whose responsibilities cross as many boundaries is the CEO. The place that records managers are assigned within the organization—whether that place is Facilities, Legal, Accounting, or IT—places automatic limits on what we can accomplish because our portfolios cannot extend beyond those of our superiors. Few, if any, of us report to the CEO. Yet assigning the records manager to report to anyone other than the

CEO limits the organization's ability to manage records throughout the life cycle.

We must now lead ourselves into managing records (see figure 7.1). We must stop following the archivists and librarians. Why we have followed the utterances of a few archivists as if they were our gurus and worshipped at the altar of library science is unclear. They do not manage business information; they manage cultural information. They do not manage the process of creation, only the process of preservation. They do not present feasible solutions to the problems we must address. They address a different set of business requirements. They do not manage information within the organization unless they are special librarians who are handling a tiny subset of information—publications and internal research. They manage cultural information and access, not business information. As history demonstrates, what we manage—business records—is as old as civilization. The notion that there are valuable cultural objects that must be managed is a relatively recent one—and a notion that is respected more in the breach than in reality, as Liberia and Hungary will attest: their histories were destroyed and carted off to other countries. Archivists and librarians are concerned with extreme lives of preservation that make our three- and six-year retentions appear insignificant in comparison.

Figure 7.1. Management Areas Records Management Crosses.

Electronic records appear intimidating because the mess created by information technology, combined with a lack of policies and procedures, is now more than twenty-five years old. When personal computers and word processors were introduced into business, cultural changes and advances in technology created copies and fragments of documents via HTML in every nook and cranny of the organization. Finding the "record copy" and destroying the copies; creating a rational file plan and connecting it to the retention schedule; reorganizing the electronic records in the various repositories; destroying those records whose retentions, according to the retention schedule, had expired; and, finally, creating policies and procedures that will work for the organization—must all be done. For a Fortune 500 company, this will take years. It is worth remembering, however, that it took 25 years to create this problem; it will take years to fix it.

One of the major changes that must take place and has many facets is cultural change within the organization. Employees must be taught that their work and their work product—the intangible asset of information—belongs to the organization. They must be taught that personal use of the organization's assets is a privilege, not a right. They must be taught that the organization cannot look the other way while they break laws or abuse others. The organization must also be taught to enforce the records management policies and procedures it creates. For many organizations, enforcing records management policies and procedures requires a Herculean effort that many supervisors and upper-level executives find distasteful because it initially appears to deal with trivial issues. Because creation of information has become easier, and the processes of creating information have become shortened with that same ease, formality and good sense are not fully engaged among the vast number of employees now charged with creating formal correspondence. We must now train everyone in the same way secretaries were trained in letter writing and format.

We discard a great deal more than we did in a previous, more paper-oriented world, before the advent of email. Only five of the more than one hundred emails I receive each day deal with business; an estimated five are correspondence with friends; most of the others are informational. Keeping the informational emails for more than a day or two makes my email inbox so clogged, I miss what is important. We decide who has the original and throw away all the copies. We must throw away drafts and previous versions that are no longer required.

The practice of records management has not changed, but the changes within our organizations must now be reflected in our practice and so the practice of records management should also change. Our role as managers has been elevated because the stakes are now so much higher for our organizations. Litigation is now part of the cost of doing business. Organizations are finally deciding that settling is more expensive than rectifying the problem. Now is the time to be a part of the solution.

NOTES

1. Performing a search at "whatis.com" on the term "compliance" brings up a slew of advertisements for storage products such as EMC Centera.

2. A good current example is *Zubulake v. UBS Warburg LLC,* 217 F.R.D. 309, 312 (S.D.N.Y. 2003); *Zubulake v. UBS Warburg LLC,* No. 02 Civ. 1243, 2003 WL 21087136 (S.D.N.Y. May 13, 2003); *UBS Warburg LLC,* 216 F.R.D. 280 (S.D.N.Y. 2003); *UBS Warburg LLC,* 220 F.R.D. 212 (S.D.N.Y. 2003); *UBS Warburg LLC,* No. 02 Civ. 1243, (S.D.N.Y July 20, 2004).

3. A current example is the conviction of Credit Suisse First Boston investment banker Frank Quattrone.

4. See, for example, George Eckes, *Six Sigma Team Dynamics: The Elusive Key to Project Success* (Hoboken, NJ: John Wiley & Sons, Inc., 2003).

Bibliography

Acland, Glenda, Barbara Reed, and Sue McKemmish. "Documenting Business: The Australian Recordkeeping Metadata Schema." Paper presented at the Fourth Australasian Document Computing Symposium ADCS '99, Cogs Harbor, New South Wales, Australia, December 1999.

Acme Visible Records, Inc. *Trade Catalogs on Card-based Filing Systems for Records Management in Business.* Chicago: Acme Visible Records, 1931.

Archi, Alfonso. "Archival Record-Keeping at Ebla 2400–2350 BC," 17–36 in *Ancient Archives and Archival Traditions: Concepts of Record-Keeping in the Ancient World,* edited by Maria Brosius. Oxford: Oxford University Press, 2003.

Armstrong v. Bush. 721 F. Supp. 343, 345 n.1 (D.D.C. 1989).

———. 139 F.R.D. 547, 553 (D.D.C. 1991).

Armstrong v. Executive Office of the President. 807 F. Supp. 816 (D.D.C. 1992).

———. 810 F. Supp. 335 (D.D.C. 1993).

———. 1 F.3d 1274 (D.C. Cir. 1993).

———. 877 F2d 690, 715 (D.D.C. 1995).

Association of Records Managers and Administrators. *Glossary of Records Management Terms.* Prairie Village, KS: ARMA, International, Inc., 1984.

Bailey, Kenneth D. "Typologies," 2188–2194 in *Encyclopedia of Sociology,* edited by Edgar F. Borgatta and Marie L. Borgatta. New York: Macmillan, 1991.

———. *Typologies and Taxonomies: An Introduction to Classification Techniques.* Thousand Oaks, CA: Sage Publications, 1994.

Ballow, John J., Roland Burgman, and Michael J. Molnar. "Managing for Shareholder Value: Intangibles, Future Value and Investment Decisions." *Journal of Business Strategy* 25, no. 3 (2004): 26–35.

Bearman, David. *Electronic Evidence: Strategies for Managing Records in Contemporary Organizations.* Pittsburgh: Archives and Museum Informatics, 1994.

———. "The Implications of *Armstrong v. the Executive Office of the President* for the Archival Management of Electronic Records." *American Archivist* 56 (Fall 1993): 674–689.

Benedon, William. *Records Management.* Englewood Cliffs, NJ: Prentice-Hall, 1969.

Beniger, James R. *The Control Revolution: Technological and Economic Origins of the Information Society.* Cambridge, MA: Harvard University Press, 1986.

Bernstein, Peter L. *Against the Gods: The Remarkable Story of Risk.* New York: John Wiley & Sons, 1998.

Bhabha, Homi K. "Signs Taken for Wonders: Questions of Ambivalence and Authority under a Tree in New Delhi, May 1817," 102–122 in *The Location of Culture,* edited by Homi K. Bhabha. London: Routledge, 1994.

Bohm, Nicholas. "Authentication, Reliability, and Risks," www.mcg.org.br/auth_b1 .htm (2003 June 16).

Bois, Yves-Alain and Rosalind E. Krauss. *Formless: A User's Guide.* New York: Zone Books, 1997.

Brandt, Per Aage. "Grounding Iconicity," in *Iconicity—A Fundamental Problem in Semiotics,* edited by B. Brogaard, T. D. Johansson, and M. Skov. Aarhus: N.S.U. Press, 1999.

Briet, Suzanne. *Qu'est-ce que la documentation?* Paris: EDIT, 1951.

Bronzite, Michael. *System Development: A Strategic Framework.* Berlin: Springer-Verlag, 2000.

Brosius, Maria. "Ancient Archives and Concepts of Record-Keeping: An Introduction," 1–16 in *Ancient Archives and Archival Traditions: Concepts of Record-Keeping in the Ancient World,* edited by Maria Brosius. Oxford: Oxford University Press, 2003.

Buckland, Michael K. "What is a 'document'?" *Journal of the American Society of Information Science* 48, no. 9 (September 1997): 804–809.

Bulkley, Nathaniel and Marshall Van Alstyne. *Why Information Should Influence Productivity.* Cambridge, MA: Center for eBusiness@MIT, 2004. ebusiness.Mit.edu/ research/papers/202_vanAlstyne_Productivity.pdf (May 6, 2004).

Cadell, Patrick. "Access and Information: European Attitudes and Anxieties." *Archives: Journal of the British Records Association* 28, no. 108 (April 2003): 3–13.

Canada, National Archives. *Records and Information Life Cycle Management.* www.archives.ca/06/0625_e.html (31 December 2003).

Chandler, Alfred D., Jr. *The Visible Hand: The Managerial Revolution in American Business.* Cambridge, MA: Belknap Press, 1977.

———. *Strategy and Structure: Chapters in the History of the Industrial Enterprise.* Cambridge, MA: MIT Press, 1962.

Chatfield, Helen L. "The Problem of Records from the Standpoint of Management." *American Archivist* 3, no. 2 (April 1940): 93–101.

Choksy, Carol E. B. "The Symbolic Document." Paper presented at the Document Academy, DOCAM '04, Berkeley, CA, October 2005.

Civil Evidence (Scotland) Act 1988. 1988 chapter c. 32.

Cisco, Susan L. and Tom Dale. *Indexing Business Records: The Value Proposition.* Silver Spring, MD: AIIM International, 1998.

Clanchy, M. T. *From Memory to Written Record: England 1066–1307,* 2nd ed. Oxford: Blackwell Publishers, 1993.

CMPros Listserv. cmpros@lists.cmprofessionals.org.

Cohn, Bernard S. "Representing Authority in Victorian India," 165–210 in *The Invention of Tradition,* edited by Eric Hobsbawm and Terence Ranger. Cambridge: Cambridge University Press, 1983.

Commission on Organization of the Executive Branch of the Government. *Paperwork Management: Part I, In the U.S. Government.* Washington, D.C.: U.S. Government Printing Office, 1955.

———. *Paperwork Management: Part II, The Nation's Paperwork for the Government: An Experiment.* Washington, D.C.: U.S. Government Printing Office, 1955.

———. *Records Management in the United States Government: A Report with Recommendations.* Washington, D.C.: U.S. Government Printing Office, 1948.

Commission on Preservation and Access and the Research Libraries Group. *Report of the Task Force on Archiving of Digital Information.* 1996. www.rlg.org/ArchTF/tfadi.index.htm (2003 June 18).

Cortada, James W. *Before the Computer: IBM, NCR, Burroughs and Remington Rand and the Industry They Created, 1865–1956.* Princeton, NJ: Princeton University Press, 1993.

Cox, Simon. "A Guide to the Dublin Core Datamodel with Some Notations for Recording Dublin Core Metadata." Paper at the Dublin Core Metadata Initiative website. 1999. www.agcrc.csiro.au/projects/3018CO/metadta/dc-guide/ (22 July 2004).

Crabbe, Ernest H. and Clay D. Slinker. *General Business,* 3rd ed. Cincinnati: South-Western Publishing, 1936.

Daum, Patricia B. "Technology and the Four-level Information Hierarchy." *Records Management Quarterly* 31, no. 4 (October 1997): 8–13.

Davenport, Thomas H. and James E. Short. "The New Industrial Engineering: Information Technology and Business Process Redesign." *Sloan Management Review* 31, no. 4 (Summer 1990): 11–27.

Davies, John K. "Greek Archives: From Record to Monument," 323–343 in *Ancient Archives and Archival Traditions: Concepts of Record-Keeping in the Ancient World,* edited by Maria Brosius. Oxford: Oxford University Press, 2003.

Day, Ronald E. *The Modern Invention of Information: Discourse, History and Power.* Carbondale, IL: Southern Illinois University Press, 2001.

Dedijer, Stevan and Nicolas Jéquier. *Intelligence for Economic Development.* Oxford: Berg Publishers, 1987.

Dewire, Dawna Travis. *Text Management.* New York: McGraw-Hill, 1994.

Diamond, Susan Z. *Records Management: A Practical Approach.* New York: American Management Association, 1995.

Dollar, Charles M. *Authentic Electronic Records: Strategies for Long-Term Access.* Chicago: Cohasset Associates, 2002.

Drouhet, G., G. Deslassy, and E. Morineau. *Records Management: mode d'emploi.* Paris: ADBS, 2000.

Drucker, Peter F. *Management: Tasks, Responsibilities, Practices.* New York: Harper-Collins Publishers, 1994.

Duranti, Luciana. *Diplomatics: New Uses for an Old Science.* Lanham, MD: Society of American Archivists, Association of Canadian Archivists, and Scarecrow Press, 1998.

——. "Reliability and Authenticity: The Concepts and Their Implications" *Archivaria* 39 (Spring 1995): 5–10.

——. "Authenticity and Integrity in the Digital Enviroment: An Exploratory Analysis of the Central Role of Trust." Paper presented at the kick-off for the InterPARES project, 2000. www.clir.org/pubs/reports/pub92/lynch.htm.

Duranti, Luciana. "Concepts, Principles, and Methods for the Management of Electronic Records." *The Information Society 17*, (2002): 271–279.

Duranti, Luciana, Terry Eastwood, and Heather MacNeil. "The Preservation of the Integrity of Electronic Records," www.slais.ubc.ca/Duranti (1999 June 15).

Eckes, George. *Six Sigma Team Dynamics: The Elusive Key to Project Success.* Hoboken, NJ: John Wiley & Sons, Inc., 2003.

Electronic Signatures in Global and National Commerce Act of 2000. Pub. L. No. 106–229, 114 Stat. 464 (2000) (codified at 15 U.S.C. § 7001 *et seq.*).

Fairthorne, Robert A. "Content Analysis, Specification, and Control," 73–109 in *Annual Review of Information Science and Technology,* edited by Carlos A. Cuadra. Chicago: William Benton, 1969.

Federal Register. *General Records Schedule 20; Disposition of Electronic Records.* 60 Fed. Reg. 44,643 (1995).

Garvin, David A. "The Process of Organization and Management." *Sloan Management Review* 39, no. 4 (Summer 1998): 33–50.

Gerstenberg, Charles W. *Principles of Business.* New York: Prentice Hall, 1918.

Gilliland-Swetland, Anne J. "Testing Our Truths: Delineating the Parameters of the Authentic Archival Electronic Record." *American Archivist* 65, no. 2 (Fall/Winter 2002): 196–215.

Goodman, Nelson. *Languages of Art.* Indianapolis: Hackett Publishing Company, 1976.

Graburn, Nelson H. H., ed. *Ethnic and Tourist Arts: Cultural Expressions from the Fourth World.* Berkeley: University of California Press, 1976.

Griffin, Mary Claire. *Records Management: A Modern Tool for Business.* Boston: Allyn and Bacon, 1964.

Gross, John W. "Inventory and Scheduling Records." *Records Management Quarterly* 7, no. 1 (January 1973): 28–31.

Guthrie, Chester L. "Federal Contributions to the Management of Records," 126–152 in *Federal Contributions to Management: Effects on the Public and Private Sectors,* edited by David S. Brown. New York: Praeger Publishers, 1971.

Haigh, Andrew. *Object-oriented Analysis & Design.* New York: Osborne, 2001.

Hall, Richard. "The Strategic Analysis of Intangible Resources." *Strategic Management Journal* 13, no. 2 (February 1992): 135–144.

Hammer, Michael. "Reengineering Work: Don't Automate, Obliterate." *Harvard Business Review* 68, no. 4 (July–August 1990): 104–112.

Hare, Catherine and Julie McLeod. *Guide pratique: Mettre en place le records management dans son organisation.* Paris: Archimag, 2003.

Headrick, Daniel R. *When Information Came of Age: Technologies of Knowledge in the Age of Reason and Revolution, 1700–1850.* Oxford: Oxford University Press, 2000.

Hedstrom, Margaret. "How to Proceed? Presenting the Results of a Working Meeting on Recordkeeping Metadata." Paper summarizing the Working Meeting on

Recordkeeping at Wolfheze and Castle Bergh, the Netherlands, 2000. www .archiefschool.nl/docs/hedshowt.pdf (3 August 2004).

Hirst, Paul Q. *Social Evolution and Sociological Categories.* New York: Holmes & Meier Publishers, 1976.

Hudders, E. R. *Indexing and Filing: A Manual of Standard Practice.* New York: Ronald Press, 1916.

Humphrey, John, Robin Mansell, Daniel Paré, and Hubert Schmitz. *The Reality of E-commerce with Developing Countries.* www.gapresearch.org/production/ ecommerce.html section 6 (2003 June 16).

Ifrah, Georges. *The Universal History of Computing: From the Abacus to the Quantum Computer.* New York: John Wiley & Sons, 2001.

———. *The Universal History of Numbers: From Prehistory to the Invention of the Computer.* New York: John Wiley & Sons, 2000.

Indiana University Project, www.indiana.edu/~libarch/ER/ (13 April 2005).

Inmon, W. H. "Toward a Unified Theory of Metadata." *Data Administration Newsletter,* Special Feature (July 2004) www.tdan.com/specialfeature.htm (10 January 2005).

International Council of Archives. *Guide for Managing Electronic Records from an Archival Perspective.* www.ica.org/biblio/guide_2b1.html (31 December 2003).

International Standards Organization. "Information and Documentation—Records Management." *ISO 15489.* Geneva: ISO, 2001.

InterPARES Project, www.interpares.org/ (13 April 2005).

Iron Mountain. *The Myth of the Paperless Office.* Boston, MA: Iron Mountain, n.d. www.ironmountain.com/resources/resources.asp?svc1_code=1&resour-ce_key=263 (3 August 2004).

Jacob, Elin K. and Debora Shaw. "Sociocognitive Perspectives on Representation," 131–185 in *Annual Review of Information Science and Technology* 33, edited by Carlos A. Cuadra. New York: Interscience Publishers, 1998.

Jacobson, James, Ivar Rumbaugh, and Grady Booch. *The Unified Modeling Language Reference Manual.* Reading, MA: Addison-Wesley, 1999.

Johnson, Ariane. "Spoliation and Electronic Discovery." *Indiana Lawyer,* June 30–July 13, 2003.

Johnson, Samuel. *A Dictionary of the English Language.* London: W. Strathams, 1755.

Jones, H. G. *The Records of a Nation: Their Management, Preservation, and Use.* New York: Atheneum, 1969.

Kahn, Randolph A. and Barclay T. Blair. *Information Nation: Seven Keys to Information Management Compliance.* Silver Spring, MD: AIIM, 2004.

Kallaus, Norman F. and Mina M. Johnson. *Records Management,* 5th ed. Cincinnati: South-Western Publishing Co., 1992.

Kerr, Orin S. "Computer Records and the Federal Rules of Evidence," *USA Bulletin* 49, no. 2 (March 2001) www.usdoj.gov/criminal/cybercrime/usamar-ch2001_4.htm (2003 June 17).

Langemo, Mark. *Winning Strategies for Successful Records Management Programs: Proven Strategies for Developing New Programs and Improving Existing Ones!* Denver: Information Requirements Clearinghouse, 2002.

Latour, Bruno. *Aramis or the Love of Technology.* Cambridge, MA: Harvard University Press, 1996.

Leahy, Emmett J. and Christopher A. Cameron. *Modern Records Management: A Basic Guide to Records Control, Filing, and Information Retrieval.* New York: McGraw-Hill, 1965.

Leffingwell, W. H. *Scientific Office Management.* Chicago: A. W. Shaw Company, 1917.

Leleu-Merviel, Sylvie. "Effets de la numérisation et de la mise en réseau sur le concept de document," *Information-Interaction-Intelligence* 4, no. 1 (2004): 121–140.

Lev, Baruch. *Intangibles: Management, Measurement, and Reporting.* Washington, D.C.: Brookings Institution Press, 2001.

———. "Sharpening the Intangibles Edge." *Harvard Business Review* 82, no. 6 (June 2004): 109–116.

Lévi-Strauss, Claude. *Les structures élémentaires de la parenté.* Paris: Mouton & Co., 1967.

Levy, Steven. *Crypto: How the Code Rebels Beat the Government—Saving Privacy in the Digital Age.* New York: Penguin Books, 2002.

Library Bureau. *Progressive Indexing and Filing for Schools.* Tonawanda, NY: Rand Kardex Service, 1927.

Liston, David M., Jr. and Murray L. Howder. "Subject Analysis," 81–118 in *Annual Review of Information Science and Technology,* 12, edited by Carlos A. Cuadra. New York: Interscience Publishers, 1977.

Litterer, Joseph A. "Systematic Management: The Search for Order and Integration." *Business History Review (pre-1986)* 35, no. 4 (Winter 1961): 461–476.

Livelton, Trevor. *Archival Theory, Records, and the Public.* Lanham, MD: Society of American Archivists and Scarecrow Press, 1996.

Losee, Robert M. "A Discipline Independent Definition of Information." *Journal of the American Society for Information Science* 48, no. 3 (March 1997): 254–262.

Low, Jonathan and Pam Cohen Kalafut. *Invisible Advantage: How Intangibles are Driving Business Performance.* Cambridge, MA: Perseus Publishing, 2002.

Lund, Niels Windfeld. "Omrids af en dokumentationsvidenskab. [Outline of a Documentation Science]," *Norsk tidsskrift for bibliotekforskning* 4, no. 12 (1999): 24–47.

Lundgren, Terry D. and Carol A. Lundgren. *Records Management in the Computer Age.* Boston: PWS-Kent, 1989.

Lynch, Clifford. "Authenticity and Integrity in the Digital Environment: An Exploratory Analysis of the Central Role of Trust." www.clir.org/pubs/reports/pub92/lynch.html (16 June 2003).

MacNeil, Heather. "Providing Grounds for Trust II: The Findings of the Authenticity Task Force of InterPARES." *Archivaria* 54 (Fall 2002): 24–59.

Mariée, M. *Traité des archives: dans lequel on enseigne le moyen de faire revivre les anciennes écritures, & la manière de procéder le plus simplement au pouillé général, pour y donner ensuite un ordre simple, laconique & constant; lequel s'applique aussi aux bibliothèques.* Paris: Cailleau, Imprimeur-Libraire, 1774.

McClelland, Frank C. *Office Training and Standards.* Chicago: A. W. Shaw, 1919.

McCord, James N. *A Textbook of Filing.* New York: D. Appleton and Company, 1920.

McKemmish, Sue, Glenda Acland, Nigel Ward, and Barbara Reed. "Describing Records in Context in the Continuum: The Australian Recordkeeping Metadata Schema." *Archivaria* 48 (Fall 1999): 3–43.

McMillan, John. *Reinventing the Bazaar: A Natural History of Markets.* New York: W. W. Norton, 2002.

McNamara, Joel. *Secrets of Computer Espionage: Tactics and Countermeasures.* Indianapolis: Wiley Publishing, 2003.

Mirkin, Boris. *Mathematical Classification and Clustering.* Dordrecht: Kluwer Academic Publishers, 1996.

Mirzoeff, Nicolas. *An Introduction to Visual Culture.* London: Routledge, 1999.

Mitchell, W. J. T. *Iconology: Image, Text, Ideology.* Chicago: University of Chicago Press, 1986.

Muller, S., J. A. Feith, and R. Fruin. *Manual for the Arrangement and Description of Archives.* New York: H. W. Wilson, 1968.

Odell, Margaret K. and Earl P. Strong. *Records Management and Filing Operations.* New York: McGraw-Hill Book Company, 1947.

Odell, William R., Harold F. Clark, Guy D. Miller, Oscar B. Paulsen, Dorothy L. Travis, and Ruth M. Twiss. *Business: Its Organization and Operation.* Boston: Ginn and Company, 1937.

Oxford English Dictionary: The Compact Edition. Oxford: Oxford University Press, 1971.

Paulk, Mark C. *The Capability Maturity Model: Guidelines for Improving the Software Process.* Reading, MA: Addison-Wesley Pub. Co., 1995.

Peirce, Charles S. "Logic as Semiotic: The Theory of Signs," 98–119 in *Philosophical Writings of Peirce,* edited by Justus Buchler. New York: Dover Publications, 1955.

Penn, Ira A., Gail B. Pennix, and Jim Coulson. *Records Management Handbook,* 2nd ed. Brookfield, VT: Gower, 1994.

Pittsburgh Project, web.archive.org/web/20000818163633/www.sis.pitt.edu/~n-hprc/ (13 April 2005).

Poore, Ralph Spencer. "Valuing Assets for Security Risk Management." *Information Systems Security* 9, no. 4 (September/October 2000): 17–23.

Postgate, J. N. "Middle Assyrian Documents in Government," 124–138 in *Ancient Archives and Archival Traditions: Concepts of Record-Keeping in the Ancient World,* edited by Maria Brosius. Oxford: Oxford University Press, 2003.

Pritchard, Stephen. "The Artifice of Culture: Contemporary Indigenous Art and the Work of Peter Robinson," *Third Text* 19, no. 1 (January 2005): 67–80.

Public Citizen v. Carlin. 2 F. Supp. 2d 1 (D.D.C. 1997).

———. 2 F. Supp. 2d 18, 20 (D.D.C. 1998).

Rangnathan, S. R. *Colon Classification.* Madras: Madras Library Association, 1933.

Read-Smith, Judith, Mary Lea Ginn, and Norman F. Kallaus. *Records Management,* 7th ed. Cincinnati: South-Western Publishing Co., 2002.

Records Management Listserv. recmgmt-l@lists.ufl.edu.

Report of the Task Force on Archiving of Digital Information. Commissioned by the Commission on Preservation and Access and the Research Libraries Group, Inc., May 1, 1996. www.rlg.org/ArchTF/tfadi.index.htm (2003 June 18).

Richmond, Phyllis A. "Document Description and Representation," 73–102, in *Annual Review of Information Science and Technology* 7, edited by Carlos A. Cuadra. New York: Interscience Publishers, 1972.

Ricks, Betty R., Ann J. Swafford, and Kay F. Gow. *Information and Image Management: A Records Systems Approach,* 3rd ed. Cincinnati: South-Western Publishing Co., 1992.

Robek, Mary F., Gerald F. Brown, and David O. Stephens. *Information and Records Management: Document-based Information Systems.* 4th ed. Lake Forest, IL: Glencoe, 1995.

Robek, Mary F., Wilmer O. Maedke, and Gerald F. Brown. *Information and Records Management.* 3rd ed. Lake Forest, IL: Glencoe, 1987.

Ross, Seamus. "Acting to Avoid Loss, But When Disaster Strikes Relying on Digital Archaeology," presented at the Managing Electronic Records Conference, Chicago, IL, November 1998.

Roth, Guenther and Claus Wittich, eds. *Economy and Society: An Outline of Interpretive Sociology,* vol. I. Berkeley: University of California Press, 1978.

Saffady, William. *The Document Life Cycle: A White Paper.* Silver Spring, MD: AIIM International, 1997.

——. *Film-based Imaging in the Document Life Cycle: FAQs for Best Practice.* Silver Spring, MD: AIIM International, 1997.

——. *Records and Information Management: Fundamentals of Professional Practice.* Lenexa, KS: ARMA, International, 2004.

Sanders, Robert L. "The Promise of Project Files: A Case Study." *Information Management Journal* 33, no. 1 (January 1999): 64–67.

Schamber, Linda. "What is a Document? Rethinking the Concept in Uneasy Times." *Journal of the American Society for Information Science* 47, no. 9 (September 1996): 669–672.

Schellenberg, T. R. *Modern Archives: Principles and Techniques.* Chicago: University of Chicago Press, 1956.

Schmandt-Besserat, Denise. *Before Writing: Volume I, From Counting to Cuneiform.* Austin: University of Texas Press, 1992.

Scholfield, Ethel E. *Filing Department Operation and Control: From the Standpoint of the Management.* New York: Ronald Press, 1923.

Schulze, J. William. *The American Office: Its Organization, Management and Records.* New York: Key Publishing, 1913.

Sedona Conference. *The Sedona Principles: Best Practices Recommendations & Principles for Addressing Electronic Document Production.* 2004. www.thesedonaconference.org/ (29 March 2004).

Sellen, Abigail and Richard H. R. Harper. *The Myth of the Paperless Office.* Cambridge, MA: MIT Press, 2002.

Sen, Arun. "Metadata Management: Past, Present and Future." *Decision Support Systems* 37, no. 1 (April 2004): 151–173.

Shenk, David. *Data Smog: Surviving the Information Glut.* San Francisco: HarperEdge, 1997.

Shepherd, Elizabeth and Geoffrey Yeo. *Managing Records: A Handbook of Principles and Practice.* London: Facet Publishing, 2004.

Silverstein, Michael. "Shifters, Linguistic Categories, and Cultural Description," 11–56 in *Meaning in Anthropology,* edited by Keith H. Basso and Henry A. Selby. Albuquerque: University of New Mexico Press, 1976.

Simpson, George Gaylord. *Principles of Animal Taxonomy.* New York: Columbia University Press, 1961.

Skupsky, Donald S. and John C. Montaña. *Law, Records and Information Management: The Court Cases.* Denver: Information Requirements Clearinghouse, 1994.

Smith, Jonathan Z. *Imagining Religion: From Babylon to Jonestown.* Chicago: University of Chicago Press, 1978.

Smith, Milburn D. III. *Information and Records Management: A Decision-maker's Guide to Systems Planning and Implementation.* New York: Quorum Books, 1986.

Stabinski, Richard and Mark Zingarini. "Calculating the Intangible Cost of Lost Records: A Legal Perspective." Webinar presented through ARMA, International, 2004.

State Records New South Wales, "The Records Continuum," *For the Record* 12. (November 1996) www.records.nsw.gov.au/publications/fortherecord/ftr12/ftr12.htm (31 March 2004).

Steinkeller, Piotr. "Archival Practices at Babylonia in the Third Millenium," 37–58 in *Ancient Archives and Archival Traditions: Concepts of Record-Keeping in the Ancient World,* edited by Maria Brosius. Oxford: Oxford University Press, 2003.

Stepanek, Marcia. "From Digits to Dust," *Business Week* 3574 (20 April 1998): 128–130.

Stephens, David O. and Roderick C. Wallace. *Electronic Records Retention: New Strategies for Data Life Cycle Management.* Lenexa, KS: ARMA, International, 2003.

Stewart, Jeffrey R. *Professional Records Management.* New York: Glencoe/McGraw-Hill, 1995.

Sutton, Michael J. D. *Document Management for the Enterprise: Principles, Techniques, and Applications.* New York: Wiley Computer Publishing, 1996.

Synott, W. R. *The Information Weapon: Winning Customers and Markets with Technology.* New York: Wiley, 1987.

Taylor, Frederick W. *The Principles of Scientific Management.* New York: Harper Brothers, 1911.

Thomas, Jr., Landon. "A Jury Assesses Morgan Stanley $604 Million," *New York Times,* May 17, 2005.

Tiryakian, Edward A. "Typologies," 177–186 in *International Encyclopedia of the Social Sciences,* edited by David L. Sills. New York: Macmillan and Free Press, 1972.

Tort, Patrick. *La raison classificatoire.* Paris: Editions Aubier, 1989.

Tufte, Edward R. *The Visual Display of Quantitative Information.* 2nd ed. Cheshire, CT: Graphics Press, 2001.

Turnbaugh, Roy C. "What is an Electronic Record?" 23–34 in *Effective Approaches for Managing Electronic Records and Archives,* edited by Bruce W. Dearstyne. Lanham, MD: Scarecrow Press, 2002.

U.K. Parliamentary Archives. *Records Management Policy Guidelines.* 2000. www.parliament.uk/archives/policy/policy1.htm (31 December 2003).

U.S. Civil Service Commission, Training Division, Interdepartmental Committee on Records Administration. *Preliminary Reports of Subcommittees on Records Administration,* October 1942. National Archives Miscellaneous Processed Document nos. 43–5.

U.S. Congress. House. *Message from the President of the United States, Transmitting Report of the Commission Appointed to Examine the Security of the Public Buildings in the City of Washington against Fire,* 45th Congress, 2nd Session, 1877. House Executive Document, no. 10.

——. *Message of the President of the United States Transmitting the Reports of the Commission on Economy and Efficiency,* 62nd Congress, 3rd Session, 1913. House Document no. 1252.

——. *Sarbanes-Oxley Act of 2002,* H.R. 3763, 23 January 2002.

U.S. Congress. Senate. *Report of the Select Committee of the United State Senate, appointed under Senate Resolution of March 3, 1887 to Inquire into and Examine the Methods of Business and Work in the Executive Departments, etc., and the Causes of Delays in Transacting the Public Business, etc.,* 50th Congress, 1st Session, 1888. Senate Report no. 507.

U.S. Department of Agriculture, Office of Plant and Operations. *Procedure Manual for Records Management.* Washington, D.C.: U.S. Government Printing Office, 1942.

U.S. National Archives. *Seventh Annual Report of the Archivist of the United States for the Year Ending June 30, 1941.* Washington, D.C.: U.S. Government Printing Office, 1941.

U.S. National Archives and Records Administration. *About Records Management, The Life Cycle of Records.* www.archives.gov/midatlantic/fed_agency_services/records_management/about_records_management.html (31 December 2003).

U.S. National Archives and Records Administration. *General Records Schedule 20; Disposition of Electronic Records*, 60 Fed. Reg. 44,643 (1995).

U.S. Rules of Civil Procedure. U.S. Code. Vol. 28 Appendix, Rule 26 (2004).

U.S. Rules of Evidence. U.S. Code. Vol. 28 sec. 803 (2004).

United States V. Microsoft Corp. 84 F. Supp. 2d 9 (D.D.C. 1999).

Upward, Frank. "In Search of the Continuum: Ian Maclean's 'Australian Experience' Essays on Recordkeeping," 110–130 in *The Records Continuum: Ian Maclean and Australian Archives First Fifty Years,* edited by Sue McKemmish and Michael Piggott. Clayton, Australia: Ancora Press, 1994.

——. "Structuring the Records Continuum, Part One: Postcustodial Principles and Properties." *Archives and Manuscripts* 24, no. 2 (November 1996): 268–285.

——. "Structuring the Records Continuum, Part Two: Structuration Theory and Recordkeeping." *Archives and Manuscripts* 25, no. 1 (May 1997): 10–33.

Uschold, Mike and Michael Gruninger. "Ontologies: Principles, Methods and Applications." *Knowledge Engineering Review* 11, no. 2 (March 1996): 93–155.

Van Lerberghe, Karel. "Private and Public: The Ur-Utu Archive at Sippar-Amnānum (Tell ed-Dēr)," 59–77 in *Ancient Archives and Archival Traditions: Concepts of Record-Keeping in the Ancient World,* edited by Maria Brosius. Oxford: Oxford University Press, 2003.

Veenhof, Klaas R. "Archives of Old Assyrian Traders," 78–123 in *Ancient Archives and Archival Traditions: Concepts of Record-Keeping in the Ancient World*, edited by Maria Brosius. Oxford: Oxford University Press, 2003.

Wallace, Eugenia. *Filing Methods.* New York: Ronald Press, 1923.

Wallace, Patricia E., Jo Ann Lee, and Dexter R. Schubert. *Records Management: Integrated Information Systems.* 3rd ed. Upper Saddle River, NJ: Prentice Hall, 1992.

Watkins, Calvert, ed. *The American Heritage Dictionary of Indo-European Roots.* 2nd ed. Boston: Houghton Mifflin, 2000.

Watson, James K., Jr., and Carol Choksy. "Digital Signatures Seal Web Deals." *Information Week* 804 (September 18, 2000): RB26–RB28.

Wegrzyn-Wolska, Katarzyna. "Le document numérique dynamique: une 'étoile filante' dans l'espace documentaire." Paper presented at *Le numérique: impact sur le cycle de vie du document,* Québec, Canada, October 2004.

Westington, Ralph. "Case Records Filing System." *Records Management Quarterly* 10, no. 2 (April 1976).

Wheaton, Kristan J. *The Warning Solution: Intelligent Analysis in the Age of Information Overload.* Fairfax,VA: AFCEA International Press, 2001.

Wigent, William David. *Modern Filing and How to File: A Textbook on Office System.* Rochester, NY: Yawman and Erbe Manufacturing, 1920.

Wilson, Tom. "Towards an Information Management Curriculum." Informationr.net/tdw/publ/papers/infmagt89.html (27 April 2004).

Withers, Kenneth J. "Computer-based Discovery in Federal Civil Litigation," 45–220 in *5th Annual Electronic Discovery and Records Management Seminar,* no editor. Little Falls, NJ: Glasser LegalWorks, 2002.

Wurman, Richard Saul. *Information Anxiety* 2. Indianapolis: Que, 2001.

Yates, JoAnne. *Control through Communication: The Rise of System in American Management.* Baltimore: Johns Hopkins University Press, 1989.

Zacklad, Manuel. "Processus de documentarisation dans les Documents pour l'Action (DopA): statut des annotations et technologies de la coóperation associées." Paper presented at *Le numérique: impact sur le cycle de vie du document* Québec, Canada, October 2004.

Zubulake v. UBS Warburg LLC. 217 F.R.D. 309, 312 (S.D.N.Y. 2003).

——. No. 02 Civ. 1243, 2003 WL 21087136 (S.D.N.Y. May 13, 2003).

——. 216 F.R.D. 280 (S.D.N.Y. 2003).

——. 220 F.R.D. 212 (S.D.N.Y. 2003).

——. No. 02 Civ. 1243, (S.D.N.Y July 20, 2004).

Index

archivists: authenticity/reliability for, 56–57; business records managers v., xix–xxi; documents for, 97–98; on electronic records, 85–86; evidence for, 69–74; goals of, 144–45, 154, 157n42; incompleteness for, 146; information subsets for, 185, 194n50; in NARS, 25–29; on records, 53–56; Records Continuum for, 146; in records management, 25–29, 50; records management v., 168–70; records managers v., 159, 202; for U.S. government, 25–29, 71, 151

ARMA International, Inc., on electronic records, 85–86

Arthur Andersen/Enron, litigation of, 54, 70, 80, 120, 146, 150, 168, 191, 201

authenticity, 52–53, 56–57, 86; appropriation in, 57; culture in, 57, 81n10; in digital signatures, 58, 81–82n14, 82n16; in email, 58, 81n11, 81n13; E-sign act for, 58–59; evidence and, 60–67; InterPARES for, 47–48, 51n15, 57, 83nn29–30; for litigation, 53–54, 57, 59–76; memoranda with, 58, 81nn11–12; study on, 89–90, 108–9nn6–7; trust in, 56–57, 59, 61–62

authenticity/reliability: business requirements on, 67–69, 83n30; in hearsay, 65–67; in metadata, 76; in tokens, 97

BCS. *See* business classification scheme

BPM. *See* business process management

business(es): archivists v. records managers in, xix–xxi; BCS in, 138–40; forms' standardization in, 17, 19–20; indexes for, 17–21, 27–28, 33; legal definition of, 73; MCP for, 185; records management from, xix, 20, 35n70; records management manuals from, 18–20, 22, 24–25, 104; terminology, 201

business classification scheme (BCS), MCP for, 138–39

business documents: correspondence in, 104–5; destruction of, 20, 22, 24, 150, 162–63; tabular information v., 104, 113

business intelligence, records management for, 50

business process(es), 202; for document control, 173–74; expectations on, 121; information organization as, 113–14, 199; innovations for, 124,

217

electronic, 102–4; filing function of, 171–72; filing software for, 171–72, 192n18; subject files v., 102
proprietary document format, non-proprietary format v., 42–43
public key infrastructure (PKI), signatures by, 58, 82n16

receipt of information, definition of, 125–26
record(s): archivists on, 53–56; authenticity of, 50; context for, 106; cultural value of, 151, 158n50; datum as, 106–7; definition of, 24, 27, 43–44, 46, 53–57, 73–74, 77–80; destruction of, 150, 153–54, 161–62; disarray in, 161; dynamic compound, 100, 108; historical, 151–52; maintenance of, 142–47, 157n39; management techniques for, xviii; management tool as, 9; memoranda in, 101; mismanagement of, 163; non-records v., 67–68, 198; *recordationem* as, 5; reliability of, 50, 52–53, 56–57; simplex, 99, 108; single, 98–99, 108; static compound, 101, 108; storage of, 16, *21, 23,* 146–48; value in, 149–54, 179; word history of, 106. *See also* business records; document(s); electronic records; hard-copy records; paper records; vital records
Records Continuum, for archivists, 146
record(s) series, 77, 136, 138–39, 180–82; access to, 139–40; class as, 79; classified elements in, 187; definition of, 44–45, 188; document type v., 188; file formats v., 188; management in, 114–15; metadata for, 179; security in, 181; sets of, 118, 120
records life cycle, 115; descriptions of, 117–19; over time, 115; phases for, 116–20, 128–29; in records management, 113–14; relationships within, 118–19
records management (RM): archivists in, 25–29, 50; archivists v., 168–70; from business, xix, 20, 35n70; business intelligence from, 50; business requirements for, 201; business size on, 8–10, 33; business terminology for, 201; change on, 120–21; class in, 78–80; compliance for, 164–65; cross-reference in, 189; decommission for, 42–43; documentation v., 78; document science v., 88–92; ECM and, 46–47, 51n14, 85–86; filing systems in, 17–22, *23,* 26; finances in, 86–87, 164; functional requirements for, 201; history, 1–5; indexes in, 189; information organization from, 170–71, 199; interviews from, 121–24; inventory in, 121–22; IT v., 169–70; jargon in, 189–90; legal regulatory and standards in, 202; life cycle management for, 25–29, 33, 44, 46, 49; manuals on, 18, 20, 22, 24–25, 104; metadata in, 177–79; NARS for, 25–29; negativity and, 150; non-records in, 68–69; "organizational informatics" v., xx; paperwork management v., 28–29; pre-mechanization, 1–5; preservation in, 11–12, 29–33, 169; priority of, 120, 156n25, 170; process-orientation of, 55; productivity from, 154; for retrieval, 31–32, 163; risk management in, 59, 120, 154, 156n25; surveys from, 123; systematization of, 20; tabulation in, 5–8, *93,* 93–94, 104, 113; teamwork from, 122–24, 136, 156n26; timeline for, *32,* 32–33; transferring in, 20, 22, 25–26, 144; translation of, 90, 109n9; vital documents in, 115–16. *See also* U.S. government, records management in

About the Author

Dr. Carol E. B. Choksy has worked in records management for more than 25 years. She has advised organizations in nearly every public industry sector as well as federal, state, and local government and NGOs on five continents. Her industry experience includes every phase of the records life cycle, particularly where technology has created problems. She has been a Certified Records Manager since 1996, and a Project Management Professional since 2006. She has been CEO of her own company, IRAD Strategic Consulting, Inc. since 1997. Dr. Choksy is an adjunct professor at the School of Library and Information Science at Indiana University, Bloomington. She also teaches courses at the IUPUI campus for SLIS. She teaches Records Management, Strategic Intelligence, Systems Analysis, Management, and Social Science Research. She has served two terms on the Board of Directors of ARMA, International (association of records managers and administrators) and is the President-elect. Dr. Choksy was educated at the University of Chicago (BA, MA, and PhD).

DATE DUE
